COMPETING DEVOTIONS

COMPETING DEVOTIONS

Career and Family among Women Executives

MARY BLAIR-LOY

Harvard University Press

Cambridge, Massachusetts, and London, England · *2003*

Library of Congress Cataloging-in-Publication Data

Blair-Loy, Mary.
  Competing devotions : career and family among women executives / Mary Blair-Loy.
    p. cm.
Includes bibliographical references and index.
  ISBN 0-674-01089-2 (alk. paper)
  1. Work and family—United States.   2. Women executives—United States.
3. Dual-career families—United States.   I. Title.
  HD4904.25.B57 2003
  305.43'658—dc21
                  2002192238

To David

CONTENTS

COMPETING DEVOTIONS

INTRODUCTION

American women today have the opportunity and experience to be highly successful in a world that previously excluded them.[1] Within the past twenty years women have started to compete for the prize jobs in American businesses. Yet during this same period, firms have increased their demands on professionals.[2] Some women, willing and able to devote long hours to their careers, have thrived in traditionally male jobs. At the same time, many women feel that mothers should devote a great deal of time and energy to their children. Many women are torn between these seemingly irreconcilable commitments to work and family.[3]

I study success stories of liberal feminism: women who have reached senior positions in a male-dominated world. Using in-depth interviews and life-history questionnaires, I analyze the ways these women struggle to reconcile work dedication with their commitment to family. Although these struggles may feel like very personal battles, I find that they are rooted in powerful assumptions about what makes life worthwhile. Cultural definitions of the conceivable, the moral, and the desirable help sculpt the capitalist firm and the nuclear family, shape personalities, and create work-family conflict.

Executive positions require an immense commitment of time, energy, and emotion.[4] Such careers are organized by a cultural model that I call the *schema of work devotion*. This cultural schema defines the career as a calling or vocation that deserves single-minded allegiance and gives meaning and purpose to life. This definition, embedded in most firms' policies, practices, and work culture, seems so obvious that many professionals scarcely acknowledge it. Employers and clients assume that high-level workers will be dedicated to their jobs and will not spend significant amounts of time on other obligations.[5]

Professional men have long experienced an intense and intimate connection to their work (Hochschild, 1997; Roper, 1994; Jackall, 1988), secure in the knowledge that their children were well cared for during their long absences from home. As a result of the legal and social changes wrought by the women's movement in the 1970s, the most blatant gender discrimination in many firms has been reduced, although not entirely eliminated. Now, large numbers of professional women can, in theory, reap the rewards of this level of career dedication.

Women pursuing demanding, elite careers, however, collide head-on with the *family devotion schema*, a cultural model that defines marriage and motherhood as a woman's primary vocation. This schema promises women meaning, creativity, intimacy, and financial stability in caring for a husband and precious children. Children are seen as fragile and deserving of a mother's tender care. Men are perceived as unable to provide the selflessness and patience that the constant care of children requires. Career-oriented women who publicly spend too much time attending to family needs violate the work devotion schema. And work-dedicated women who evade or delegate family responsibilities violate the family devotion schema. And so, work-family conflict is born.

The schemas of work devotion and family devotion are powerful but not deterministic. My study identifies two maverick groups of women trying to shape these schemas into new models. Their efforts are made possible by access to new ideological and material resources, but they also face much resistance. Their endeavors may eventually help redefine the institutions of the nuclear family and the capitalist firm in ways that reduce the conflict between involved parenting and elite careers.

The business and popular press often treat work-family conflict as an individual problem, a psychological challenge, or a personal choice. For example, in its widely read 2001 issue listing the 100 best companies for working women, *Working Mother* magazine suggests that women can achieve work-family balance if they establish clear priorities, develop better communication skills, set limits, and learn to say no (Finnigan, 2001). Similarly, Sylvia Ann Hewlett's book *Creating a Life: Professional Women and the Quest for Children* advises women to strategically choose a partner early, have children before age thirty-five, and find an undemanding career (Hewlett, 2002: 301–302). Employees often agree that work-family balance is a personal and psychological challenge (Becker and Moen, 1999). For example, a female finance executive I interviewed maintained, "It boils down to very personal choices."

It is part of American culture to view work-family issues as private, personal, and amenable to individual solutions for people who are clever enough to figure them out.[6] This culture of individualism offers the illusion that we can solve these dilemmas by ourselves, without having to join with others to examine assumptions and challenge social structures.

Focusing only on individual decisions and personal choices ignores the question of why our choices are so limited. When it comes to work-family balance, broad historical, social, and cultural forces shape our few options. Moreover, these same forces shape how we personally react to the options we have.

Social scientists are trained to examine the historical, social, and cultural environment that shapes our choices and our attitudes toward them. But unfortunately, much social science research posits a peculiar type of individual: one who is either excessively strategic or excessively reactive. These studies assume that people confront work-family dilemmas by strategically weighing the costs and benefits of time at work versus time at home or by reacting to various incentives generated by the marketplace and the family. Even literature that avoids succumbing to this simplistic economic model still makes the naive assumption that the concepts of "work" and "family" each have a straightforward meaning and an obvious, a priori set of demands.

Yet depending on the cultural and social context, people do interpret these concepts differently and have widely varying perceptions of how much time and energy they require. People develop a sense of what are legitimate job and family demands by filtering and interpreting their experiences and exigencies through different cultural models of the meaning of work and of family. Individuals are in fact not separate and distinct from job and family demands. It is overly simplistic to say that people "juggle" or "negotiate" work and family obligations as if their identities were distinct from the work or family to which they are responding.[7]

Of course some behavior is strategic, and some is reactive, but the way people grapple with work-family conflict is more complex than that. Work-family balance is not merely an economic equation, weighing the family's need to pay the bills against a child's needs for time with a parent. Work-family conflict is not only an individual struggle to balance an employer's demands with a spouse's demands.

This book argues that, at its heart, work-family conflict is not merely an economic or a cognitive tug-of-war. Instead, work and family responsibilities define, for many adults, our deepest social and personal identities. Work-family issues are fundamentally rooted in shared, powerful, cultural understandings. To confront work-family conflict is to grapple with profound issues of moral commitments and social and individual identity, as shaped by the cultures and communities in which we are immersed. This book portrays women actively embracing, rejecting, and reformulating normative and emotional definitions of who they should be.

Work-family balance hinges on the cultural definition of what makes a meaningful and worthwhile life. Conflict between work and family is a wrenching contradiction between powerful cultural understandings of who we are as competent and moral adults. These cultural understandings shape our most personal understandings of what we owe our careers, our families, and ourselves. Moreover, these cultural models have real consequences for people's lives. They help define the expectations of employers, clients, and spouses. They shape careers, they open or close off opportunities, and they influence couples' decisions about who builds a full-time career, whether or not to have children, and who is primarily responsible for family caregiving.

Schemas of Devotion

This book analyzes work-family conflict in terms of cultural schemas. In my usage, schemas are the shared cultural models we employ to make sense of the world. These schemas are frameworks for viewing, filtering, understanding, and evaluating what we know as reality. Constructed by societies over time, they gradually become largely unquestioned. Schemas are objective in the sense of being shared, publicly available understandings. They shape social structure, the patterns and activities of groups and individuals in institutions, firms, and families. They are also subjective and partially internalized, thereby shaping personal aspirations, identities, and desires.[8]

I focus on particularly compelling cultural models, which I call *schemas of devotion* (Blair-Loy, 2001b). These are cognitive maps that help define and organize our thoughts and assumptions. They are also moral and emotional maps: like articles of faith, they evoke intense moral and emotional commitments. The family devotion and the work devotion schemas emerged most strongly in the people I studied, but other types of devotion schemas may be more salient in other populations.[9]

I first delineate these schemas as ideal types. The term "ideal type" means abstract and general rather than preferable or perfect. These ideal types are my analytical constructions that emphasize the schema's defining characteristics.[10] The later chapters show that there are patterned variations in people's real-world understanding and use of these abstract models. Table I.1 outlines the main tenets of these schemas as ideal types.

As an ideal type, the family devotion schema assigns primary responsibility for home and family to women. It mandates a stable mar-

Table I.1 Central Tenets of the Family Devotion and Work Devotion Schemas as Ideal Types

	Family Devotion Schema	Work Devotion Schema
Hierarchical, complementary relationship between	Husband and wife	Employer/supervisor and elite employee
Mandate	Homemaking is a calling. It demands and deserves single-minded focus and allegiance.	Career is a calling. It demands and deserves single-minded focus and allegiance.
Life is meaningfully spent	Time-intensive, emotionally absorbing care for child(ren) defined as vulnerable and sacred. Also care for husband and household.	Time-intensive, emotionally absorbing dedication to employer and career advancement. Breadwinner for family.
Reciprocal relationship between schemas	Caring for husband, household, and children enables husband to fulfill work devotion schema.	Financial rewards enable wife to stay home or work part-time so she can fulfill family devotion schema.
Rewards	Fulfillment, meaning, creativity, intimacy, secure livelihood, community with other mothers.	Advancement, financial security, status, interesting work, collegiality, intensity, and transcendence.
Traditional gender of person fulfilling schema	Female	Male

riage between a man and a woman with different and complementary life callings. It promises women fulfillment, meaning, creativity, intimacy, and a secure livelihood in caring for husband and children.[11] This cultural schema prescribes a model of motherhood that is intensive, emotionally absorbing, and centered on one's precious child or children (Hays, 1996; see also Skolnick, 1991).[12]

As an abstract model, the work devotion schema, traditionally masculine, demands that one give an immense time commitment and strong emotional allegiance to one's firm or career. This model developed in part due to the pressures of capitalism but has since become semi-autonomous from economic factors and has a normative force of its own (cf. Schor, 1991). Work has become an important source of "meaning, justification, purpose and even salvation" (Hunnicutt, 1988: 313).

This cultural model is characteristic of the financial services industry studied in this book, an industry that demands extremely long hours from its most senior employees. To its devotees, the work devotion schema bestows far more than a good income. It also promises a strong sense of competence, identity, belonging, and meaning.[13] The demands of the work devotion schema make it virtually impossible for those with significant care-giving responsibilities to reach the peak positions in an organization (cf. Britton, 2000; Moen, 1992; Acker, 1990, 1992). As long as professionals were predominantly male, with a wife caring for the family at home, the family devotion schema and work devotion schemas were complementary cultural models defining the complementary institutions of the capitalist, male-dominated business firm and the nuclear family.

What happens, though, when *women* dedicate themselves to their work? When they hold professional degrees from the best schools and commit long hours to their careers over a period of many years? When women are inspired by their work and are highly invested in their firms' success? When they either choose not to have children or hire full-time caregivers to help raise them?[14]

Other researchers have characterized these women as biological females who act as "honorary" or "social men" (Heilbrun, 2001: B8; Acker, 1990: 139). Hochschild (1997) asserts that employed mothers are discovering what men have long known—that time at work is preferable to time spent at home. But these claims are so oversimplified as to be misleading. Women who have succeeded in male-dominated organizations and occupations still have to confront powerful cultural notions about what constitutes an appropriate and fulfilling life.

Rather than dismissing these women as "honorary men," I try to understand them. To comprehend fully *why* women maintain demanding careers in the first place, we need to understand the emotionally charged cultural understandings that inspire, organize, and justify work dedication as well as the conflicting cultural understandings of the importance of involved motherhood. I study how a group of exceptionally successful women interprets their world through competing cultural models of a worthwhile life.

Two Groups of Women

To study these processes, I selected two groups of women who started out as unusually career-oriented and successful. My respondents are, by definition, atypical. They are on the extreme end of the distribution of employed women. They enjoy unusually generous resources (graduate educations, autonomous and creative jobs, supervisory power, and lucrative salaries) yet face high barriers. Their jobs demand extremely long hours in a turbulent, competitive industry. Their careers have required many years of full-time dedication. Many of my respondents are the only or one of a few women at the top of their firms. Many have overcome gender discrimination to get where they are yet still feel the need to prove themselves. These women face an unusually stark conflict between career success and involved parenthood.

The extreme nature of these women's situations is useful because it highlights those cultural models—normally taken for granted and scarcely acknowledged—that organize competing loyalties to work and to family. Their predicament throws into sharp relief the work devotion schema, the family devotion schema, and the conflict between them. These cultural models, in a more diluted form, also shape the life decisions of more typical women.[15]

I conducted in-depth interviews with and collected life history questionnaires from the two groups of women. (The appendix describes the methods and sample in more detail.) To preserve confidentiality, I refer to all respondents and their family members and organizations with pseudonyms.

I call the first group the *career-committed group*. This group includes fifty-six predominantly white female finance executives who have flourished in a highly competitive industry that demands very long work hours. They are all members of a professional organization that admits only high-ranking women in finance-related fields. Most are senior employees and partners in firms that provide financial services (including investment banks, commercial banks, public accounting firms, consulting firms, brokerages, and corporate law firms). Some hold finance-related positions (for example, treasurer and chief financial officer) in companies that buy the services of financial services firms. They have all reached senior levels in their firms, and their job titles include senior vice president, chief financial officer, managing director, partner, managing partner, and chief executive officer.[16]

Since launching finance careers, no one in the career-committed group has ever stopped working for pay and only two have ever worked part time. All have bachelor degrees. Eighty-six percent have professional degrees, predominantly from elite business and law schools. Just over a third have children.

I call the second group of women the *family-committed group*. This is a sample of twenty-five white women who left full-time, promising professional careers when they had children. They left their careers after a median of nine years of full-time work as senior managers in finance, marketing, consulting, and health care, or as corporate attorneys. Thirteen had attained ranks as high as those reached by members of the first group; the others were well up the ladder but had not reached executive levels before leaving their positions. Ten women are now full-time homemakers; the others combine involved motherhood with some kind of employment. All have bachelor degrees, and 84 percent have advanced business or law degrees, again mostly from elite schools. All have one, two, or three children living at home with them.

I use the terms "career-committed" and "family-committed" to distinguish the two groups. Of course, women in the career-committed group love their families, and women in the family-committed group are also invested in paid work or volunteer pursuits. These terms do not imply a value judgment. Dedication to work and commitment to family are emotionally charged topics in American culture. My job as a social analyst is not to declare that one group is right and the other is wrong, but to analyze how these cultural schemas and the institutions they define limit and shape women's choices and their evaluations of them.

Competing Devotions to Career and Family

Coser and Coser see the firm and the family as "greedy institutions" with "omnivorous" demands for "exclusive and undivided loyalty" (Coser, 1974: 4; see also Coser and Coser, 1974). The Cosers argue that those in power in these institutions (for example, bosses or husbands) extract the scarce resources of people's time and energy by instilling and maintaining demands for loyalty and by cutting people off from competing loyalties to other institutions.[17]

I agree with the Cosers that employers and husbands benefit from their employees' or wives' devotion and that women can be devoured by greedy institutions. But I argue further that the professionals and homemakers are also actively involved in maintaining these institutions. Many of the women I interviewed give of themselves to their firms and families as a way to create fulfilling lives and to gain power and status. They also enforce this allegiance among their coworkers and subordinates or friends and neighbors.

Many of these women are inspired by and committed to their work. Their identities are forged by their interactions with colleagues and by the work itself. For example, Rachel Kahn described the excitement, community, and sense of invincibility her career provided:

> The pace, getting up in the morning with a rush of adrenaline ... Every day we'd be coming into work to do impossible things. The whole team would work to do it. And we were succeeding ... There were no barriers to what we could accomplish ... to forward the mission of the organization.

Similarly, Sarah Jacobs discussed how her work gave her a sense of identity:

> This profession gives me, in a lot of ways, a real piece of me, and the longer you do it, the more it gives you ... It's been enormously good for me and not just financially. I mean, in terms of who I think and know I am.

Yet the women interviewed also wrestle with an alternative definition of meaningful life, the magnetic pull exerted by the cultural model of devoted motherhood.

Competing devotions to career and to family are rooted in the contradictory definitions of and demands on high-level professionals and involved mothers. All the women I talked to had to confront this conflict one way or another. Almost two-thirds of the career-committed group dealt with this conflict by not having children. The family-committed group responded by leaving full-time jobs. Many of them discovered that a life dedicated to family caregiving was wonderfully rewarding. For example, Vicki Orlando's intense experience of motherhood drained her job of its meaning:

Here was this just wonderful, little person. I was totally surprised. I was not prepared for how wonderful motherhood
was . . . Yeah, I thought work was cool. I liked having secretaries
and all that money. But here's this little baby. She is also very
cool. After a year, emotionally, I didn't want to go back. I was still
nursing her.

Vicki ended up relinquishing the high-powered job she had loved.
She stayed home with her daughter for several years and then took a
much less demanding, part-time position in another organization.

About half the women in the career-committed group, like Sarah
Jacobs, continue to be proud of their career dedication. These women
tend to be those who have reached the highest levels of their organization; work devotion seems to be a cause and a consequence of career success. And about half the women in the family-committed
group, such as Vicki Orlando, remain deeply satisfied with the decision to center their lives around family.

But half the women in each group have grown ambivalent or re-
sentful about the sacrifices they have made in order to be devoted executives or devoted mothers. For many, the sense of divided loyalties
is painful. Some career-committed women mourn the children they
never had. Others, who have maintained demanding full-time careers
after their children were born, are profoundly dedicated to their work
but agonize over spending so little time with their children. Some
women in the family-committed group grieve for the careers they
have sacrificed.

Despite conflicting feelings, all the women continue to resolutely
express their dedication to career or to family. This devotion continues to give their lives meaning, both personally and as members of a
community.

For example, Rachel Kahn had loved her demanding job as president
of a mid-sized company. She also wanted children. After trying unsuc-
cessfully to conceive, she and her husband decided to adopt. Shortly af-

ter adopting one girl, they became pregnant and gave birth to another girl. Rachel then felt that her daughters needed more time with a parent. Her husband was unwilling to cut back on work, so she quit her job and set up a part-time, freelance consulting business out of the home. She is a creative, energetic, and loving mother who spends a great deal of time with her three- and four-year-old daughters. Yet she admits:

> A part of me is not totally satisfied with it. I don't devalue people who do take care of children. I admire preschool teachers immensely. But my skills are different, *my calling is different.*

In the Hebrew Bible and in traditional Protestant culture, one's calling was understood to be ordained by God. Even in secular society, a calling is a deep sense of vocation, the life task one feels particularly suited for and fulfilled by (Weber, 1958a, 1958b). Rachel's choice of words illustrates how work-family conflict can be a dilemma as deeply moral and emotional as a crisis of faith.

Later in the interview, she confesses:

> I've never hated a job as much as I hate this . . . But the quality of the kids' lives would be so different if I didn't do this. It's a decision I made when I decided to have kids . . . It's a responsibility I took on. I was not prepared for . . . this sleep deprivation, constant demands, boredom, lack of stimulation.

Transitions

Several important points are illustrated by Rachel Kahn's transition from passionate dedication to her job, to devotion to the children she had wanted so badly, to bitter resignation about her career sacrifice and the drudgery of child rearing. Rachel had invested fully in the work devotion schema, found her career immensely rewarding, and expected the same commitment from her subordinates. She strongly believed that it would be wrong to leave her children in day care for twelve hours or more a day, which her job would have required. Despite hating the life of almost full-time caregiving, she saw any other choice as morally reprehensible. She manages her grief over her lost career by offering it up as testimony of her devotion to her children. Many family-committed mothers like Rachel believe that full-time employed mothers have insulated themselves "from their hearts," walled off their children from their love, and severed themselves from their own humanity. In contrast, some career-committed mothers contend that women who abandon their careers after childbearing foster neediness in their children in order to justify their own lack of work dedication.

Rachel was resigned to the fact that her husband refused to take on more of the child rearing, due to his devotion to his own career. The family devotion schema mandates a traditional gendered division of labor, with the wives specializing in caregiving and the husbands investing in breadwinning. Most of the family-committed group thought the arrangement was based in biological predispositions. Some were angry about it, but all of them accepted it. Moreover, their husbands' work devotion paid the bills so they could dedicate themselves to their children.

In contrast to neoclassical economic theory of the family (Becker, 1981), the people in my study did not make decisions about which spouse should cut back on work to specialize in family care based on maximizing family income. When Rachel was working full-time, she was earning more than twice her physician husband's income. In fact, almost two-thirds of the women in the family-committed group had earned full-time incomes greater than or equal to their husbands'. Decisions about maximizing family utility are refracted through the devotion schemas' definitions of a moral and worthwhile life. A related finding is that many employers' decisions to risk losing their valuable executives rather than to allow them to work part-time for a reduced salary were not economically rational for the firms.[18]

The power of the devotion schemas to affect people's actions is

shown by Rachel Kahn's continuing the relationships and actions ordained by the devotion schemas, despite a private crisis of faith.[19] (In a
related finding, about half the career-committed group had seen their
work devotion flag after feeling extremely overworked or betrayed by
their employers. Yet they continued to act like devoted executives,
while they privately fantasized about one day leaving their companies
for nonprofit work or retirement.)

Finally, Rachel's comments illustrate how the actions of individuals
help reproduce a society in which talented, ambitious women continue to face a clash between cultural models of a worthwhile life. Like
many women in both groups, Rachel says, "I feel guilty whatever I do."
She cannot serve two masters. By being faithful to one devotion
schema, she betrays the other. She fears that by giving up her career,
she provides her daughters with a martyr as a role model and endan-
gers the independent, pioneering women they could grow up to be.

Chapter Overview

Chapter 1 delineates the ideal type or abstract model of the work devotion schema in more detail and shows how it is lived out in the lives
of the career-committed group. Although most women in this group
initially had fervently accepted the work devotion schema, about half
have grown skeptical of its promises. Those who continued to embrace the work devotion schema reached the very highest levels in the
group; ongoing work devotion was likely a cause and consequence of
advancement. Yet even those who became wary of or even felt betrayed by the work devotion schema continued to organize their lives
according to its dictates.

Chapter 2 delineates the ideal type of the family devotion schema
and then presents its manifestation in the lives of women in the family-
committed group. Some women joyfully carry out its dictates, while
others, like Rachel Kahn, fulfill its obligations rather grimly.

Although these devotion schemas are powerful, they are not immutable. Chapters 3 and 4 consider groups of mavericks who try to transform the work or the family devotion schema into a new cultural model.

Chapter 3 demonstrates how some women in the family-committed group have threatened the champions of work devotion by carving out part-time arrangements in their firms. These women have been treated by their employers and coworkers as heretics and barred from the firms' highest ranks. Some have even left their jobs after their bosses have indicated they would rather lose their talent and experience than tolerate part-time arrangements from senior professionals. This chapter illustrates how violators of the work devotion schema are isolated or banished, despite their economic value. The work devotion schema is tenacious, yet there is a possibility that part-time elite workers may gradually moderate the requirements of work devotion to make the schema more reconcilable with raising families.

Chapter 4 analyzes differences in career and family formation across three cohorts in the career-committed group. Members of the oldest cohort were born during the World War II era, members of the middle cohort were born during the early baby boom, and the youngest women were born during the mid–baby boom. Unlike their older colleagues, the youngest women entered career tracks that were, after the mid-1970s, at least officially, gender-blind. They dedicated themselves to their careers and married relatively late, after amassing the high incomes that gave them power in family decisions and after men had begun to share in the cultural idea of gender-egalitarianism. Unlike their older colleagues, the youngest cohort has access to new ideological and financial resources, made available by the women's movement and their own late marriages and career success. These resources enable them to revise the cultural definitions of family devotion and children's needs in ways that accommodate career commitment.

For women to maintain an intense career commitment in the face of American culture's emphasis on family devotion, they require the material resources of work experience, income, and status before marriage, and the subsequent ideological resource of an egalitarian marriage. The youngest career-committed women have also crafted a definition of children as resilient and independent, although this definition rests uneasily with their co-existent view of their children as vulnerable and deserving of a mother's care.

Chapter 5 examines why some mothers stay in demanding, executive careers, while for others childbearing leads to a turning away from full-time careers. The latter group (the family-committed women) married younger and had a shorter career tenure before marrying, on average, than the mothers in the career-committed group. Firmly establishing herself in an important career before marrying may make it less likely for a woman to leave that career after childbearing.

Moreover, before leaving their full-time careers, the family-committed group was twice as likely as the career-committed women to report that family crises had occurred. In contrast, mothers in the career-committed group, who maintained these careers after childbirth, were more than twice as likely to describe unexpected positive occurrences at work, such as a promotion. A confluence of negative work and family contingencies may help predict businesswomen's turning points out of full-time, demanding business careers. Alternatively, a different constellation of positive work events may help encourage new mothers to maintain full-time careers.

However, there is no simple formula for predicting which events will either pull a woman out of her full-time career or inoculate her against this turning point. This is because work and family contingencies are viewed through the lenses of the different devotion schemas. Women from the career-committed group, already committed to the work devotion schema, were more likely to interpret negative work and family events as less corrosive of their career commitment and less harmful to their children than were women from the family-committed group.

Chapter 5 also shows that family devotion is the default schema of even the most career-committed women in this study. The family devotion schema's prescription of work and domestic roles for men and women ensures that these women's husbands are unable or unwilling to respond to family emergencies. If unexpected crises require that family members need more nurturing than paid caregivers can provide, even the most intensely career-committed and successful women are likely to abandon the career track to provide that nurturing while their lower-paid husbands continue working. The family devotion schema imparts meaning to the women's renunciation of their careers and absolves their husbands from making a similar sacrifice. It both engineers and interprets an abrupt turn of fate.

Chapter 6 points to the broader implications of this research. It explicitly addresses and advances sociological theory on social and cultural structures, institutions, human agency, and gendered inequality. It also considers the extent to which findings from this extreme case shed light on the work and family situations of more typical Americans. More broadly, it shows how people's actions are profoundly shaped by gendered cultural schemas that organize our categories of thought, beliefs, and emotions. This chapter also discusses implications for employers and workers. It notes the ineffectiveness of work-family policies without a transformation of the work-devotion culture currently devouring American managers and executives. Finally, the appendix presents details on the samples and methods.

Overall, this book analyzes how human action is both enabled and constrained by cultural schemas within historically specific time periods. It examines the power and the limits of competing devotion schemas as resourceful women conform to, defy, or attempt to reconcile them. These schemas are in flux yet also retain a tenacious grip on our hearts and minds.

1

THE DEVOTION TO
WORK SCHEMA

Schemas of devotion promise to provide meaning to life and a secure connection to something outside ourselves. The devotion to work and the devotion to family schemas are institutionalized: they create taken-for-granted rules of thought and behavior in everyday life (Meyer and Rowan, 1977). They also inspire moral and emotional commitments.

Families and firms are "greedy institutions" (Coser, 1974). If it were just a question of survival, families and companies would not demand so much of their members. They do so based on cultural schemas that give life structure and meaning. For example, a household of biologically related individuals does not inherently require an adult, usually a wife, to give most of her time and energy to her spouse and children. The schema of devotion to the family is a white and middle-class cultural model, rooted in the nineteenth century and flowering in the postwar baby boom era, specifying that it is desirable and worthwhile for women to spend most of their adult lives intensively caring for their families.

Similarly, one may work in a firm in order to earn money to live, but biological survival does not require sixty-plus-hour workweeks, all-night negotiations, extensive travel, or the willingness to use social connections for business ends. This is a middle-class, traditionally masculine, twentieth-century, urban model of an upwardly mobile managerial career (Whyte, 1956). "In the midst of organizations supposedly designed around the specific and limited contractual relationships of a bureaucracy, managers may face, instead, the demand for personal attachment and a generalized, diffuse, unlimited commitment" (Kanter, 1977: 63).

To comprehend *why* people launch and maintain demanding careers in the first place, we need to study the cultural understandings that inspire, organize, and justify career dedication. Without an analysis of powerful and partially internalized cultural schemas, we cannot fully understand why senior and autonomous professionals feel compelled to devote very long hours to their jobs.[1] As highly successful, career-committed women, female finance executives let us see the cultural schema of work devotion in its most distilled form.[2]

I examine work devotion as a cultural schema that orients female executives toward a preoccupation with their own advancement, defines their priorities, and evokes a passion for their careers. In contrast to scholars who emphasize employment as a domain of autonomy and independence (for example, Gerson, 2002) or commodification, the women I interviewed find work to be a site of intense relationships and personal transformation. The work devotion schema is the ideal dimension of social structure, the symbolic aspect of the institution of the capitalist firm (Sewell, 1992; Friedland and Alford, 1991). It gives meaning to and is shaped by the material dimension of the firm—the resources and patterned relationships of evaluation, compensation, and promotion.

First, I describe the work devotion schema as an ideal type or abstract model, my analytical construction of the schema's defining characteristics. Next I show how it actually inspires and makes sense of career-committed women's lives. Then I consider what happens when firms break their implicit promises to executives, and why some women continue to have faith in the schema while others grow disenchanted. This analysis reveals how the work devotion schema is interwoven into the organizational structures of advancement and reward.

Work Devotion Schema as an Ideal Type

For managers and executives, the work devotion schema is the symbolic dimension of the late twentieth–early twenty-first-century American capitalist firm. This cultural definition is buttressed by material resources and patterns of relationships. At a general level, long work hours among professionals are supported by the 1938 Fair Labor Standards Act, which distinguished between hourly workers, eligible for overtime pay, and salaried workers, who are exempt from this extra compensation (Schor, 1991; Jacobs and Gerson, 1998). This law, combined with high salaries and expensive benefits, created a broad economic incentive for employers to hire fewer elite workers and expect them to work longer hours.[3] Assessing elite employees by the "face time" they put in (Fried, 1998; see also Hochschild, 1997) or by the number of "billable hours" charged to particular clients (Epstein et al., 1995) reinforces the expectation. The fear of losing out in a competitive and turbulent economy compounds this pressure.

However, this model of intensive work commitment has become semi-autonomous from purely economic considerations and plays an analytically distinct role in shaping people's understandings and actions (Wuthnow, 1996; cf. Schor, 1991; Hunnicut, 1988). At the same time, the cultural definition of work devotion remains empirically linked to a firm's practices of evaluation, compensation, and advancement. I illustrate this later in the chapter by showing that the career-committed women at the pinnacle of their organizations tend to be the most zealous disciples of work devotion. Firm resources flow to those with the most devotion, and their devotion is reinforced by the firm's faithfulness. The work devotion schema makes executives' long hours meaningful. It defines what executive careers should be like and what, for the most successful respondents, these careers *are* like.

In other words, people who are preoccupied with career advancement rely on a shared schema to tell them that these concerns are meaningful and worthwhile. In his study of the lives of middle managers, Robert Jackall points out that "striving for success is, of course, a moral imperative in American society. In the corporate world, this means moving up or getting ahead in the organization" (1988: 43). The work devotion schema articulates this moral imperative that orients managers toward concern with their own advancement.

As a general model or ideal type, the work devotion schema implies a relationship between employer and manager, in which the manager's allegiance will be rewarded with upward mobility, financial security, a positive sense of identity and recognition from peers, challenging and autonomous work, collegiality, and even transcendence. This schema shapes respondents' objective job descriptions and opportunities at the same time as it influences their ambitions and desires. The schema creates normative expectations among managers and employers. It is assumed to operate until it is violated.

Devotion is generally first induced early in a manager's career by the employer's demands for wholehearted allegiance. If the manager provides allegiance and proves her trustworthiness, the firm will reward her with salary raises, promotions, and social status.[4]

As the organization bestows more rewards, it also makes increasing demands. Promotion into senior levels brings managers into the organization's elite corps and gives them responsibility for leading the organization toward its goals. As the senior manager continues to express fealty to the firm, she receives growing rewards, including increasingly challenging and autonomous work. These responsibilities may require longer hours and closer involvement with colleagues and clients. Her work may take on a single-minded, emotional intensity that fuses personal and professional goals and inspires her to meet these goals. In some cases, this intensively devoted work and close association with colleagues allow her to lose herself in her work and at the same time induce a powerful sense of transcendence.[5]

The work devotion schema serves the employer's economic interests, which are more or less tightly linked with those of senior managers through bonuses, stock options, or shares. Yet the devotion schema has a power beyond motivating productivity or veiling exploitation. The schema supports some behavior that actually contradicts economic rationality. For example, many firms are willing to tolerate high turnover among senior women rather than allow senior executives to violate the work devotion ethos by working part-time. All career-committed respondents seemed to incorporate some version of the schema initially. In about half of these cases, their devotion to work has strengthened over time and has been amply rewarded. Their commitment remains firm.

In other cases, the centrality of the work devotion schema is most apparent when it is violated. Some employers break the schema's promises, such as by demoting a partner or laying off an executive during a lean year. Coworkers can betray an executive's trust. Sometimes firms simply demand too much and exhaust a manager's dedication. Because the work devotion schema is central in organizing the executive's role, its fracture can be devastating.

Elements of Work Devotion

The central elements of the ideal-typical devotion to work schema are the senior manager's *allegiance* to the firm, the firm's *provision of an array of rewards,* the *intensity* and evocation of a sense of *transcendence,* and the senior manager's *single-mindedness* about her responsibilities.

Allegiance

Martha Ungbarsky, the CFO of an investment bank, expressed her allegiance to her firm with hard work, long hours, and fidelity: "I devoted my life to my career . . . I don't have any other commitments." Alice Witt, a senior vice president at another investment bank, says that management is expected to signal allegiance by financially investing in the firm: "I'm a stockholder in the firm. Whenever you become a

VP, you start owning stock. Owning it is supposed to be a good thing. You show your confidence in the firm."

Allegiance can also entail a loss of geographic freedom. Relocations are common among the women I interviewed. For example, Amy Peterson, then a partner at one of the largest public accounting firms, was asked to relocate from a small city to New York City, where there was a need for her specialty. She felt compelled to go, even though she and her husband were "outdoorsy people" and hated to leave their beloved rural estate and farm animals:

> So they said, we really want you to go to New York . . . I went there kind of almost feeling I had to . . . You can say no maybe once or twice but then basically they'll say, if you don't go where we need you, it's not in the spirit of partnership, and maybe you should think about doing something else . . . My career was the most important thing to me at the time, so we left.

She dragged her husband off to New York with her, where they both felt unhappily constricted by the urban lifestyle.

Rewards

For senior executives, allegiance to employer and career promises a multiplicity of rewards. Respondents appreciate their jobs' financial compensation as well as value rewards more intrinsic to the work itself.

Financial Security and Independence

Financial rewards play a large part in respondents' decisions to enter and to stay in finance-related occupations. These rewards are generous. Career-committed women in for-profit firms earned $125,000 to $1,000,000 in 1993.[6] In past years, some made millions from the sale of stock; others look forward to future wealth when they sell current stock holdings. Monetary rewards are important in other ways as well. Money does far more than provide a comfortable life. It also promises security in a chaotic world, cements one's membership in a high status group, and provides a secure retirement. Many respondents cherish their incomes because these incomes give them independence from men who might otherwise limit their autonomy. Women from the first cohort (born around World War II) and the second cohort (early baby boomers) were more likely than younger women to explain their decision to move into a lucrative career by their wish to avoid financial dependence on a man.

For example, the general manager of a financial services company, Louise Finch, ruefully remembered her economic dependence on her former husband while she earned a masters degree in library science in the late 1960s. "I had to ask my husband for money during my masters program. I will never do that again. I will never be a vulnerable person again." Similarly, the corporate attorney Sarah Jacobs remembers how she had chafed under her former husband's control over finances:

> I hated having someone tell me what I can spend or not spend or ask me if I balanced his checkbook. Or said, gee, it's too much money to spend X on a blouse. Or, why didn't you go to seven different stores for a refrigerator where you could have gotten it cheaper? I consider that a basic element of control.

Leaving her husband and advancing her career were interrelated actions that led to her financial independence and "control" over her life.

Management consultant Mindy Stone still shudders when she remembers her mother's economic vulnerability after her parents' marriage ended. She shudders more violently when she recollects her own past economic dependence on a deteriorating marriage while she took a long, unpaid maternity leave.

> He moved out, but he still paid the bills. He could always threaten not paying them or paying them late; he used that as a stick . . . But after several months, I really wanted a divorce. It became a dependency thing. I was dependent on him. This was absolutely what I had wanted to avoid.

The incomes produced by finance-related jobs were valued as protection from men using their economic power "as a stick" to limit the women's autonomy. While executive men as well as women presumably value the consumer goods, high social status, and comfortable retirement that a high income buys, women particularly cherish the resulting freedom from patriarchal authority.

Status

Respondents frequently reported the desire for promotion to a higher level in the company. For instance, Penny Smith, now partner in a national public accounting firm, recalls being motivated by the hope of making partner and by enjoying the status of a recognized expert.

> After I reached the manager level, I saw making partner was a possibility, and I worked my buns off. I was very determined . . . Once you start to specialize and learn an industry, you really get tied up in it. It becomes a big part of you . . . I gave speeches and wrote articles. It's an ego thing, it gives you good self-esteem, if people see you as a recognized expert.

The desire for prestige may be common among men and women. But the desire to be recognized as an expert with her own achieved social status may have more salience for women, who traditionally have made do with the reflected social status of the men in their life.

For example, Laurie Goodman, a former treasurer of a Fortune 500 company, discussed how she had been motivated throughout her career by the desire for status and recognition.

> It seems that for an awful lot of my career, I was fighting to get recognition and fighting to get the promotions and fighting to get ahead. When I became treasurer of United Foods, it was great fun when people would say: "And what do you do?" And I would say: "I'm the treasurer of United Foods." And they'd go: "*The* treasurer?"
> You know, it was an impressive position, and you could see that in the reaction people gave you. I felt like I finally made it . . . I felt like I had gotten to the point where people had to recognize that I was an important person like the guy next to me was important, a senior executive kind of thing.

Senior jobs in finance-related fields accorded these women respect and an achieved status. This recognition was not based on being a prominent man's wife or secretary but on being important oneself, "like the guy next to me was important, a senior executive."

Similarly, Sarah Jacobs contrasts her work as a mother in which "ultimately, the child's success is his own, not yours," with her work as a celebrated corporate attorney, in which her achievements are hers alone. Her career represents her independent accomplishment. "It is my space. It is my alley. This career is mine and no one else can own it, only I can own it, and I needed that." Sarah elaborates further on the importance of professional recognition:

> With all the therapy I've been through, [I realize that] you're supposed to feel terrific within yourself. But it helps that outside people sort of recognize your professional accomplishments. Pat you on the head and say you're really good . . . In business, the gratification is much more constant [than one gets in motherhood]. The other lawyers think you're fabulous. The

clients think you're fabulous. Fabulous deals have been brought
into the city and you're the attorney chosen to do it.

A successful career constitutes a sphere in which respondents' identities are not defined by their relation to family members. It is a sphere
in which their triumphs are their own.

Challenging Work and Exciting Opportunities

Respondents frequently mention the interesting opportunities that
their companies provide them. Their hard work is rewarded by more
hard work, but it is work they find interesting and absorbing. For instance, one partner in a financial services firm told me about her
rapid advancement:

> It couldn't have been any faster. Virtually every opportunity is
> available. It's a meritocracy. By your own hard work you can
> prosper. My first year, one of the younger male partners gave me
> a lot of opportunities. He sent me out there to sink or swim. It
> was a terrific opportunity . . . There's enough newness in this
> work that it keeps it intellectually challenging. You can't find in a
> book how to do this deal. Instead there are these personalities
> and these goals.

Autonomy and creativity are also valued rewards. A banker explains what she likes most about her job: "I like the variety, the creativity, the independence. The fact that our work is discretionary. We
self-determine the best way to meet our general objectives." Alice
Witt, a senior vice president in an investment bank, initially fantasized about quitting her job and living full time in her lakefront vacation home. When I asked her what keeps her from doing that, she
said: "When all is said and done, I like having an interesting and challenging job to go to every day." Similarly, Dorothy Jones, the treasurer

of a Fortune 500 company said, "I basically do my own thing. There's a lot of creativity on the job. I like the idea of being considered the authority in my area for this company."

Collegiality and Community

Several women discussed how much they enjoyed the time they spent with their coworkers. According to Frances Swing, a Fortune 500 vice president, organizations exist so that people can be in relationship with other people. She said: "Emotional capital, relationships—that's why organizations exist. Otherwise, we'd all be at home with our faxes and our modems. That's why people want to work in organizations." Workplace relations were not always auspicious for respondents but when positive, they were highly appreciated.

Yvonne Smith glowingly described the colleagues she had in her previous organization: "It was the best group of people I ever worked with: smart, aggressive, open-minded. It was great." The people I interviewed also derived satisfaction from their connection to clients. For example, one banker described her relationships with long-term clients as "the great satisfaction of this practice. Keeping involved with their businesses and getting to know them well. You form fun, gratifying relationships." Another banker told me that she became personally invested in her clients and in the success of their businesses. She considered herself the "defender" of certain clients to whom she had become "personally attached."

Intensity and Sense of Transcendence

The rewards associated with elite jobs do not do justice to the compelling nature and the emotional charge of the schema of devotion to work. Rather than simply appreciating the status that their jobs accord, some women invest themselves completely toward the goal of promotion. More than just enjoying their challenging tasks, some respondents speak of being thrilled by their work. Rather than merely valuing their workplace colleagues, some feel urgently committed to those colleagues and to the firm's success.

In short, intensity is another key element of the work devotion schema. Intensity is the emotional quality, the lifeblood, that makes the rewards of status, challenge, and collegiality so compelling. Respondents describe the emotional charge to the long hours and hard work they give their employers. They speak of being "totally consumed by" their work; they cite their "drive" to be promoted. Intensity evokes the torch of excitement that fuses corporate and personal goals and the rush of adrenaline that rouses the energy to meet these goals. Carol Baker, an investment firm president, said, "I find the stock market absolutely thrilling. I really love it."

Public accounting firm partner Amy Peterson reported that her hard work was motivated by a "consuming drive" to make partner. She describes an intense, exciting workplace environment: "You work really hard, and it's a cultural thing too. There's an adrenaline flow and there's a big deal going on. It's much more than a job and it demands much more than a job." The corporate culture consumed her but also held out the promise of a new, exalted identity, that of partner in the firm.

Rachel Kahn, a family-committed group member who left her job as executive director of a large HMO when she had children four years ago, also uses the adrenaline metaphor to describe what she misses most about her former position.

> The pace, getting up in the morning with a rush of adrenaline . . . Every day we'd be coming into work to do impossible things. The whole team would work to do it. And we were succeeding . . . There were no barriers to what we could accomplish . . . to forward the mission of the organization.

She personally received "positive feedback" at work that was intimately connected to fulfilling the "mission of the organization." The fused goals of personal and corporate fulfillment were realized through her connection to her "team." Working together, she and her colleagues transcended limits and accomplished seemingly impossible tasks.

Another family-committed group member, Yvonne Smith, recalled the intensity of the career she recently relinquished to care for her children. She remembered long hours, stimulating work, and plenty of opportunity.

> I was there Christmas Eve day until 7 P.M. I was usually there until 11 P.M. I worked all the time. I was very challenged, stimulated. I had a lot of drive and ambition . . . I got promoted very early . . . I always found a lot of career success, a lot of attention and credibility.

But Yvonne Smith describes her career as more than simply garnering the rewards of challenge, promotions, and recognition. She characterizes her career as ecstatic. At mid-career, Yvonne left the Fortune 500 company she worked for to become general manager and president of a small company.

> [When I joined the company,] it was a $200,000 business in sales. I built it up to a $3,500,000 company in three years . . . We had a really fun team. It was complete euphoria. I used all my skills. That's the most fun you can ever have, running your own small business. We were a cohesive group . . . I worked with some very impressive women. It was a fun, great group.

Her job claimed all her talent, energy, and dedication. In return it gave her the euphoria of successfully working with like-minded devotees toward a common goal.

The schema of devotion to work contains within it a compelling normative force and a promise to bring the worker into a communion with like-minded believers. The descriptions from Rachel Kahn,

Yvonne Smith, and others describe the emotional charge, the euphoria, and the sense of transcendence realized in a group of people intensely working toward a common end. These reports are similar to Emile Durkheim's classic account of the religious ceremony of Australian native groups, in which "the very fact of the concentration acts as an exceptionally powerful stimulant" and the participants are raised to a level of exaltation (Durkheim, 1965: 246–247). My respondents credit the group dynamism and cohesiveness for their tremendous success. Rachel Kahn's colleagues came together every day "to do impossible things . . . there were no barriers to what we accomplished . . . to forward the mission of the organization." Yvonne Smith's company grew by a factor of seventeen in under four years. Their association with their colleagues "raises [them] outside of [themselves]" into an "environment filled with exceptionally intense forces" that transform and empower them (Durkheim, 1965: 465, 250).

Renowned rainmaker Sarah Jacobs explained her meteoric rise to the partner status in a prestigious law firm by citing her intense effort ("I busted my ass") and her sociable connection to business associates. The long hours she put in were as vital for cementing relations with colleagues and clients as for the number of deals she closed. Her drive was based on more than personal ambition. In the law firm, she discovered a mentor to revere and new facets of an identity to cultivate:

> I really worshiped my mentor . . . [When I made partner,] it was thrilling . . . This profession gives me, in a lot of ways, a real piece of me and the longer you do it, the more it gives you . . . It's been enormously good for me and not just financially. I mean, in terms of who I think and know I am.

Sarah admits that she thinks her work is "sometimes obsessive." Yet it is an obsession that makes sense in light of the schema of devotion to work. In immersing herself in the long hours and intense, sometimes worshipful relationships, Sarah says she has been given "a real piece of me." In losing herself in her work, she has found herself. In Durkheim's words, Sarah Jacobs feels "dominated and carried away by some sort of external power which makes [her] think and act differently"; she believes she has become "a new being" (Durkheim, 1965: 249).

Vicki Orlando, a family-committed group member now home full time, had a litigation practice in a large, corporate law firm.

> My job was terrific. My mentor was very smart. He was also demanding. He gave you a lot of responsibility. Those years, they were very intense years . . . People were winning and losing all the time. I decided I had to start winning from day one.

Her job was "terrific" and "intense." She also earned a lot of money for her firm. In a whirl of activity, she won several cases. The intensity strand of the devotion to work schema provides the sense of urgency in meeting the demands of the job. "I was simply exhausted for years. I kept going with caffeine." Her employer's demands had become incorporated into her demands of herself. She says:

> I was a compulsive overachiever. All the strokes were there for me. I was performing for everybody—the evaluation committee, my mentor. It was my highest hour . . . All I knew is that I was working hard and that I was succeeding.

Reminiscent of Sarah Jacobs' description of her work involvement as sometimes "obsessive," Vicki looks back on her litigation practice as "compulsive" overachievement. But like Sarah Jacobs' obsession with work, Vicki Orlando's compulsion makes sense when seen through the lens of the devotion to work schema. At the time that she was practicing law, she regarded her work as more than intense, stimulating, and all enveloping; she also found it transcendent. Her professional achievements enabled and legitimated her personal success. It was her "highest hour."

Single-mindedness

The schema of devotion to work stands in tension with other commitments. Allegiance to a job with extreme demands required Vicki Orlando to maintain a single-minded focus on her professional responsibilities.

> My husband [at the time] and I both worked very hard . . . All our friends were in the office. We had no other interests. We worked on Saturdays and were exhausted on Sundays. It was a totally stimulating and all encompassing job . . . You have no casual clothes because you are never casual. You don't read. Holidays are a nuisance because you have to stop working. I remember being really annoyed when it was Thanksgiving. Damn, why did I have to stop working to go eat a turkey? I missed my favorite uncle's funeral, because I had a deposition scheduled that was too important.

Within the "stimulating and all encompassing" perspective of the devotion to work schema, hobbies, holidays, and even deaths in the family become nuisances. Vicki, who had been an English literature major, stopped reading for pleasure. Any nonwork activities paled in significance compared to her pressing professional responsibilities. She also shielded herself from all nonwork obligations. She was childless at that time and paid others to handle the mundane details of living.

> Money helps too. It insulates you from chores. You don't go food shopping. Someone comes and picks up the dry cleaning. Secretaries handle a lot. I was able to function like a man with a wife at home. I would be so exhausted if I had to do housework or buy groceries.

This single-minded focus on work is an experience generally reserved for males in her social class "with a wife at home."[7]

Like all other career-committed women, Vicki Orlando could only sustain her career by contracting out household chores to others. Two-thirds of the work-committed group did not have children; their work commitment remains undivided. Those who are mothers subcontract out childcare labor to others so they can fulfill the demands of work devotion. For example, Harriet Simpson, a managing partner in a large law firm, maintained: "I started from the premise that I had to have a full time, live-in childcare person. When Elizabeth was little, we had a live-in nanny, always." Law firm partner Anne Fogelquist stated in a matter-of-fact tone: "I see my [eighteen-month-old] daughter for fifteen minutes before I leave. Her care giver comes in, and I head for the train." Anna Lake, a managing director of a real estate investment company, said: "My husband and I go through some periods of intense work schedules. We are thinking about hiring someone to take over for the nanny when we can't get back in time."

The actions of the mother who sees her baby for fifteen minutes in the morning and the parents who hire a babysitter to relieve their full-time nanny make sense in light of the devotion to work schema. In the past, men commonly justified their absence from the home by the social legitimacy of their bread-winning role and their vocational calling. Now some executive women are doing the same thing.

Critiques of the Work Devotion Schema

All respondents in the work-committed group *initially* shared some version of the devotion to work schema. For about half of these women, their fidelity has been generously rewarded and their commitment to their firms has grown over time. However, the other half of the career-committed group has seen one or more strands of the schema broken. Their dedication has either turned to ambivalence or, in the case of six women, completely soured.[8] The disillusioned women explained their feelings to me in terms of fatigue, deteriorating rewards, disenchantment with top management's practical ethics, or experiences of rejection or betrayal.

Fatigue

Older respondents were most likely to be exhausted by years of hard work. For example, a banker in her fifties complains: "I'm burned out at work . . . It might be fun to do more playing and less working." Although these women dream about the time when they can do more "playing," they admit they will probably give several more years of hard work to their organizations. The schema of devotion to work is not easily abandoned.

Environmental Turbulence and Deteriorating Rewards

In addition to being wearied by long hours, some respondents maintained that their businesses were becoming more grueling in an increasingly competitive industry. For instance, Ursula Mann, a managing director of national repute in a large consulting company, groped for her coffee cup at our early breakfast meeting.

> I worked until 11:30 last night and the night before . . . [Working until] 10:00 or 10:30 is not uncommon. Our business is not nearly as much fun as it once was . . . [Our potential clients are] constantly out shopping for services, which means you get a lot of chances to bid on stuff, but also, you're always being bid against, so you're spending a lot of time writing proposals. You're getting half as much money or a third as much money for the work you're doing than you did a few years ago . . . You're getting a lot less money for doing the work. It's really making people tired.

Ursula continued:

Also, the consulting firms have been shrinking because of the [smaller profit] margin and, with the firms shrinking, a lot of them, then you end up with some downsizing, you end up with everybody stabbing everybody's back . . . [People are thinking:] "If somebody's going to go, I want it to be you, not me." It seems like, generally, in our industry, it's just in a very tough time, and it's had its toll on a lot of people.

Although Ursula continues to offer her firm hard work and long hours, the work devotion schema's promised rewards of income, security, and collegiality are diminishing. In response, her commitment is waning, and she fantasizes about leaving the firm to teach in a university.

I heard several refrains of Ursula's story of writing more proposals for less business and working harder for fewer dollars. The past twenty-five years have seen many mergers and acquisitions among companies, a corporate real estate recession, a stock market crash, increased competition from globalization and technological advances, and continued industry consolidation.[9] All of these developments reduce the client base of consulting, public accounting, and other service firms. They also make surviving clients anxious to pay lower fees for their services.

Disenchantment

As some respondents have ascended the ranks of the corporation, they have become disillusioned with what they regard as the values of those running the firms. I illustrate with Angela Rossi who had followed her original boss, Tom, from firm to firm until she worked for him as a managing director of a large bank. These geographic and organizational relocations helped her land on her feet in a turbulent industry and also underscore her loyalty to her boss (cf. Roper, 1994). During our interview, she told her secretary to hold all calls "except from Tom." Tom did call, apparently to chat about a coworker. When Angela was not speaking to Tom during the interview, she spoke a great deal about him. For her to talk about her career was to talk about Tom. Late in the interview, she mused that her loyalty to her boss is not fully reciprocated.

> I've gotten close to the top of the organization, and I'm not sure I like what I see. Nothing grossly illegal but immoral . . . My boss [Tom] is one of five men at the top. They are all incredibly ambitious. My boss would go to bat for me as long as he didn't put himself at risk. I have a hard time with that from a moral perspective. I don't always see them doing the right thing. They rationalize it.

It is growing harder for her to tolerate having her dedication repaid with Tom's unwavering concern for his own interests. She has become "less trusting" and more politically astute but is unwilling to adopt the ethical worldview she witnesses at the pinnacle of the organization. She hopes to be "financially secure" enough in the next five years to leave the bank for a nonprofit organization.

Lisa Mignetti is an example of someone who stopped climbing the organization because she did not like the view emerging from the heights. She explained why she left her position as vice president at a Fortune 500 company to start her own consulting business:

> After you get to a certain level, it's not developing the best strategic plan, it's the sheer competitiveness of it—who can kill everyone else. You have to be able to devote everything to the company. Most women are not willing to do that.

Lisa discusses a growing disenchantment with the political maneuvering and stark competition required to get and keep power in the corporation. She says that once she had proven she could achieve a certain stature in the organization, the job's generous financial compensation lost its allure.

Are women more likely than men to become disillusioned? In other words, is this process of disenchantment gendered? Lisa Mignetti contends that most women are unwilling "to devote everything to the company." Yet we have seen numerous examples of women who have fully embraced the work devotion schema. When I asked Lisa whether she thought there were gender differences in corporate disillusionment, she said:

> Men derive a lot of their self-esteem from their position and title. Women are less inclined to do that. I get adequate self-esteem from knowing that I do a good job. I only want enough money to live well. I don't need a million dollars each year. But men think the size of their penis is equal to the size of their paycheck. Symbols are more important to them.

She believes that women are less likely than men to be seduced by the notion that the work devotion schema's rewards of income and status are worth any sacrifice.

Several critics of the work devotion schema generalize their own skepticism to the entire female gender:

> Women's values are more multi-dimensional. Women need more than just financial success to be happy. Men see that as women being less committed. Women see it as being more balanced.

In contrast, others maintain that women's "balance" and lack of total commitment to the firm is a consequence, not a cause, of their trouble reaching top positions. For example:

> When you keep banging your head against the wall and working as hard as you can, you're totally consumed and driven and you

don't get the rewards that a lot of men get, it causes you to become "balanced" much more quickly.

Executive vice president Audrey Weyler remarked that women, unlike middle class men, have more of a choice about whether they want
demanding careers: "Men don't think about it. They keep on plug-
ging." In contrast to manhood, womanhood has not traditionally
been defined by the devotion to work schema; women thus have the
potential for more cultural leeway to question and to reject it (cf.
Fiorentine, 1987).

Yet the women who have done the cultural work to embrace the
work schema, despite its traditional lack of fit, and who have resisted
the temptation of the devotion to family schema, are among the work
schema's most enthusiastic adherents. Although some female critics
of the work devotion schema may derive critical insight from their social experiences of being female, I suspect that most women executives may be more faithful to the schema than their male counterparts
because they have sacrificed more for it.

Rejection and Betrayal

Some executives wholeheartedly devote themselves to their organizations and are repaid by being cheated, laid off, or subjected to discrimination or sexual harassment. A few respondents reported being
defrauded by employers or business partners. For example, Cornelia
Runge had been a junior partner in a real estate development company. When the company was sold a few years ago, the senior partner
absconded without returning the junior partners' investments.

Most of the older women and some of the younger women had stories of explicit or implicit gender discrimination. The most traumatic
episodes occurred when women were faithfully serving their companies and were then blindsided with an unexpected rejection. For
example, Jane Buckingham began working at a national public accounting firm in the late 1960s. She had worked hard, relocated to a

new city upon request, and anticipated further promotions. Eleven years later, her career was derailed when she was denied consideration for partner. She explained:

> I'd been at the public accounting firm for eleven years and done exemplary work. My evaluations were always excellent. I would've been the first woman partner in my division. They weren't ready for it. After you'd been manager there for four to five years, they'd tell you whether you'd be partner material. One year before I would've been admitted, they took my name off the list. They said I "lacked interpersonal skills." In other words, I wore a skirt to work. I had no idea this was going to happen. I felt like I was kicked in the stomach.

Jane Buckingham had been playing by the rules of the devotion to work schema. She gave her company dedicated and "exemplary" work; they gave her "excellent" evaluations, raises, and promotions. A year before she expected to be named the first female partner in her division, the firm suddenly decided she lacked the "interpersonal skills" to become partner and fired her.[10]

If we generally accept Jane Buckingham's interpretation of these events, the firm's discriminatory actions in the late 1970s are not particularly surprising. What is most striking about the story is Jane's behavior and emotions: her complete dedication to the firm, astonishment at being rejected due to her gender, and subsequent anguish and embitterment.

A decade later, she took a job as the chief financial officer (CFO) of a bank known for its frequent reorganization of senior management. When she was fired this time, she was neither astonished nor anguished. She reported:

> One day the CEO got tired of me and fired me. This time I was not a victim. I called my lawyer, and we took him to the cleaners. My experience at the public accounting firm taught me that you

had to be in charge of your life. I used to think of the firm as a family. That's what they tell you. Baloney. They will take your twelve years and then you're out on the street. I learned that I would never be a helpless victim again, and I'd never expect a company to take care of me. Big companies are shit places to work, whether you are a man or a woman.

Jane Buckingham had already learned to be skeptical of the devotion to work schema's promises. This time she responded to the firm's rejection not with gut-wrenching distress but with a counterattack. Because her gender seemed to be irrelevant to losing the CFO position, her critique of the devotion to work schema has broadened to a denouncement of all large firms as "shit places to work" for women and for men.

While her boss's fickleness reportedly cost Jane Buckingham her CFO job, broader economic trends also contribute to firms' failure to keep the promises of the work devotion schema. We saw earlier that Ursula Mann, a nationally prominent managing director of a consulting company, has so far weathered her consulting firm's contraction in the late 1980s and early 1990s. Yet she acknowledges that downsizing and backstabbing have taken their "toll on a lot of people." Shrinking revenues in service firms can be devastating for more vulnerable managers.

To illustrate, Amy Peterson was a young rising star at a Big Six public accounting firm until she was demoted from partner to manager during the economically troubled early 1990s. She was among numerous new partners who were demoted during that time. She maintains that, in a competitive environment, public accounting firms no longer make good on their implicit promise of financial rewards and secure partnership in exchange for intensive work.

Public accounting firms really count on promises of big rewards, probably to middle class people who had never dreamt of making that much money in their life. And so you work really hard . . . When the recession hit, the social contract was clearly broken . . . It was naive of me to have thought that if I did a really good job and did everything the firm wanted, that they would take care of me . . . I think the goal that all of us were willing to put in all those crazy hours for was joining the club [partnership] with the assumption that once you were in, it was a lifetime membership . . . After working so hard to achieve a goal, you think you're entering this club and you realize that you've entered a pool of sharks.

Rather than accepting her fate as due to an economically troubled industry, Amy Peterson blames the greed of the firm's senior partners. What stung most was her realization that she had sacrificed so much of her life to join the elite ranks of an organization that turned out to be run by "sharks and cannibals." She discovered that her own contributions were irrelevant to the success of the organization and that she was deemed expendable by the partners in charge, who remained primarily interested in making "more than they ever made before."

Women may generally be more vulnerable than men to losing their positions in a contracting industry (cf. Epstein et al., 1995). Amy Peterson argues that male senior partners tend to be more comfortable mentoring other men (cf. Kanter, 1977). Her lack of guidance and personal ties to powerful partners left her more vulnerable in an increasingly competitive environment. Because building extensive networks, establishing trust, and working intensively with coworkers and clients are such crucial parts of the job, the lack of solid workplace relationships hurts women professionally (Blair-Loy, 2001a).

Four respondents discussed experiences of unwelcome sexual attention from male bosses. This recently happened to the only female senior colleague of an investment banker named Alice Witt. According to Alice, her colleague was even more devastated by her colleagues' lack of support for her afterward than by the harassment incident itself. The CEO gave her harasser a medical leave of absence and asked the woman not to discuss the incident with anyone, and she said nothing. However, Alice continued:

> But the guy [the harasser] called everyone in the group and trashed her. So now, she said, many people in her group don't talk to her. Monday she told me she was going to resign today, after her horrible year. I felt so bad. She could have sued the hell out of the firm. She just wanted to do her job, and now she's the victim, and she has to leave. Either you report it and you have to leave, or you don't report it and you have to leave. I felt bad—angry, sick. She became aware of four others who had been harassed . . . You go along and you think: "This is pretty good. I'm well liked by management." Well, don't kid yourself.

Assuming that this account is reasonably accurate, it is not particularly surprising that an incident of sexual harassment occurred. What is striking are the actions and emotions of the harassment victim and the narrator. After experiencing the harassment and the CEO's lukewarm response, Alice Witt's colleague reportedly continued to subscribe to the devotion to work schema. She wanted to be a "good corporate citizen," part of the team, and just do her work. It was not until well after the episode, when the team stopped speaking to her, that she resigned. The worst aspect of her "horrible year" was not the harassment incident *but rather the experience of being rejected by her colleagues.* Alice's response to the story is to feel "bad—angry, sick." Like Jane Buckingham's sense of being kicked in the stomach when she was denied consideration for partner, Alice is sickened and surprised at the corporate community's disloyalty.

Most older respondents and some younger ones have experienced episodes of a marked lack of welcome from their male colleagues, such as being excluded from business golf outings or finding a rotting fish waiting in a desk drawer upon return from vacation. When this lack of acceptance occurs, it damages women's prospects for developing and maintaining business. It also engenders feelings of loneliness and deprives women of the reward of collegiality.

Ambivalence

The demoted public accountant Amy Peterson asks, "are you willing to give up personal and family and other interests for a reward that is not very solid any more?" For about a third of the career-committed group, the answer to that is equivocal. Their ambivalence was most apparent when I asked about future plans. For instance, Audrey Weyler said:

> Realistically, I don't see myself working here at 50. I'll only do this for five more years and then I'll pursue some non-paying endeavors. It's too bad. There are people here looking at me to go to the very top. I'm the closest woman to the president. It's been great, but in five years I'll be ready to do something else.

But a few minutes later, she said, "Now I don't have to work for financial reasons. But as long as it keeps being interesting, I'll stay here. I enjoy being involved in corporate boards." My attempts to point out an inconsistency in her statements and to ask her to clarify her intentions were fruitless. Audrey did not acknowledge a contradiction and continued to affirm both her exhaustion and her intent to stay "as long as it is challenging." Like many women I interviewed, she did not seem to be an introspective person; rather than worrying about internal contradictions, she continued to articulate the requisite ambition under the devotion to work schema in addition to her desire to leave the firm.[11] She and other discontented work-committed group members do "emotion work": they induce some feelings and suppress others to make them appropriate to the situation (Hochschild, 1983, 1979).

After relaying the story of her colleague's sexual harassment and rejection, the investment banker Alice Witt talked about wanting to quit. A few moments later, I asked her what she wanted to be doing ten years from now. I hid my surprise when she enthusiastically told me: "I'd like to be president of our firm. It's a very challenging job." Alice Witt was shocked and sickened by the treatment of her female colleague precisely because it breached the schema's promises. At the same time, she continues to assert—and to believe on some level— that she wants to become president of the company, which is the required attitude of aspiring managers.

This remark illustrates the external force of the work devotion schema. It is part of the workplace culture, imposed by upper management, and eventually more or less internalized by managers moving up the ladder. Like Audrey Weyler, Alice Witt does the emotion work to summon the feelings appropriate to her structural position as an executive. Despite the evidence of her colleague's downfall and regardless of her partial disillusionment, Alice continues to hope and believe that her abiding fidelity will be rewarded.

Who Are the Critics and Who Are the Faithful Adherents?

For fifty of the fifty-six women in the career-committed group, I was able to make a clear judgment about whether each respondent had embraced the devotion to work schema early in her career and whether she continued to embrace it or had rejected it at the time of the interview. All fifty seemed to initially incorporate some version of the devotion to work schema. The schema remains basically intact for twenty-six respondents. Dedication has shifted to ambivalence for eighteen women. And for six more individuals, belief in the schema has been shattered.

As an interpretive tool, I used simple cross-classification tables to explore associations between faith in the work devotion schema and several variables: the year in which respondents entered finance, promotion rate, turbulence in the firm or industry, and job level. (For a discussion of these variables, see Blair-Loy, 1999.) Promotion rate is weakly related to the intactness of the work devotion schema. But job level has the closest relationship to whether women retain faith in this schema. In my data, women who had reached the very highest levels in their organizations (for example, chief executive officer, chief financial officer, managing partner) were *more* likely than women at relatively lower levels to continue to fully embrace the work devotion schema, *less* likely to regard it with ambivalence, and *less* likely to have completely rejected it.[12]

Due to the small sample size, we must interpret these analyses as preliminary and heuristic. Further research should more fully examine the correlates, causes, and consequences of work devotion. But the results here echo many other studies, which have found that work commitment is correlated with level in the job hierarchy in other populations of workers (Lincoln and Kalleberg, 1990: 80–81, 115, 120).

My findings suggest that the ideology of work devotion becomes purer at the top of the firm. This could be true for several reasons. The schema is deeply embedded in most firms' reward and promotion structures. The most ardent believers may be most likely to be promoted and in turn become the senior managers who expect similar effort and loyalty from subordinates. High-ranking managers get to shape their firm's version of the schema to serve their own interests. Additionally, more powerful members of the firm can ensure that they receive the rewards promised by the schema. For example, they may be able to insulate themselves from layoffs related to industry consolidation. Moreover, those who have moved ahead the furthest are more likely to consider the schema to be a fair and accurate description of reality.

Executive women (and perhaps executive men as well) who reach the highest levels are those who have lived by a set of stringent cultural rules and assumptions. According to Clifford Geertz (1973: 124), these rules serve as both a description of and model for reality, as both a gloss and a template. The greater material resources that accrue to people expressing the most work devotion help ensure that this schema will persist, despite competing cultural models such as the family devotion schema and the ideology of work life balance supported by many human resource professionals, policy makers, and academics. The expectation that executives and aspiring managers put in extremely long hours remains a stable social structure of managerial work (cf. Acker, 1990).

Industry consolidation and downsizing may have the potential to weaken the work devotion schema.[13] However, top managers have been less vulnerable than middle managers or nonmanagerial workers to downsizing in the 1980s and early 1990s (Osterman, 1996: 9). And despite an erosion of loyalty between employers and many workers, core managerial and professional employees are still expected to display work devotion. For example, according to Kunda and Van Maanen (1999: 74–75):

> Employers may rely on a thinner, presumably more select cadre of managers and professionals, but they still expect an intense continuing relationship with them governed by the rules of exchanging emotional investment for corporate benefits . . . Major corporate decisions such as restructuring, outsourcing, plant closings and downsizing . . . are choices made by people at the top of the corporate hierarchy.

Respondents like Amy Peterson, who lost jobs earlier in their careers, did experience disillusionment with the work devotion schema. But the senior executives studied here are, as a group, largely insulated from the threat of layoffs. The most powerful, protected, and ideologically pure executives remain in positions that reaffirm their own work devotion. They also wield the power to enforce at least outward conformity to the work devotion schema among their subordinates, to whom they may offer diminished rewards in return for their dedication.

*   *   *

Whether the women I interviewed ultimately believe in the work devotion schema or renounce it, they never regard it with indifference. These women resolve the contradiction between work and family devotion in different ways. We will see that some members of the family-committed group, who had relinquished full-time business careers after childbearing, asked their employers to allow them to work part time. By requesting reduced hours, senior managers revealed their infidelity to work devotion and risked being banished from their organizations. Nonetheless, they continue to challenge the reigning work devotion ideology and disobey the commandment of single-minded devotion to their careers.

2

THE DEVOTION TO
FAMILY SCHEMA

For many professional women, the catch in working full-time with children is employers' demand for single-minded allegiance. Executive-level jobs do not easily accommodate involved motherhood.[1] This chapter examines family devotion from the perspective of the family-committed group, twenty-five women who left promising full-time business careers after having children.

The group includes ten women who gave up paid work completely, five who do part-time freelance professional work from their homes, and ten who work part-time for corporations.[2] These women invested a great deal in their education and careers. All have bachelor's degrees and 84 percent have professional degrees. They had a median of nine years of full-time professional experience before they relinquished full-time careers.

First I describe an ideal type or abstract model of the family devotion schema's defining characteristics. Next, I show how this cultural model inspires and makes sense of the lives of women in the family-committed women's group. Twelve women (almost 50 percent) find living in accordance with the family devotion personally fulfilling, while the remaining carry out the schema's mandates more grimly. The family devotion schema contains within it a definition of childhood and a model for how wives and husbands should divide the household and paid work. Among the family-committed group, this division of labor defies economists' notions of an economically rational household. Two-thirds of these women had earned full-time incomes similar to or greater than their husbands, yet the women, not the men, are the ones who cut back on work to focus on family. Through the lens of the family devotion schema, this decision makes sense. Its definitions of appropriate domestic and breadwinning roles are presented as rooted in biological sex differences. Its mandates are affirmed by a community of like-minded devotees. While family devotion is lived out most consistently by the ten family-committed women who completely relinquished careers for homemaking, it also profoundly shapes the commitments and decisions of respondents who are employed part-time.

Family Devotion Schema as an Ideal Type

Like the work devotion schema, the family devotion schema is a compelling framework for viewing, filtering, understanding, and evaluating what we know as reality. Both schemas are objective: they are shared, public understandings with real consequences. They are also subjective and partially internalized: they shape our cognitive understandings, our desires, and our views of right and wrong. As Kathleen Gerson (1985: 193) notes, "women face a set of dichotomous choices in which work and family commitments are posed as competing alternative commitments." For professional women in demanding jobs, the competition between cultural models of work and family devotion is particularly keen.

As an abstract model or ideal type, the family devotion schema assigns responsibility for housework and child rearing to women. It prescribes that women spend most of their adult lives intensively caring for their families (Hays, 1996; D'Emelio and Freedman, 1989; Coser and Coser, 1974).[3] This schema presumes a heterosexual, permanent, reciprocal marriage, in which wives are dependent on husbands for livelihood and social status, while husbands rely on wives for physical and emotional care of themselves and their children (Skolnick, 1991; Stacey, 1990; D'Emelio and Freedman, 1989). The schema stipulates that women find fulfillment in the creativity and intimacy of "intensive motherhood" (Hays, 1996: 129). Women's devotion to the family trumps all other commitments. Even if they also do paid work, their primary duty lies in giving their children absorbing and time-consuming care. The ten family-committed group members who completely abandoned employment embody family devotion at its most consistent. But family devotion is also the polestar around which part-time workers orient their commitments, desires, and decisions.

The family relationships prescribed by the family devotion schema are assumed by many in our society to be rooted in biological sex differences. This assumption makes gendered family relationships seem natural, inevitable, and taken-for-granted (Lorber, 1994; cf. Douglas, 1986). Yet at the same time, the family devotion schema's definition of a meaningful life has been challenged by the 1970s women's movement and the influx of married women and mothers into the labor force. Nonetheless, the family devotion schema maintains a strong grip on many people's hearts and minds.[4]

Elements of the Family Devotion Schema

The family devotion schema helps orient priorities among family-committed women, despite their track records as dedicated and financially successful professionals.[5] Many do not seem to question their understanding of appropriate breadwinning and domestic roles for men and women. For example, a public accountant I call Ellen

THE DEVOTION TO FAMILY SCHEMA

Lake left her job shortly before the birth of her first child. Toward the end of the interview, I asked whether she had ever contemplated an alternative household arrangement.

I: Did you ever think about or discuss the possibility that Bill would be the one to stay home with the baby?
R: We never considered that he would stop working. His career is going gangbusters.

Nina Lombardi, a former corporate attorney with a degree from a prominent law school, is now home full-time with her two children. She had a similar answer to that question: "I never thought about [my husband] staying home. It didn't occur to either of us. He didn't want that role. And I wanted so much to stay home."

Rebecca Feinstein earned a degree from a top-five law school and relished her corporate legal practice. When her first child was born, she shifted to part-time. She offered a similar response to my query:

I: Did you ever think about or discuss the possibility of your husband being the one to work part-time?
R: We never even thought about it. He was always more career-committed than I was . . . My husband and other men get their main source of satisfaction from their careers. That is not my source of self-image and satisfaction. It is more important for me to take care of my kids right now.

These couples take the family devotion schema for granted. They apparently never questioned that the wife rather than the husband should be the one to cut back on work to spend time with the children. Moreover, many in the family-committed group longed to stay home with their children; they take much pleasure in living out the schema's dictates.[6]

Rewards

The devotion to family schema implicitly promises a rich array of rewards to wives and mothers whose primary allegiance is to the family. The term "rewards" is misleading, however. As an ideal type, family devotion is not entered into for instrumental gain but because it is understood to be a worthwhile, natural, and desirable way for women to live their lives. Financial support, meaningful responsibilities and creative tasks, and intimate connections to cherished human beings are viewed as the felicitous outcomes of a responsible woman's commitment to her family members' well-being.

The family-committed women in my group are privileged mothers, married to high-earning professionals. They live in affluent suburbs with good schools. Unlike some of Kathleen Gerson's (1985) working-class respondents, who reluctantly took up full-time motherhood after becoming discouraged with dead-end jobs, the highly educated members of my group chose to leave promising careers to care for their children. Their workload is limited by their small family size (a median of two children) and their use of housekeepers and babysitters. On the other hand, they are busily engaged in transmitting an upper-class cultural capital to their children. They chauffeur children to far-flung music lessons and sports practices, monitor homework, volunteer in the schools, and maintain large houses.

Despite their comfortable surroundings, the devoted mothers in the group are committed to an almost ascetic life path of transcending self-centeredness for the sake of others' well-being. Many implicitly view their motherhood as a calling, a deep sense of vocation that contributes to the greater good (Weber, 1958a, 1958b).

Financial Support

The ten family-committed women who are home full time rely completely on their husbands for financial support. Most of the fourteen part-timers are partially supported by their husbands: as part-timers they now earn, on average, about a third of the family income.[7]

Several of these women told me they had to lower their living standard when they left the full-time work force but that this "cut in overhead" or "change in lifestyle" was well worth the time it gave them with their children. I asked whether they felt that the decrease in or disappearance of their incomes had changed the balance of power in their marriages.[8] The majority quickly denied that it had and insisted that their husbands highly valued their contributions at home.

Some women expressed relief at being freed from the burden of breadwinning. Susan Pflanz, a former corporate attorney who is now home full-time, confided:

> Working in a law firm, you're always waiting for something bad to happen. I still have this nightmare that I didn't enclose something in a FedEx package that's going to cost someone millions of dollars. There's constant stress. I don't know how I could keep stuff together at home and at work.

She is planning to look for an undemanding part-time position after her son starts school; "I want a job I can leave at work when I leave."[9] Emily Lutzenheiser, a former senior manager at a Fortune 500 company, commented that caring for children "might sound humdrum, but I like it. I worked hard for so long. It's like a vacation."

However, some admitted to feeling uneasy about their economic dependence. For example, former marketing executive Mary Warshawski said:

> You have to work through the fact that you're financially dependent on your husband. You have to contribute. My contribution is working around the house. You go through a period when you are uneasy about being supported. Your husband takes on a

new dimension. He's not only your husband. He's also the father of your children. You need him to support them.

Others expressed concern over a shift in the balance of power in the marriage since they gave up their full-time jobs and complained that their husbands did not fully appreciate their domestic work. A few high-earning part-timers said that their job enabled them to mitigate their economic dependence and maintain some marital power. For instance, Rebecca Feinstein, who now earns about a third of the family income, maintains:

> It does give you more bargaining power in a marriage if you earn more. Men don't really value what mothers do. The fact that I bring in a salary probably gives me more clout . . . If I hadn't gone back to work at all, the power balance in our marriage would've changed.

Many in the family-committed group relish the freedom from maintaining a full-time job. Without this obligation, they feel able to be the kind of involved and creative mothers they think they should be.

Meaningful and Creative Work

According to the family devotion schema, an involved motherhood is vital and creative. Christine Colarullo renounced her lavish corporate life as a management consultant in order to nurture her two children's development. She and the children read, play music, and cook together.

> An ideal evening is when we play games as a family. Or we put on little concerts. Everyone gets an instrument, and my son conducts. We read an hour a day together. It's a nice bedtime ritual. And there are Montessori things. I try to get my kids involved in preparing dinner.

Rachel Kahn traded in her executive director position at a large health maintenance organization (HMO) for intensive motherhood. She devotes hours to creative play with her preschool daughters.

> I have a lot of energy with them. In one day we'll make biscuits, then we'll paint something, then we'll move the living room furniture around and make tents. By the end of the day, the house is a complete disaster area.

Lisa Dunbar, an attorney, is thankful for the time her part-time schedule gives her with her two children. "I wouldn't trade [anything] for those afternoons at the swim club . . . I went to see my daughter's butterfly migration parade for kindergarten. I get to do things like that."

Marsha Dickens, a part-time attorney with her own practice, was already a mother of two when she adopted a four-year-old girl from Russia. She has reduced her hours even further so that she can spend more time with her adopted daughter. She explains:

> But the fact that Anna is here is really the thing that made me decide to work this year only three [short] days a week, because Anna is learning how to speak English and also learning how to be in a family, which she's never been in before. That just seems like so much that she has to do, that she really needs her parents around as much as possible.

Marsha says that her daughter needs "her parents around as much as possible." In practice, that means that Anna's *mother* will devote more time to her nurture. Marsha feels that caring for her children, including teaching Anna English and the love and constancy of family life, is highly significant work. Although she works part-time out of the home, caring for her children is, for now, her calling, the essence of a life well lived.

Intimate Connections with Cherished Human Beings

Another outcome that the family devotion schema promises mothers is a close emotional bond with their children. A former banker, Naomi Schumacher, quit her job because she could not bear to leave her infant as her maternity leave drew to a close. She explained:

> I was having unexpected feelings, yearnings. It's hard to say without sounding sappy. The baby made me so happy to be with her. It was a love that was different from any I had had. A bonding connection that was new and different and deep. After two months, we started interviewing nannies . . . There was nothing wrong with these women. But they were other women who were picking up my baby. I watched these women bonding with my baby. I broke down into tears. I sat my husband down and bawled like a baby. I said, I can't do this. I can't walk out of the house. For what? For a stupid job?

The job she had previously relished was now "stupid" because it would drag her away from her beloved child. Going back to work would force her to attenuate the intense connection she and her son had forged.

Vicki Orlando, who left a stunningly successful career at a large corporate law firm after her daughter was born, talks of being knocked off her feet by her baby.

> I fell in love with her. Here was this just wonderful, little person. I was totally surprised. I was not prepared for how wonderful motherhood was . . . She was an amazing thing. Yeah, I thought trials were cool. I liked having secretaries and all that money. But here's this little baby. She is also very cool. After a year, emotionally, I didn't want to go back. I was still nursing her.

Although Vicki had thrived at work, she found raising her daughter even more fulfilling. Her daughter, now in elementary school, struck me as an affectionate and precocious child. As I watched her and her mother playing together in their charming old suburban house, I could see that the love affair was still going strong.

Twelve family-committed members (48 percent) struck me as very content. A common refrain was that their part in the family devotion script was a far more satisfying one than their husbands'. Out earning a living, their husbands were missing out on the close rapport they enjoy with their children. Susan Pflanz remarked, "I feel sorry for my husband who can't sit here all day with them." Similarly, Nina Lombardi said:

> I see it with my husband. He adores our kids. But he travels a lot. He doesn't feel the same bond. He doesn't feel the same conflict over being away from them that a mother would.

Nina believes her husband never had the chance to develop the intimate connection to their children that she has. Thus, it does not break his heart when he is away on business for several days at a time.

Naomi Schumacher, who now stays home with her two children, drove me from her suburban house to the train station at the end of our interview. Just before I got out of her car, she riveted me with an intense gaze and said:

> It's a trade-off; I realize that . . . But I have something my husband can't have. I have the option to stay home with my kids. As soon as he was born with a penis, he lost the option to stay home with them. He loves his children. My children love their father. But he has a different relationship with them. He's not there when they come home from school, bubbling over with enthusiasm about what they did that day. If I worked, I would have the same relationship with my kids that my husband has. But I didn't want that kind of relationship. And I'm very happy, because I get to be with them. I'm very happy.

Some of the women in this group enjoy a congruence between their family's well-being and their own. Their focus on home and family makes their children more secure, eases their husbands' lives, and engenders a sense of personal happiness and serenity. For instance, Nina Lombardi remarked:

> I've never been happier or more at peace . . . I feel almost guilty that I have such a wonderful life. I spend time being with people I love. I love my life. I'm sure that looking back, this will be the greatest time of my life. I don't regret it. I know the pressure that people who are working feel.

I characterize the remaining thirteen women in the group as discontented.[10] Yet even they cling faithfully to the family devotion schema. They consider their own happiness to be irrelevant compared to their children's needs for their day-to-day, intensive attention.

Definition of Childhood

One strand of the family devotion schema is a mother's emotionally invested, tender care for her children. The schema thus contains an implicit definition of childhood. To be an appropriate object of mothers' time and attention, children are understood as naturally fragile, needy, and deserving of a mother's devoted care. This is a historically constructed cultural model of childhood that first emerged in the eighteenth and early nineteenth centuries (Hays, 1996; Zelizer, 1985; Aries, 1962).[11]

Today, there is debate in the social scientific literature about whether and under what conditions mothers' employment is harmful to children. Overall, most scholars have not found a consistent negative effect of maternal employment on children's well-being, and some studies have found a positive effect. However, the conditions of the mother's employment (number of work hours, nature of the work), family variables (the age of the child, the father's employment, family income), and the quality of the child's care and supervision may affect the relationship between maternal employment and children's well-being (see Perry-Jenkins, Repetti, and Crouter, 2000, for a review of recent studies).

I did not study my respondents' children and here do not make an argument, one way or the other, about whether children are best served by intensive motherhood. Instead, I am arguing that the definitions of childhood develop over time in particular societies and subgroups of societies. These definitions are part of schemas of devotion, which shape social institutions and mold personal understandings, feelings, and beliefs.

The cultural definition of children that the family-committed group holds sacred contrasts with the cultural definition of children as autonomous and resilient, a view developed by some career-committed mothers. In both cases, these definitions are highly charged; their advocates are personally invested in them and condemn those who do not share their beliefs.

Susan Planz explains that she protects her children from having to learn independence too early:

My kids haven't been forced to be adaptable. My daughter, she's 9 and doing more things now, but my son [age 5] doesn't like to go places without me. I haven't pressed them too hard, figuring they'll get there eventually.

Because they are able to provide the devoted care that they believe children need, mothers in the family-committed group can describe their own children as happy, healthy, and "normal." Christine Colarullo noted, "I'm very proud that my kids are happy little campers. If my son didn't have someone here to give him TLC [tender loving care], he'd have some problems." Linda Giovanni proclaimed, "I've been home since the third one was born. You should see this kid. He's so happy and self-assured. He's not clingy at all. I wonder if that's because I've been home." Yvonne Smith is pleased to see her children's "moral development," which she believes that only a mother can instill.

Even respondents who work part-time can to a large extent adopt and act on the family devotion schema's definition of children. They adamantly distinguish themselves from full-time employed women, whom they believe fail to provide day-to-day intensive nurturing.[12] For example, part-time executive Deborah Stein walks her young son to school each morning. Similarly part-time legal counsel Angie Jacobson, a mother of two preschoolers, says, "Your kids need you more as they get older. They don't need you to change their diaper anymore, but they need you in terms of being more important that you're available to go on a class trip." Part-time corporate attorney Rebecca Feinstein believes that children continue to need much of their mothers' time, even after they are in school: "Now that my daughter is starting school, she needs me to help her with her assignments. I want to go to her school functions, to her soccer games, to her ballet performances."

Similarly, if corporate attorney Donna Schmidt worked full-time, she would not be able to escape the office until late in the evening. As a part-timer, she is able to leave the office before 6:00 P.M., even though she does have to go back to the office from 9:00 P.M. to midnight. She believes—and acts on the belief—that her preschoolers need their mother to fix them dinner and put them to bed.

Reaffirming the Family Devotion Schema: The Negative Example

As compelling as schemas of devotion are, they need continuing public reaffirmation to remain convincing and legitimate. Members of the family-committed group are surrounded by old friends and former colleagues who have maintained demanding business careers after having children. Members sustain their conviction by forming friendships with other former businesswomen, who share their commitment to involved mothering. They collect and retell stories of the harm that full-time employed mothers inflict on their families.

These shared stories are a way of drawing symbolic boundaries that distinguish these women from full-time employees, whom they deem to be inferior mothers. Symbolic boundaries are the types of lines that people draw when they categorize other people as less worthy. ˌhis "boundary work" reveals and reinforces broadly shared prejudices "shaped by the cultural resources that people have at their disposal and by the structural situations they live in" (Lamont, 1992: 2).

For example, Christine Colarullo observed that mothers with demanding careers "assume that kids are less needy than they really are, that they can be more like adults. They just send them off to programs, sit them in front of TVs." Similarly, Angie Jacobson criticized a neighbor for not letting her children get enough sleep. Angie recounted a recent telephone conversation with this woman.

I said, "I think I hear your kids in the background." It was 8:30, and my kids were in bed. And she said, "well, we never get home until 8 or 8:30," and her five-and-a-half-year-old goes to bed at 9:30, and her two-and-a-half-year-old goes to bed at 10:30 or 11:00. She said, "If they went to bed at 8:00, I would never see them."

Other women in the family-committed group declared that children they know who lack primary caregiving mothers are "not well adjusted," "emotionally abandoned," "out of control," and "bouncing off the walls." My respondents morally condemn full-time employed mothers for ignoring their children's inherent vulnerability.

With no prompting from me, seven family-committed respondents (28 percent) relayed elaborate narratives about families that suffered due to the mother's employment. For example, Ellen Lake told me about a dual-career family she knows.

The older girl is four, and she's out of control. She bounces off the walls. When they were at our house, each parent told the

other one what to do, but nobody told the girl to stop. It's sad for
their daughter. But Donna loves her job. I'd rather [not work
but] have a healthy family with well-behaved children.

Ellen defines the problem to be that "Donna loves her job," not that
Donna's husband loves his job.

Elizabeth Cruz reported that when she was still employed, the one
senior woman with children in her firm left them in daycare all week.
She occasionally showed them off at work, treating them "like trophy
kids." Yvonne Smith related that since her next-door neighbors both
worked demanding jobs, their young children had "no parental guidance" and were turning into delinquents. Similarly, Susan Pflanz told
a cautionary tale about her neighbor's disastrous return to full-time
work after her maternity leave ended.

Christine Colarullo described a four-day visit from out-of-town
friends:

It was the worst four days in our entire lives. They have two
kids, ages two and four. Both parents work; they are lawyers. The
kids are raised by nannies. They are really unhappy. It was a
nightmare. It took our family a month to recover from that
visit . . . Their mother kept telling me that the kids were doing
fine. But they wouldn't be crying themselves to sleep if they were
happy. That session was so eye-opening for me. It reconfirmed
for me why I'm home.

These stories paint these children as truly troubled: emotionally
abandoned, crying themselves to sleep every night, or juvenile delinquents. People in the family-committed group conclude that these
perceived woes derive from the mother's alleged absenteeism rather
than from another cause such as a father's absence, marital discord
among the parents, health problems, learning disorders, or being bul-
lied at school. And while family-committed members probably know

some full-time employed mothers who have healthy and happy children, they do not gather and retell stories about those families. Their cautionary tales hammer home the point that children are vulnerable and terribly scarred by their *mother's* full-time commitments outside the home. Christine Colarullo said that her story of the nightmarish four-day visit from friends "reconfirmed for me why I'm home." These narratives are resounding affirmations of family-committed members' faith in the family devotion schema.

According to these stories, these full-time commitments away from the family scar the mothers as well as the children. Christine Colarullo said of her houseguest's visit that her friend's misery was as great as her children's. Working full-time and flaunting the family devotion schema had only brought the friend guilt. "My friend was so guilt ridden. She had so many rationalizations. It was pretty sad." Nina Lombardi portrays a full-time employed friend as equally unhappy:

A friend of mine is still [at my old firm] full-time. Every time I talk to her, she's miserable. She agonizes over whether she should let go or if she should continue working. She's always conflicted.

Because the family devotion schema defines a woman and her family as having congruent interests, these stories portray employed mothers as simultaneously undermining their children and sabotaging themselves.

Emotions and Identities

These narratives reinforce the women's sense of membership in a superior category and helps them cultivate the emotions and priorities they believe a good mother should have. Rebecca Feinstein thinks that mothers who are employed full-time must have, like men, "less guilt" and "lower standards for what the kids can do." Vicki Orlando criticizes full-time working mothers for leaving their children when they are sick. "A sick kid tears at our heart, if you're open to that. A lot of people just drop them off at some sick kid place. [They] are insulated from their hearts."

Several family-committed women stated flatly that "you can't have it all"; they believed that the conflict between having a "high-powered" career and being a good mother is irreconcilable. One woman said, "you can't work a demanding job full-time *and* have kids that are centered and secure." Another declared, "I don't care what anyone says. With the juggling routines, it's the *kids* who lose out. Who cares about the parents? It's the kids who lose out." A mother's sacrifice of all other major commitments for the sake of her family is worthwhile, because her vulnerable, deserving, beloved children need her.

Rachel Kahn articulated this well. "At a gut level, kids need to see their parents. They feel safer with their parents than with anyone else." Here, Rachel uses the gender-neutral term "parents" to describe the people children need to be with to feel secure. In practice (according to Rachel Kahn's account), the parent who primarily provides emotional security to these children is the mother.

There are disciples of each devotion schema who hold up violators of the schema as negative examples who injure their children. My point is not to argue whether one or the other of these definitions of childhood is more or less accurate or better or worse for children's well-being. My position is that these definitions are emotionally and morally charged. They are more than post-hoc rationalizations of what a woman wants to do anyway. They help define and make sense of what she finds desirable and compelling.[13]

The Gendered Division of Labor in the Family

Family members decide how to divide up all the work that needs to get done—earning an income, managing the household, caring for children, cleaning, cooking, and shopping. The work devotion schema assumes that the worker has a family-oriented spouse at home. The family devotion schema presupposes a husband who can economically support the family. As we have seen, people in the family-committed group castigate full-time employed mothers but they do not criticize full-time employed fathers. They believe male work devotion is appropriate and provides the family incomes that should allow women to devote themselves to their children's day-to-day nurture.[14]

Day-to-Day Childcare and Household Management

Family-committed women who are home full-time do most of the childcare and household management themselves. Their domestic work is supplemented by occasional babysitters and housecleaning help. For example, Nina Lombardi cares for her two young children, takes care of the home, and does other domestic chores. She elaborates, "I pick stuff up at the cleaner, get groceries. I mow the lawn."

Women employed part-time for corporations work fairly long hours in order to justify their work dedication despite their reduced-hour status. Their jobs require that they be available to their clients and coworkers whenever needed. Thus, most part-time respondents rely on full-time, paid child care. Despite their considerable professional responsibilities, women in the family-committed group staunchly fulfill the family devotion schema's requirement that they manage the household and oversee their children's day-to-day care. They share the breadwinning with their husbands but remark on how their husbands, consumed by work devotion, fail to share substantially in their homemaking responsibilities.[15]

To illustrate, part-time corporate attorney Cindy Kroeger manages her children's caregiver and handles the day-to-day schedule changes and contingencies of family life:

I bear the brunt of it in the sense of making the arrangements when something goes awry, [such as when] a housekeeper is sick or a kid is sick and the housekeeper isn't expected till later or whatever. I was the one who usually called my friend or my mother.

Cindy says she tries to get her husband to do more at home but remains frustrated that he lacks the initiative to anticipate the children's needs in advance.

And then sometimes I get frustrated and I yell at [my husband] and say, "you call." And he would. But the difference between us is that, he would do whatever I asked him to do, but *I* had to *ask* him. I knew it had to be done; he didn't. It's like, men sit back and wait . . . He doesn't have the initiative to say, "I better figure out that our son will need a dentist appointment." Or "I better figure out that next Tuesday [we should tell the housekeeper] we're gonna be late." . . . [He doesn't] *anticipate* need.

She explains her husband's lack of leadership in domestic matters by his immersion in his work. Like other women she knows, she is more focused than he is on the children's day-to-day well-being.

I think that part of it is what's on your mind. You only have so much time and so much mind. And [my husband is] a very, very good lawyer and his mind is always thinking about that stuff. I'm much more apt to be thinking about my kids than I am about work and I think that's the difference . . . He *is* very concerned about the kids. He's just more distracted by work . . . Most of my friends at work have very, I think, equal marriages and the husband takes his responsibility for the kids as seriously and doesn't think it's the woman's job. Yet in the end, it's always the woman who bears the burden.

Assuming Cindy Kroeger's report about her husband is reasonably accurate, he is a loving father and a good breadwinner. In daily life, he defines his primary commitments and concerns in terms of the work devotion schema. Cindy resents this and tries, without much success, to get him more involved at home. But she ultimately is resigned to his inattention to family caregiving: "In the end, it's always the woman who bears the burden" of keeping her family's needs forefront in her mind.

Rebecca Feinstein's interview follows a pattern similar to Cindy Kroeger's. Rebecca first tells me about all of her domestic duties.

> When we are looking for new nannies, it's generally my respon-
> sibility to find them, because I work part-time, quote un-
> quote . . . Someone comes in every other week to clean . . . I do
> the other stuff around the house. I help Sarah [the nanny] with
> the laundry. It's up to me to find someone to replace the cleaning
> lady, to hire the babysitters when it's the nanny's night off. I
> make the doctor and dentist appointments. I fill out the school
> forms. I check for homework in the stuff they bring home . . . I
> do all the letter writing and present sending to my family and to
> [my husband's] family.

She then tells me that her husband, who "has to work until midnight five or six days a week," does not worry about being apart from the children the way that she would.

> It bothers him when he's working a lot and doesn't see them. But
> he expects that that's just the way it goes. He doesn't have the
> same guilt that I have. He doesn't worry that it's going to hurt
> them. His father was like that too. I always think that any behav-
> ior problems they exhibit are because we don't spend enough
> time with them. My husband says I'm crazy.

In the same vein, part-time executive Kim Fox first narrates a long list of things she does to keep children and the household running smoothly.

Household management is a nightmare. Mostly, I try to get people to come do stuff. We have an older house. It needs a lot of work. I spend a lot of time driving the kids to the dentist, to birthday parties, to all their activities. Each child has two activities. Margie [age six] has ballet and gymnastics. Liza [age four] has gymnastics and art. I also have to make play dates for each girl . . . It's a *mammoth effort* to get this family moving.

Then she explains that her husband is "immersed in his work" and does not pay the kind of attention to the children and the home that she thinks is necessary.

There's a lot going on; I have a lot to juggle. It doesn't get done well when I'm not here. Duane is immersed in his work. He doesn't think to look in Margie's school folder when she gets home from school, to see if there's homework she needs to do or papers he needs to sign. I don't know if it's just my need for perfection, but there's always a lot to do.

Kim Fox echoes the feelings of Cindy Kroeger and Rebecca Feinstein when she says that her husband's work devotion swallows up so much energy that he is unable to focus on the day-to-day welfare of his children.

These litanies of tasks and complaints highlight the mother's unique caregiving role under the family devotion schema. On the one hand, family-committed members working part-time are proud that their professional responsibilities do not diminish their constant level of care for their children. On the other hand, many also complain about their heavier domestic burden.

But this nascent critique of their husbands' inability to focus on family caregiving dissipates as they acknowledge work devotion's first claim on their husbands. Their appeal for more of their husbands' attention at home is no match for the firm's demand for the men's time and energy. Their status as intensive mothers who do not work full-time depends on their husbands' successful breadwinning. Ultimately, these women view the gendered division of family labor as inevitable, even if it does not always seem fair.

Economics of the Family Division of Labor

Gary Becker (1981) has made the influential argument that families make rational, economic decisions to maximize family income while also efficiently providing adequate care at home. Given a family's need to earn money and to take care of the children and home, the spouse with the highest earning potential will specialize in paid employment, while the spouse with lower earning potential will specialize in family caregiving, perhaps while also working a less demanding and lower-paid job. According to Becker, this process is in theory gender-neutral, but mothers are in fact much more likely to leave the labor force or to work part-time than fathers because women generally earn less or have lower earning potential than men. Thus, it makes good economic sense for men to focus on their careers while their wives focus on family.

It is true that women generally earn less than men in the United States and that women with children are particularly hit with a "motherhood penalty" in wages (Budig and England, 2001; Crittenden, 2001; Waldfogel, 1997). But these trends are not necessarily the *cause* of subsequent decisions by couples that women will focus on family rather than career, as Becker argues. Instead or in addition to this process, these trends could be a *consequence* of the cultural models of the gendered division of labor that orient potentially high-earning women toward home rather than toward the workplace.

To really assess Becker's argument, we must look at the cases in which wives earn as much as or more than their husbands do. Recall that in the family-committed group, eight women (32 percent) had earned full-time incomes considerably larger than their husbands' and another eight women had earned full-time incomes roughly equal to their husbands' incomes.

In this sample, couples' decisions about who should specialize in the labor force and who in family caregiving are not simply governed by who can earn more money. Instead, economic decisions are filtered and refracted through the lens of the family devotion schema. This schema specifies that women, regardless of their earning potential, are particularly suited for and find unique fulfillment in dedication to family caregiving. It did not even occur to many of these couples to arrange for the husbands, instead of the wives, to shift to part-time status or stay home. This is even true for some of the wives who substantially out-earned their husbands when both worked full-time.[16]

For example, consider Deborah Stein, a chief operating officer at a large organization, who shifted to part-time after having a child. Her husband's full-time job commands only half her part-time salary. Despite her much higher earning potential, Deborah is committed to the marriage and motherhood models implicit in the family devotion schema. Her husband is frequently out of the country on business. I asked her if she ever resented being saddled with most of the domestic work.

I: Did you ever feel, gee, maybe my husband should take on some more of this burden at home? If he's in Japan, basically you are a single mom much of the time.

R: Right. Well, we are both pretty traditional people in spite of the fact that I am often doing untraditional things. The truth is, my husband loves his work. For him to make a change would be change of such magnitude, such importance to him personally, that—the price associated with that would be very high.

I: For him?

R: For both of us . . . I know people who the dad just stays home and is largely responsible for the childcare and stuff, and that's just not my husband, that's not his personality. That's not what he's all about. And in truth, I wouldn't be so happy with that either, because I adore walking my son to school in the morning. I adore it.

Deborah Stein illustrates how the devotion schemas suffuse subjectivities and shape decisions. According to Deborah, her husband's very "personality" is molded by a devotion to work, whereas she attains great satisfaction from being the primary caregiver for her son. She initially downplays the fact that she also loves her work, because that emotion does not fit with her part in the family devotion script.[17] Only as the interview drew to a close did she admit that she also loves her career and feels terribly torn by working part-time. That shift has endangered her future career advancement and may even cost Deborah her current job. But ultimately, the fact that her earning potential is much greater than her husband's is irrelevant. She and her husband are "traditional." They subscribe to the gendered work and family roles sanctified by the devotion schemas.

Many of my respondents' husbands appear to be more successful and therefore justified in specializing in breadwinning *only because* their wives gave up their full-time careers. For example, Nina Lombardi mused that a benefit of leaving her job is that she no longer outperformed her husband at work.

David and I had worked at the same [law] firm; we had been competing. Although it is a bigger burden for him to earn all the money, he no longer has a competitor. I had been getting better grades and was making slightly more money. He was very supportive of me being at home. It may have been part of his life plan too, to have a wife at home.

Now that Nina has taken herself out of the competition for breadwinning, her husband David can shine in that role.

My argument is not that couples' decisions about the division of labor are irrational. Rather, I contend that we must pay attention to the cultural models that define economic rationality. There is actually a reciprocal causal relationship between Becker's argument and my own. Gendered cultural schemas help shape gendered organizations, gendered careers, and gendered personalities, a trend that creates the gender gap in pay and the motherhood penalty in income. These pay iniquities provide further justification for many couples' decisions to have the husband specialize in breadwinning while the wife specializes in family caregiving. Generally speaking, social interactions based on cultural assumptions within institutions push women and men into appropriate caregiving and work roles in a series of events over their lives. At each step, this process may be contested and incomplete; but the cascade of all these experiences, one after another, creates a remarkable social conformity in the gendered division of labor (cf. Jacobs, 1989). Because this process usually works so well, in a sample of typical women the cultural engine driving this conformity is largely invisible.

My extreme case of exceptionally successful professional women brings the power of these gendered schemas of devotion to light. The devotion schemas help set up social institutions and shape gendered personalities such that many women are likely to be oriented toward family care (sometimes combined with part-time work) and men toward the workplace, regardless of their actual earning potential.

Discontented Intensive Mothers

The discontented women in the family-committed group carry out their responsibilities under the family devotion schema more grimly. Early in the interviews, they recited everything they liked about involved mothering, as if dutifully fulfilling an expected obligation. As the conversations wore on, however, they began revealing ambivalence, resentment, and sometimes anguish. They nostalgically re-member the financial independence, status, challenge, collegiality, and intensity they had enjoyed as full-time workers. They are more likely to chafe under the gendered division of labor. Moreover, these family-committed women find the rewards of the family devotion schema to be less fulfilling than promised. They feel betrayed, rather like the career-committed members who feel they have missed out on the culturally promised rewards of work devotion.

Discontented family-committed group members do not experi-ence the same congruence between their own and their families' in-terests that the more contented mothers feel. The family devotion schema helps the discontented mothers come to terms with and even sanctify this incongruity. It defines an adult's personal happiness as ir-relevant compared to a child's well-being. In a sense, the discontented mothers' devotion is even purer than that of the contented mothers, because they understand themselves as sacrificing their personal ful-fillment for the sake of their children, an act of abnegation affirmed by communion with fellow believers.

The most common complaints I heard from the family-committed group were boredom, isolation, and career sacrifice. The discontented mothers found the supposedly creative work of intensive mothering to be "boring and mind-numbing." In addition, some women wres-tled with a sense of terrible isolation, unease over economic depend-ence, and a concern that their work at home was not fully valued by their husbands.

Carol Walker left her banking job four years ago when she and her husband adopted Jack. Shortly after that, she became pregnant with another child. She now spends her days caring for her two preschool-ers and doing volunteer work, while her husband shoulders the breadwinning responsibilities. Our interview was scheduled for a Sat-urday afternoon. Carol was twenty minutes late to pick me up at the train station near her suburban home because, as she apologetically explained, Jack had detached and lost the hands to his robot. She had a sense of humor and a generous spirit but was also caught up in the chaos of her life.

Carol drove us to a diner, where we ordered coffee. She confided: "When Jack came, it was a horrible adjustment . . . It's the same routine everyday. It's really boring. I'm still adjusting to that. My other jobs were never so routine."

She then spoke at length about feeling subservient to her husband ever since she left her banking job. She told me that her and her friends' involvement in volunteer work irritated their husbands, who expected them to spend their time keeping house and watching the children. She and her friends felt forced to sneak out to do the volunteer work they loved and then rush home to straighten up before their husbands returned from work. Carol admitted that this subterfuge made them feel childish and subordinate. She added, "if he were my boss rather than my husband, he would have fired me long ago." From my vantage point he may as well have been her boss, as she nervously cut our interview short and whisked me back to the train station. She was terribly worried about inconveniencing her husband, who was home "babysitting" the children for her that afternoon.

Another example of a discontented mother is Marsha Dickens. Marsha works three short days out of a home office as a freelance attorney. She first told me how important it was that she spend more time with her children, especially her daughter recently adopted from Russia. Later she bluntly discussed how tedious it was to be home with her three preschoolers all day.

> It's boring. You can't do anything, really. You can do a few things. Like yesterday, I put a license plate on my car and washed two potty seats. That was my day's accomplishment. Now if you're satisfied (laughter) with that one achievement, you're gonna do okay.

Not only does caring for children interrupt other tasks, but also she finds childcare itself to be terribly monotonous. Nonetheless, she continues to regard the work as extraordinarily important.

Other family-committed group members described the life of intensive mothering in more brutal terms. For example, after first expounding on all the creative activities she and her two preschoolers do together, Rachel Kahn talked about motherhood as drudgery.

I've never hated a job as much as I hate this. It's not fun. But the quality of the kids' lives would be so different if I didn't do this. It's a decision I made when I decided to have kids . . . Mostly I feel resigned to it. It's a responsibility I took on. I was not prepared for how much it would be. It's relentless. This sleep deprivation, constant demands, boredom, lack of stimulation. You can't prepare for what that feels like day after day after day.

She believes that mothering children according to the family devotion schema's model is an irrevocable "responsibility" she took on when she had children. But she says that if she had realized what intensive motherhood entails, she would have forgone having children in the first place.

If I knew then what I know now, I could've made the decision not to have them. If I knew then how hard and demanding it was going to be. When I first had them, I kept wondering, why didn't anyone say? Why didn't anyone tell me how hard it would be?

Although the discontented family-committed women love their children, they find childcare oppressively monotonous in part because they are comparing their lives as mothers to their former lives as elite workers. It is the discontented mothers themselves who question the gendered rules of the family devotion schema. Why is it, they ask, that to care adequately for the children they define as vulnerable, deserving, and beloved, the mother's career is the one that is almost always sacrificed?

Rachel Kahn complained that despite the agreement she and her husband had originally made to share childcare equally, he thought the daycare center should provide most of it. The consequence of his work devotion is that she has taken on most of the children's nurturing.

> My husband is an ophthalmologist . . . He's more career committed than me—but that's not fair. What is it that makes the woman more willing to give up her career? Of the two of us, I was more ambitious, I made more money, I reveled in the corporate scene. But there's no question. When the kids came, I am the one who gave up my career. If the kids are sick or there's childcare problems, I'm the one who jumps in. I'm considering quitting [my part-time freelance] work until the kids are in school.

In effect, she says that the family devotion schema's model of child rearing has penetrated her psyche far more deeply than it has her husband's.

> Guy is a highly involved father . . . [But] if I wanted to work 80 hours a week, that would be fine with him. I have a standard of how many hours I can leave the kids with a non-parent. He doesn't.

With a spark of anger, Rachel added: "He'd be happy to leave them in day care all day." Her husband's solution to work-family conflict, put the kids in day care, is no help at all, because it would violate her beliefs about who she is as a mother and how she can treat her children. So Rachel fulfills the family devotion schema's intensive mothering demands while her resentment simmers. She says:

> But I worked hard to get my career together, to put myself through graduate school and to prepare myself for what I thought was going to be a really influential career in health care. If I didn't have children, I would be doing something pretty exciting. That expectation hasn't been reached, which fuels my resentment.

As employment opportunities continue to expand for women, the more likely they are to be doing "something pretty exciting" and the more they are sacrificing under the family devotion schema.[18] Rachel Kahn had relished being the executive director of a large health maintenance organization, which brought her a higher income than her husband's. Similarly, Yvonne Smith's full-time career had been more successful and lucrative than her husband's. In her mid-thirties, she was having "a blast" running a small, highly profitable company. But her biological "clock was ticking," and she decided to try to have a child. She said:

> I was astonished that I got pregnant right away . . . [But] I loved my career so much . . . I always assumed I would go back. I'd hire a great nanny and just go back. I tried that. If I had really found a fabulous nanny who stayed with me for years, . . . I might have kept working. I don't regret what's happened. The children are better off. But even with a fabulous nanny, those nagging questions, they always come up.

A series of unsatisfactory nannies and her son's medical problem "forced" Yvonne "to re-assess" the decision to continue as the company's president, which required long hours and frequent travel. She finally decided to quit her job for the sake of the children. But she claims that she doesn't "regret" it because the "children are better off."

Under the family devotion schema, the mother sacrifices other major commitments for the sake of the children. Yvonne believes this is appropriate.

> I'm comfortable that this is the best thing that could have happened for my family. It may not be the best for me and my career. I've taken the complete brunt of it. I really miss working. I'm most happy when I'm working. But it means so much to the kids to have me home.

She says she continues "to mourn the loss" of her career at the same time she believes "that it was the best thing for the children." Like many family-committed respondents, she insists that unlike men, women simply "can't have it all." I asked whether she feels it is unfair that highly talented and career-oriented women cannot have both families and high-powered careers. She responded tensely:

> Sure, I have the sense that it is unfair. But there is nothing you can do with that feeling. There's nothing I can do with that. It doesn't lead anywhere. I don't let myself feel that too much, because I can't do anything with it.

Like Rachel Kahn, Yvonne Smith tries to control her resentment and not let herself "feel that too much," to keep it from boiling over while she devotes herself to her children. Hochschild (1989, 1983, 1979) analyzes how particular social structural situations put a premium on the individual's capacity to do "emotion work," to induce or suppress feelings to make them appropriate to the situation. Yvonne's emotion work is doubled: she represses her resentment and contains her grief at the same time that she evokes the involved mother's expected level of interest in her children's accomplishments and compassion for their feelings.

Christine Colarullo struggles to do the same emotion work. A former consultant who traveled worldwide meeting with senior executives, she is now home full-time raising children aged three and six. Her husband, also a consultant, travels a great deal and is rarely home. Christine first told me how much she enjoys playing musical instruments and reading with her children. But later in the interview, she confessed that the boredom, "intellectual rot," isolation, and constant demands of involved motherhood can be unbearable. She continued:

> Sometimes I really want to scream. I've learned to nip that in the bud before it gets too bad . . . [Sometimes] I'd like to drop off the face of the earth.

She strives to manage her resentment by attending book discussion groups and going for long walks. Despite her unhappiness, Christine insists that it is morally reprehensible for mothers to be employed full-time if they are not financially compelled to do so.

> When I meet mothers who don't spend time with their kids, I make judgments. I think it's a travesty the way a lot of kids are raised this way . . . Breaking the glass ceiling, if that's your goal in life, then you should raise dogs.

She states adamantly: "Who cares about the parents? It's the kids who lose out."

At first hearing, Christine Colarullo, Yvonne Smith, Rachel Kahn, Carol Walker, and the other discontented women sound like apostates in admitting that they at times hate the job of intensive motherhood. Yet in the next breath, they affirm their belief in the family devotion schema, which helps them persevere despite their unhappiness. They believe a mother's personal happiness is irrelevant compared to the well-being of her child. This strong affirmation of the fragile, sacred child gives the family devotion resiliency and tenacity, despite the personal toll it takes on some mothers.

Hochschild (1979: 566–567) argues that "Rules for managing feeling are implicit in any ideological stance . . . Deep acting or emotion work . . . can be a form of obeisance to a given ideological stance." Family-committed discontented mothers do not simply repress their resentment, boredom, loneliness, and sense of injustice. They grieve for their former careers. Yet they manage their emotions in a manner more profound than simply suppressing them. They offer those feelings and sacrifices up as part of their devotion. They can regard themselves as even more faithful mothers, because they have transcended their own personal unhappiness to serve their children.

As we saw earlier with the part-time employees, the fledgling critique that the discontented women begin to make of the gendered division of labor rarely becomes fully articulated or acted upon. For example, Christine attacks not fathers but "*mothers* who don't spend time with their kids." She believes that it is career-dedicated mothers, not fathers, who deserve to raise dogs. Any notion that women's caregiving responsibilities as mandated by the family devotion schema are "not fair" or "unbearable" dissolves in the face of their husbands' consuming work devotion, their definition of children as needing and deserving highly involved care, and their dependence on their husbands' incomes to finance their family devotion.

Naturalization of the Family Devotion Schema

The family devotion schema is a cultural model that remains compelling, despite its violation of the economist's assumptions about family economic rationality and despite the career sacrifice it demands of high-achieving women. Cultural schemas are constructed gradually by society over time. Often, their emergence is abetted by powerful groups whose interests they serve. The schemas often become semi-independent from the social conditions that generated them and become causally important in their own right (Alexander, 1988; Weber, 1958b). But to become powerful and persuasive, these schemas need to become naturalized, which means people take them for granted and can barely imagine an alternative. These cultural definitions are then assumed to be part of the natural order of things (Douglas, 1986).

Many people in the United States believe that the division of labor mandated by the family devotion schema is based in biology. This belief stands in contrast to arguments made by social scientists who study gender and families. Scholars have shown that cultural models of appropriate roles for men and women vary widely over historical time and across places. They advocate a social construction of gender argument: Views of appropriate roles for men and women are constructed by people interacting with one another in particular societies. These scholars maintain that it is not a biological instinct tied to female chromosomes or hormones but instead the *social experience* of primary caregiving that creates what our society knows as "mother-hood." In other words, it is the lived experience, normatively upheld by the rest of society, of caring for children that creates the bonds and feelings we know as "mother nature."[19]

The current social organization of our families, particularly since the industrial revolution when men left the family farm to work for wages in towns and factories, is that women are primarily responsible for children's care. But if our society were organized so that men, rather than women, were required to have primary and intense re-sponsibility for children, that cultural rule would become naturalized instead. In this hypothetical situation, most Americans would come to assume there was something called "father nature" and take for granted a father's natural, instinctual bond with his children.[20]

Like many Americans, the women I interviewed assume that women's caregiving responsibility is part of a biological process. They believe that biology makes the caregiving role natural.[21] For example, Mary Warshawski, a former marketing executive now home with three boys, said: "Every mother wants to be home with her baby. It's mother nature. It's an animal instinct." Similarly, former banker Eliz-abeth Cruz is now home with three young children. She answered my question about whether she had ever considered alternative domestic arrangements:

> We joked about my husband staying home. We were making the same amount of money. But we didn't talk about it seriously. There are mechanisms of nursing a child. You can't get away from the fact that women bear children. My mom was home with us.

Elizabeth believes that just as biology had dictated her mother would raise her, it also decreed that she would stay home to bear, nurse, and raise her own children, notwithstanding her MBA from a top-five business school and former promising career.

Yvonne Smith is a former consultant who has an MBA from another top-five school and whose full-time salary had been three times that of her husband. She commented that mothers are simply biologically better at being the "primary parent."

> My husband would not be as good of a parent being a primary parent. He would find it very difficult . . . He'd be very antsy to get back to work. It would drive him crazy. This is typical of males versus females. Moms can put their own needs below others in the family. Most fathers are not as able. Some of it is the biological attachment between the child and the mother. How the child is born, the experience of nursing . . . It's impossible for me not to completely accept that commitment [of being the primary parent]. I can't look the other way.

Yvonne believes that although her husband is well suited to obey the work devotion schema, the "biological attachment" between mother and child, intensified by the experiences of childbirth and nursing, compels her to fulfill the responsibilities mandated by the family devotion schema. Her conviction that it is natural for women to forfeit their career aspirations helps Yvonne come to terms with sacrificing her own career ambitions.

Susan Pflanz concurs that the domestic and employment roles for men and women mandated by the family devotion schema are biologically based. Musing about why most men do not do more caregiving work, she says:

> Maybe it's genetic too. I'm more biologically connected to my children. I have more of a link with them than my husband does. Men love their children; they would do anything to take care of them, to protect them. But the day-to-day stuff is harder for men.

The social construction of gender argument is just not very convincing to these women, who have found the biological explanation so useful for making sense of how they spend their lives. For example, Cindy Kroeger had learned the social construction of gender argument when she was a sociology major in college. But she now explicitly rejects it. She said that her experience of raising two sons has taught her that the social scientists are wrong, and that innate gender differences explain her sons' aggressive behavior.

> As a sociologist, I used to think that there was a lot more environmental stuff going on and that the differences between men and women could easily be attributed to socialization, and I have since changed my views on that. It's part of observing two male children and seeing how different they are at young ages. They're hunters (laughter). We gave them unisex toys. They only wanted the gun. We didn't want them to have guns. That's all they wanted; they turned every stick or baseball bat into a gun.

She believes that just as men are biologically programmed to be hunters out making a living, women are naturally the nurturing caregivers at home, whether or not they also have jobs. She sees this pattern among her employed women friends, who strive for egalitarian marriages but still end up doing most of the domestic work. The biological explanation makes sense of this pattern and legitimates it as unalterable.[22]

According to this viewpoint, a life lived in harmony with the natural order of things also creates the most personal happiness for women and children. Linda Giovanni, a part-time banker, explained that:

> My one-year [maternity] leave was great. Studies show that women are happier if they stay home [after childbearing] for at least a year and then don't go back full-time. I've read that several places. And I know its true because I've lived it!

Family-committed women firmly believe that the domestic roles prescribed by the family devotion schema are validated by biology and scientific studies and further confirmed by personal experience. This belief gives the schema the legitimacy of a cosmic plan and embeds the schema into a net of assumptions that can scarcely be questioned.

Despite the conviction that an involved motherhood is what nature intended, family-committed members recall the transition from full-time careers to a new status as homemakers as far from effortless or natural. Women discussed the brutal shock of just being "somebody's mom" rather than a highly respected professional or executive leading an exciting life. They experienced isolation, alienation, and boredom until they joined a communion of like-minded family devotees.

Seven of the ten full-time homemakers explicitly discussed the importance of making connections with other business and professional women who had embarked on similar homemaking vocations. This community became critical for affirming their own faith in the family devotion schema and for maintaining their sanity.

For instance, Nina Lombardi commented on the rocky transition from her corporate law firm position to being home full-time with her new baby:

> The first few months I was in shock. I went from working day and night, being on this career track, to just being at home. But I quickly built up a support network with Vicki and some other moms.

Recall Mary Warshawski's early remark that "every mother wants to be home with her baby. It's mother nature. It's an instinct." Later in the interview, she told me that staying home all day with her first baby had been agonizing until she developed relationships with similar mothers:

> It was an awful transition, staying home. I was lonely, alienated. It was terrible. It took me six months to get used to it. Until I finally met other women, other professional women who wanted to stay home with their children. First of all, you have to find a

playgroup. That is why playgroups are so popular, so mothers can keep some semblance of sanity.

On a sunny fall morning, Mary and I met in a café in her suburban town and then ran some errands. Throughout the morning, we bumped into three women, with children in tow, whom Mary knew socially. They discussed the upcoming community harvest festival, which Mary was coordinating. In the six years since she was last in the labor market, she has built up a supportive community of other mothers who share with her a life organized around dedication to family and civil society.

Rebecca Feinstein, now working very hard at a nominally part-time job, would agree with Mary Warshawski that the experience of motherhood becomes most meaningful when placed in the context of other mothers who cherish time spent serving family and community. She nostalgically remembered her thirteen-month maternity leave: "I loved being home with my baby. It was great. I got involved with the community. I got involved at the temple. I didn't miss work at all." Similarly, Carol Walker survived the loneliness and boredom of raising young children by plunging herself into a network of mothers who do volunteer work in the community.

As Marsha Dickens put it, spending time with other women who share your commitments is "the thing that sort of saves people." These communities are doing the work of the social construction of gender. Although these women give the credit to biology, it is their communities of like-minded mothers rather than their genes that create and affirm devoted motherhood.

Tension between the Family Devotion Schema and Late-Industrial Trends

The family devotion schema is in tension with several late-industrial trends, including the rise in mothers' labor force participation, the increase in divorce, and the increase in women's career opportunities and aspirations sparked by the second wave of feminism. Women's labor force participation has grown steadily throughout the twentieth century, but since 1950 the sharpest increase has occurred among mothers of young children (Bianchi, 1995; McLanahan and Casper, 1995; Hayghe, 1997).

Rising female labor force participation set the stage for the revival of feminism in the 1970s, which in turn encouraged women's employment in traditionally masculine occupations (Shu and Marini, 1998; Giele, 1995; Klein, 1984). The federal government finally began to enforce women's employment and education rights in the early to mid-1970s. Title IX of the Education Amendment of 1972 and other legislation contributed to the soaring female rates of enrollment in business and law schools in the 1970s (Spain and Bianchi, 1996).

Most of the women I interviewed entered the labor force after the passage of legislation prohibiting explicit gender discrimination in schools and workplaces, and during a time in which liberal feminism encouraged women's aspirations toward well-paid and male-dominated occupations. My respondents took advantage of these new resources and gender-egalitarian schemas. They pursued advanced degrees in business and law and then built careers in prestigious, male-dominated occupations. Women in the career-committed group are on the leading edge of this trend, as they maintain uninterrupted, full-time careers and climb to positions of corporate power (Blair-Loy, 1999).

Family-committed women, especially those who are home full-time, have turned away from their investment in education and early careers to focus on caring for children and volunteering in their communities. Yet most mothers are employed today; the numbers of full-time homemakers in the United States have plummeted. For example, between 1976 and 1996, the proportion of working mothers with their youngest child between the ages of six and seventeen jumped from 55 percent to 77 percent. Over the same period, the proportion of mothers of preschoolers in the labor force increased from 38 to 62 percent, while the proportion of women with children under age one in the labor force soared from 31 to 55 percent (Barnett, 1999).

A common factor supporting mothers' labor force participation is economic necessity, especially given the stagnation of male wages since the early 1970s (Levy, 1995). Most married couples now depend on two incomes (Jacobs and Gerson, 2001; U.S. Bureau of the Census, 1998.) Despite their generous salaries, my respondents' husbands may begin to feel financially pinched when they are surrounded by dual-earning couples.[23]

A few of the women home full-time said that their husbands were tiring of shouldering the breadwinner responsibility alone. For example, Nina Lombardi, whose two children are now in school, feels pressured by her husband to re-enter the labor force.

> Until recently, I felt supported by [my husband], and that he valued my contribution. But last year we were struggling financially . . . He was stressed about money. I felt a lot of guilt . . . I get mixed signals from him, like I should be contributing financially. I'm not feeling this from inside me . . . For the time being, I like being home. I wish this could last forever, because it's a wonderful life.

She still immensely enjoys her role in the devotion to family schema, but her husband is growing weary of being the sole provider.

Similarly, Naomi Schumacher says that her husband "keeps asking me when I will go back to work. He tries to sit me down and have a discussion about my long range plans." Both women are so far resisting a return to the labor market. But in an era in which over two-thirds of women with young children are employed, these respondents are staying home on borrowed time. Even for women married to high-earning husbands, the family devotion schema's promise of financial support for caregiving wives may have an expiration date.

Schemas of devotion are embedded in and stabilized by supporting
ligaments and tissues of relationships and institutions. For professional women to abandon or curtail promising careers, some do profound emotion work to cope with this loss. Just as the work devotion
schema depends on a complementary but unequal relationship between employer and manager, the family devotion schema depends
on a complementary but unequal relationship between husband and
wife. Often, these human relationships and cultural schema each reaffirm and legitimate the other. But when the relationships, as ordained
by the schema, start to break apart, the schemas are threatened as well.
Similarly, a change in schemas can threaten the work and family relationships they govern.

3

REINVENTING SCHEMAS: CREATING PART-TIME CAREERS

Many in the career-committed group take their allegiance to their employers for granted, rarely questioning how much the firm demands of them. For these women, work devotion renders life meaningful and rewarding. This cultural definition is tremendously powerful in shaping their worldview, and it is reinforced by their bosses, coworkers, and the ways that the firm's resources seem to flow to those who express the most dedication to the company.

Yet despite its power, the work devotion schema does not fully determine the aspirations of every professional. Some career-committed women grow disillusioned with its promises. And the twenty-five women in the family-committed group, invested in family devotion, openly defied the work devotion schema by leaving full-time positions after having children.

This chapter studies the fifteen family-committed women who work part-time in high-level positions. They see themselves as both committed professionals and as devoted mothers. They are trying to transform the organizational policies and workplace cultures rooted in the work devotion schema by openly dividing their commitment between work and nonwork endeavors.

Their bosses and many coworkers strongly oppose their efforts and define part-timers as uncommitted, second-class corporate citizens. The opposition of supervisors and colleagues is rooted not in economic rationality but in the defense of an established cultural order in which they are deeply invested.

Despite this antagonism, these part-timers continue to challenge the work devotion schema's dictate that professional worthiness can exist only among full-time workers. They hold fast to their roles and identities as dedicated workers *and* highly involved mothers, while refusing to abandon either source of meaning in their lives. At the same time, this chapter illustrates the tenacity of both work and family devotion schemas.

The Meaning of Part-Time Work

The extent to which professional women desire to work fewer hours is an area of spirited debate among social scientists.[1] Even workers who desire to reduce their hours may not be interested in jobs labeled as "part-time." Part-time positions are often regarded as "mommy track" ghettos lacking career advancement possibilities. For instance, part-time lawyers in the U.S. are considered "time deviants" uncommitted to their work; this stigma limits the number of attorneys who desire to and who are able to negotiate reduced workloads (Epstein et al., 1999; see also Williams and Calvert, 2001; Women's Bar Association of Massachusetts, 2000). And in a study of professionals in a large financial services firm, less than two percent of the sample worked part-time, while a quarter said they would like to work part-time but felt they could not, partly due to fears about the effect on their careers (Wharton and Blair-Loy, 2002).[2]

These findings suggest that the number of hours worked per se is less important than the *meaning* of these hours. Many would probably relish extra time for spending with family or for errands, sleep, or leisure. But the experiences of the women I interviewed suggest that asking for a work arrangement defined by the organization as "part-time" is treacherous.

In the family-committed group, eleven women had attempted, achieved, or were currently trying to create part-time arrangements. Of these, ten reported resistance from employers and coworkers to working part-time. This resistance ranged from feeling unwelcome to being denied promotion to losing a job.

This opposition is not rooted purely in an economic cost-benefit analysis. Generally, turnover costs to replace professional-level employees are very high (Williams and Calvert, 2001 or Women's Bar Association of Massachusetts, 2000; Williams, 2000; Hochschild, 1997).[3] Flexible working arrangements can help decrease turnover and increase productivity (Barnett and Hall, 2001; Williams, 2000; Galinsky and Bond, 1998; Tilly, 1992; Morgan and Tucker, 1991). And specifically, the women I interviewed offered their companies a good economic deal.[4] Instead, employers' hostility to part-time arrangements is rooted in the implicit belief that these managers and professionals had violated the schema of devotion to the company by publicly splitting their allegiance between work and non-work responsibilities.[5]

Giving Employers a Good Economic Deal

The twenty-five people in the family-committed group have a history of high career commitment. All have bachelor's degrees. Twenty-one (84 percent) have professional degrees (MBAs, JDs), many from prestigious schools such as Harvard, University of Chicago, Wharton, Northwestern, Yale, Georgetown, and Columbia. These women had left full-time business careers after a median of nine years of full-time work. All had last worked full-time between 1986 and 1992, when they earned a median of $70,000.[6] Eight women had earned full-time incomes substantially greater than their husbands', and another eight had earned full-time incomes roughly equal to their husbands'. Even as part-timers, four women continue to earn more than their husbands' full-time salaries.[7]

Respondents working part-time for corporations continued to offer their employers full-time dedication and made great efforts to be available whenever necessary.[8] Overall, they tried hard to justify their dedication and value, despite their violation of the work devotion schema's assumption that commitment equals full-time, undivided attention to the firm. Former banker Linda Giovanni (now home full-time) discussed the part-time arrangement she had arranged:

> I made or exceeded my performance requirements and did more than a lot of full-time people. It was a great deal for them [my employer]. They were paying me three-fifths salary, and I outperformed a lot of my full-time counterparts. I wanted to prove myself and worked really hard. I did almost as much as I did before I was part-time.

Similarly, communications firm executive Kim Fox was adamant that "you have to be totally committed" for a part-time arrangement to work.[9]

Part-time women emphasized the importance of being "available," "accessible," and "flexible." For example, Cindy Kroeger explained: "You can't practice law three days a week. I mean, not big deals. You can't do real work. You can't say to a client, 'oh, gee, I don't meet on Friday.'" Similarly, Donna Schmidt insisted, "You have to be flexible. There will be times when you have to work full-time for a while and maybe even weekends . . . [There may be] a three-month trial in San Francisco." The women also stressed the importance of availability even when they are at home with their children. Cindy Kroeger claimed that her clients had accepted her part-time status because it never inconvenienced them: "I give them my home phone, and they call me here, and they fax me here, and I'm very accessible."

Their official part-time status notwithstanding, many continue to work very long hours, especially during peak business periods. Rebecca Feinstein, an experienced attorney with a JD from Harvard, shifted to part-time after her second baby was born. She said that when she returned to work after her maternity leave, the heavy workload meant that she worked over sixty hours a week for a six-month period, despite her formal part-time status. "My hours were awful when I returned . . . I said goodbye to my baby on Sunday night and was back again on Saturday morning." Work is less hectic now, but she still "constantly" works far more than her official 60 percent schedule. For other women, long hours are a regular part of a nominally part-time schedule. For instance, Kim Fox travels for business one or two nights each week. Donna Schmidt routinely comes home after a full day at the office, gives her two preschool children dinner and puts them to bed, and then returns to the office between 9:00 P.M. and midnight. After all, she says, "I'd rather it come out of my hide than theirs."

Like full-time career-committed women, most part-timers in the family-committed group hire full-time childcare to meet the work devotion's demands of constant availability to employer and client. For example, Lisa Dunbar told me that "I've always had full-time childcare . . . I always make it possible for me to work late or come in early, or travel if I have to." Likewise, Jane Leiserson explained that "you have to be flexible. I have always had full-time childcare arranged. If a meeting comes up, I'm definitely there." Similarly, Rebecca Feinstein explained that she has always had a weekly housekeeper and a full-time, live-in nanny. "I have to have someone who lives in my house because my hours are so unpredictable. Sometimes I have to work until midnight." Cindy Kroeger told me, "I always had a full-time housekeeper, so that I didn't have the problem of saying, 'I really should be there on Friday, but I don't have anyone to take care of the kids' . . . I always had someone come in five days a week just in case I needed them." After our interview in Cindy's home, she introduced me to her housekeeper and nanny, a young woman who smiled pleasantly as she folded laundry and kept an eye on the two children.

Family-committed women working part-time for corporations and firms make remarkable efforts to fulfill the work devotion schema's mandate of commitment and availability. They are a bargain for their employers, often, as Donna Schmidt put it, "bringing home a part-time salary and working full-time." They are grateful for their official part-time status and eager to prove that they are as valuable as their full-time colleagues. Despite these heroic efforts, their part-time status almost always provokes hostility from employers and coworkers.

Employers' and Coworkers' Resistance

Ten of the eleven women who requested a part-time arrangement encountered some resistance—ranging from moderate to severe—to their requests. The sole woman who reported a universally positive experience had an implicit understanding with her boss that she would work full-time again when her children were all in school.

Levels of Resistance

Five of the eleven women seeking part-time work encountered moderate resistance. For example, although Rebecca Feinstein's boss had refused to "work with a part-timer," she was able to change to another practice area in her law firm. When Kim Fox first presented her proposal to share one full-time job with another manager, her boss's boss was "infuriated" and warned Kim: "If it doesn't work out, you will never work in this organization again." This hostility was troubling, especially given Kim's exemplary work performance to date. But at least the boss did not fire her or prohibit the arrangement.

When respondents discussed these relatively moderate forms of antagonism, two themes emerged. First, they said that their commit-

CREATING PART-TIME CAREERS   97

ment was questioned. Second, as Rebecca said, "You are a little bit of a second-class citizen." Attorney Lisa Dunbar, who officially works 80 percent of a full-time schedule, claimed that her coworkers question her commitment to the law:

> I am the main support of my family . . . But they assume, "she likes to keep her hand in, she likes to dabble in the law, but she may decide to do flower arranging tomorrow" . . . And that kind of hurts.

Similarly, Kim said that, before going part-time, her resumé "looked like the totally committed manager." Once she began job-sharing with another manager, her coworkers' reaction was: "How can they be committed? They're just part-timers."

Relations with coworkers are further strained by the necessity of being as efficient as possible. For example, Rebecca muses, "I don't have time to gossip. I'm very efficient at work. I don't have time to call someone and chat for twenty minutes." Similarly, Angie Jacobson notes that when she is in the office, she just puts her head down and plows through the work. This means that she misses "out on all the camaraderie." These comments illustrate how the work devotion schema is not a model for workplace productivity and efficiency as much as a cultural model that defines worthy identities (the "committed" full-time worker) and communities (the collegiality and shared vision of like-minded work devotees).

Negative reactions from coworkers rob these part-timers of the work devotion's promised rewards of collegiality and reinforce the moral equation of full-time work with commitment and worth. The flip side of this understanding is that part-timers are less committed, less worthy, and deserve to be treated like second-class citizens. But once we step outside of the assumptions embedded in the work devotion schema, this equation of work commitment with official full-time status seems much less obvious. These highly educated and experienced part-timers I interviewed put heroic efforts into cramming a huge workload into a reduced schedule and to being available whenever business demands it.

Four women encountered particularly strong opposition to their attempts to work part-time. One example is Deborah Stein. When I interviewed her at a downtown café, she struck me as one of the most poised, powerful, and impressive women I had yet met in my research. She has a Wharton MBA, over twenty years of business experience, and was working as chief operating officer of a large organization. She had reduced her schedule to 75 percent time a year earlier. She told me that ever since shifting to part-time, she has been "in the dog house" with her boss, feels very "vulnerable," and expects she will have to leave the firm.

Another impressive woman, Angie Jacobson, has a JD from the University of Chicago and over fifteen years of full-time experience as an attorney. She told me that she had previously worked as in-house counsel for a Fortune 500 company and wanted to reduce her hours after her first child was born. She describes how difficult it was to convince her supervisors to allow her to work part-time.

> It was a horrible meeting because they tried to cross-examine me about, "Do you think you'll be able to concentrate on work when you're here or are you just going to be here thinking about your baby?" All these cuckoo questions. It was very intrusive, but I felt that I had asked for something kind of extraordinary and that I had to put up with it or whatever. Eventually, he said yes. So, I went back three days a week.

Under the work devotion schema, such an arrangement was indeed "extraordinary." Angie was the highest-ranking employee at the company to work part-time. She did so for a year and a half, during which she received good reviews, raises, bonuses, and no indications of any problems. She became pregnant with her second child and, as a courtesy, informed her boss. When she was about seven months pregnant, her supervisors asked to talk with her.

> They said, "we need to talk to you. We have decided to eliminate your part-time position." And there I was, clearly pregnant. And they said, "but we love you, we think you're just wonderful. And we want you to come back full-time and we think this is a really good time." I remember they said, "we're the only big food company that has a senior attorney who's part-time" . . . So they gave me two weeks to think about it.

The apparent absurdity of these supervisors telling a visibly pregnant part-timer that because she is so wonderful she must work full-time (or not at all) makes sense when we see that she was openly violating the allegiance required in the devotion to work schema. Her pregnancy signaled that she would not be returning to full-time status any time soon and had powerful commitments outside the workplace.

Angie Jacobson later learned from a coworker that the CEO had strongly disapproved of her part-time status all along. Her colleague informed her that:

> The CEO felt very strongly that if you were really on the team for the company, it had to be like the most important thing in your life, and that you were really expected to eat and sleep and dream work and do everything for it. And he had said no part-time people.

This report of the CEO's views is a clear expression of the schema of devotion to work. Using his metaphor, senior managers are either on the team or off the team. Part-timers are not on the team. They are not true believers. The CEO's policy here was to uphold the devotion to work schema and banish those who dishonored it. Angie left the company and finally found a lower-status job in the legal department of another corporation.

Sacrificing Upward Mobility

All but two of the eleven women who negotiated part-time arrangements with firms said they had relinquished the chance for upward mobility. In most cases, there was a symbolic boundary making the most revered jobs—for example, equity partners in law firms or vice presidents in large corporations—off limits to those unwilling to dedicate themselves completely to the firm.[10]

Four part-time respondents are attorneys in law firms, and all four are officially or unofficially ineligible to be promoted to partner as part-timers.[11] For example, Cindy Kroeger has worked seven years full-time followed by thirteen years part-time at a large law firm. With her advancing seniority, her title was finally upgraded from associate to "of counsel," but she is ineligible to make partner. She explains:

> I am sort of this hybrid, neither here nor there. It was a way of acknowledging that I was senior. I was beyond an associate, but as long as I was part-time, they weren't willing to make me a partner . . . It will be a cold day in hell before anyone becomes a partner there.

Cindy added that she is feeling increasing pressure from the firm to return to full-time status and is growing more dissatisfied with the work assignments she receives. Because she has lost one of the core rewards of the work devotion schema, the chance to do meaningful work, she has just decided to accept a job offer at another firm. She is happy to be leaving her current organization but worried that the new firm would also pressure her to increase her hours. She explained:

> They wanted me. They did *not* want me part-time . . . I held my position and they eventually accepted me on my terms. We'll see how that works when I start in January, because maybe they did [accept my part-time status] but not really.

Other part-timers I interviewed also lost the opportunity to move upward in their firms. For instance, the director of a large financial services company explained that since she started working part-time, she relinquished the possibility to advance in her career. "I am in the top 5 percent of my company, but I'm not a vice president, and I'll never be there. I don't know any vice presidents who are working part-time."

In contrast, Kim Fox is one of two family-committed women who have crossed the symbolic boundary cordoning off part-time employees from the most revered positions in the firm. About a year before I interviewed her, she and her job-share partner Lisa were the first part-timers in their very large corporation to be promoted to the executive level. After Kim and Lisa received their promotion, they had to work with colleagues who, as Kim describes, were "horrified when we got this executive position." Kim believes she and Lisa have survived the hostility so far because "our chairman has been very supportive" of job-sharing at their firm. Now each works three-and-a-half to four days a week. She says that they are "the poster children for [our firm] as a flexible and family friendly company." Nonetheless, she continues to worry that they are in a "vulnerable" position at the company.

Forgiveness for Transgressions

If part-time professionals were willing to move back to full-time status, employers and coworkers were sometimes willing to forgive them. For example, Donna Schmidt worked full-time for nine years as an attorney in a large firm and had been considered on-track for partner. After her first child was born, she cut back to part-time. She returned briefly to full-time status but went part-time again after her second child was born. During her four years at part-time status, she officially worked 80 percent time. But "nervous about being stuck in the part-time ghetto," which she characterized as "dangerous and sad . . . [and] unfulfilling," she made sure she was available full-time, including weekends, whenever client business required it. She added:

"If you want to move up, and to work part-time, you have to be able to work full-time when you have to."

Working part-time made her ineligible for promotion to partner. I interviewed her about the time she had decided to return to full-time status for "career and promotion reasons." Her hope was that if she worked full-time intensively for several months, she would again be considered partnership material. I telephoned her several months after our interview to ask how her quest to make partner was going. She elatedly told me she had been promoted and more soberly added that this was on the condition that she promise never again to work part-time.

This struck me as a lot to ask of a fairly young mother of two preschoolers. But from the work devotion schema framework, it makes sense. The partnership decided to forgive her earlier violation and accept her into its hallowed ranks only if she would never again violate the doctrine of single-minded allegiance to the firm.

Paula Moore, the only family-committed woman who reported a universally positive experience with working part-time, reports a similar expectation that she return to full-time status. As a part-timer, she had reached the level of senior vice president in a medium-size company and was the most senior woman in the organization. She credited her continued advancement to an extremely supportive boss and to her tacit promise that she would come back to work full-time. I checked back with her after the interview, and she had indeed returned to full-time status. She explained, "As my daughter was starting first grade, I recognized that the time was right to do it . . . I didn't want to wear out my welcome in terms of being tolerated or dealt with differently, . . . and I started working full-time." She recognized that her unorthodox arrangement would not be tolerated indefinitely.

Contemplating Heresy

Those who give their lives to the company are considered true believers. They are promised full membership in its dedicated corps. But those who violate the precepts of allegiance are heretics who risk being eased out of their senior jobs or out of the organization altogether.

All but one family-committed group member had already left full-time work by the time I interviewed them. They told me about their after-the-fact interpretations of this process. Frances Swing is the one person in the family-committed group currently working full-time. She is planning to ask for part-time status and gives us the valuable perspective of someone contemplating making this heretical request before it occurs.

Frances has had a stellar career. With an engineering degree and a Harvard MBA, she rose quickly through the ranks of one of the nation's largest diversified industrial firms. As of the interview date, she is directing a key corporate division and reports to someone who reports to the chairman.

Frances also has a career-involved husband, two young children, and a new pregnancy. She does not think she can continue to perform her job full-time and care for a third child. She is planning to approach the chairman, the president, and the director of human resources, with a proposal that she work part-time. But she anticipates that it will be difficult to convince them:

> Even if I could show them an economic model and a job responsibility model showing that it would be of value to the organization to have me 60 percent of the time, they'd have a hard time relating to someone who's not there full-time. It is a big emotional hurdle . . . The people involved in this decision are all men in their fifties, who have always had spouses at home. Most of their kids are grown—they are all removed from the young children scene.

I asked her to elaborate on her supervisors' resistance to an economically sound proposal.

They will think it's not fair. Even if we've adjusted my compensation. It's hard for guys to think that someone can get the level of responsibility I have, who's not as dedicated as we guys are. They think I'm being given something special, because a man would die for that kind of job and wouldn't ask to go part-time. This argument is a red herring, but it has a real hook to it. They ask, if she *doesn't buy into it all* the way like I do, why should I let her have this job? Even if it's good for the organization. It's hard for them to stomach the idea. It's hard for them to give the status that they attribute to these jobs to someone who's not bleeding for the organization . . .

All I can do is say, "measure what you're getting with me, and decide if it's worth it." But I know it's not that rational. That's naive. Emotional reactions are still there.

Based on Frances' account, her company is full of devout adherents to the work devotion schema, who "buy into it all." She expects that her supervisors will be unable to make a rational cost-benefit analysis devoid of their commitment to this schema. She anticipates an emotional reaction based on her repudiation of the schema of devotion to the company that they hold sacred. These devotees are also willing martyrs: "a man would die for that kind of job"; they do not want to give a high-status position to "someone who's not bleeding for the organization," someone who is a nonbeliever.

I tried out this analogy with Frances:

I: Tell me what this analogy sounds like. It's like there's a close-knit group of people all worshiping a god, making sacrifices to it, and then someone like you is a doubter. That threatens the others' beliefs. Does that sound right, or not really?

R: I never thought about it like that. But it makes sense. It definitely calls into question their priorities. They see me enjoying my kids, openly looking forward to being with them. I like being here, but

I look forward to seeing them. This calls into question these guys leaving their families as much as they do. I have more flexibility within the organization than they do. I have more license to say no. It's partly because I'm willing to put myself on the line. And it's partly because I'm female . . . I like your worshiper analogy. They all feel they have no choice—it's imposed upon them. My pushing the system implies that they have a choice as well. Their sacrifices are suddenly not prescribed to the same extent.

Frances already challenges her male colleagues' public commitment to the company by her open interest in her children. For example, her office is decorated with her children's artwork. On business trips, she says good night to her colleagues early and announces that she wants to talk to her children before they go to bed. So far she has gotten away with tweaking the work devotion schema because she is competent, senior, and female. But working part-time poses a much greater threat to the work devotion schema and to her colleagues' sacrifices to that schema than do finger-painted office decorations and phone calls home. Frances predicts she has a 50 percent chance of negotiating a part-time arrangement with her company.

The allegiance requirement of the work devotion schema demands that trusted managers climbing the ladder equate the success of the company with their personal success and fulfillment. Hard work, long hours, relocation on demand, and expressed fidelity to the organization above all other commitments are required to manifest that allegiance. The company should at least appear to be "the most important thing in your life." One is "expected to eat and sleep and dream work and do everything for" the company, including, figuratively, "bleeding" and "dying." These demands are predominantly made by male senior executives who, as Frances notes, have wives at home and are "removed from the young children scene." And these demands can only be fulfilled by employees who can also act as if young children are not a major part of their lives.[12]

Most family-committed women knew that asking for a part-time schedule would jeopardize their chances of advancement, their coworker relations, and maybe their very jobs. They knew that doing so would violate the "moral imperative in [corporate] American society . . . moving up or getting ahead in the organization" (Jackall, 1988: 43). Given the compelling power of the work devotion schema and employers' monumental resistance to part-time work, how did these women decide to try to negotiate a part-time arrangement?

Despite the power of social structures, people are not completely determined by them. People do exercise a certain degree of agency, which is the capacity "for desiring, for forming intentions, and for acting creatively" (Sewell, 1992: 20). This is especially likely to happen when they live at the intersection of social structures with competing or multiple meanings. People are able to question previously taken-for-granted social arrangements when they can view them through the lens of an alternative cultural schema and when they have the material resources (for example, sufficient household income from their husbands) to act in new ways. In these cases, human agency is enlarged.[13]

Conflicting Expectations

Although the family-committed group members were immersed in the work devotion schema, they were also mothers and had to grapple with the family devotion schema. Ten family-committed women indeed found the family devotion schema's definition of reality highly compelling and left the labor market to dedicate themselves full-time to family caregiving. But the remaining fifteen women resisted succumbing completely to either schema's mandates. Within the clash of competing schemas, they struggled to create a new definition of a meaningful life.

This process was initialized by different factors for different women. Childbirth and nursing alone did not activate a conversion to a new life more consistent with the family devotion schema. These biological experiences had to be given meaning by others. Respondents accustomed to a high-powered, professional life generally reported feeling terribly isolated, lonely, and bored when first home full-time with an infant. They required a connection with a community of like-minded believers to help affirm the value of dedicating one's days to family care and civic involvements. However, these connections were harder for women working part-time to forge. They had less time to spend cultivating those ties, less time for playgroups and for volunteering, and were not always fully welcomed by at-home mothers.

We have seen that even family-committed women working long hours at part-time jobs are primarily responsible for the housework and childcare. Because all but one of the family-committed women had already left full-time work at the time of our conversations, I cannot determine how they divided domestic work with their husbands when they worked full-time. My impression, though, is that many of these women had always had marital relationships that assumed they were primarily responsible for domestic work and family caregiving.[14] Especially after having children, many found it increasingly difficult to shoulder their family responsibilities while also maintaining full-time, demanding careers. For these women, meeting the expectations of a good mother and a committed professional became impossible.

Recasting Identities

Cultural schemas pattern interactions and expectations of colleagues and spouses. They also shape personal identities. Several women in the family-committed group struggle with relinquishing their single-minded focus on their careers. They remain ambivalent, still pulled by loyalty to their previous vocation yet also do deep "emotion work" (Hochschild, 1979) to induce feelings appropriate to their new social structural situation. For instance, Jane Leiserson articulated the painfully competing tugs of work and family devotion:

Going part-time was a difficult decision. First, I knew I wouldn't advance in my career. How much would that matter to me? I finally decided that it doesn't. I've plateaued out. That's fine. Work is a priority for me, but I'm not going to dedicate my entire life to it, in lieu of family. It's tough. I went to graduate school. I see my classmates pass me by. I knew I wouldn't progress any higher. I had to realize that it's OK.

Despite the great meaning work has for her, Jane self-consciously forsakes the work devotion schema's demands that she "dedicate" her "entire life" to work. She does the emotion work to "realize that it is OK" to renounce her desire for the rewards of career advancement. Although she continues to put in long hours at her job, to be available whenever the company needs her, and to rely on full-time childcare, she also relishes the extra time she has to spend with her two daughters.

Rebecca Feinstein describes a similar, self-conscious process of renouncing the work devotion schema's claims:

I do feel pangs . . . Sometimes I think maybe I made the wrong decision. You have to weigh everything . . . [But now my career] is not my source of self-image and satisfaction. It is more important for me to take care of my kids right now.

Kim Fox insists she has never regretted her decision to shift to part-time. But then she adds: "But sometimes, I've had twinges. I'm not someone who'd be content to work at a lower level, just to earn money. I need to feel like I'm doing something enjoyable, challenging, and difficult."

Deborah Stein spent much of the interview relating her joy in spending more time with her son, now that she works part-time. Toward the end she dropped into a confessional tone and admitted the "terrible struggle" of giving up her identity as a full-time professional.

Despite the long hours and dedication that these part-time employees continue to put in, they still regard the shift to part-time status as a threat to their work identities. No matter how much energy they—as individuals—put into their work, they participate in a workplace culture that defines the part-time worker as an uncommitted, second-class corporate citizen; unworthy of ascension to the firm's most venerated positions.

The Best of Both Worlds?

Family-committed part-timers unveiled and challenged taken-for-granted cultural models, defied powerful employers, risked losing significant professional rewards, recast their identities, and forged new emotions. Once they redefined their cultural assumptions, jobs, and personal commitments, was it all worth it?

The biggest advantage is that their official part-time status put a check on the otherwise all-consuming hours demanded of their full-time colleagues. This gives them at least a little more time with their children. To illustrate, Lisa Dunbar tries to avoid going into the office one day each week, generally on Wednesday. As a full-time attorney, she never could have gotten away with that work schedule. This sanctioned time away from work allowed her to watch her five-year-old's butterfly migration parade at school and gives her afternoons with her girls at the swim club.

Thus, respondents working part-time can to some extent adopt the family devotion schema's definition of children as precious, fragile, and completely deserving of a mother's care. For example, Deborah Stein walks her young son to school each morning. Angie Jacobson, mother of two preschoolers, says, "Your kids need you more as they get older. They don't need you to change their diaper anymore, but they need you in terms of being more important that you're available to go on a class trip." Rebecca Feinstein believes that children continue to need much of their mothers' time, even after they are in school. "Now that my daughter is starting school, she needs me to help her with her assignments. I want to go to her school functions, to her soccer games, to her ballet performances." If Donna Schmidt worked full-time, she would not be able to escape the office before six most evenings. As a part-timer, she is able to believe—and act on that belief—that her preschoolers need her to eat dinner with them and put them to bed, even though she does have to go back to the office from 9:00 P.M. to midnight.

In some ways, the family-committed women viewed these reduced-hours arrangements as the best of all possible worlds. Some women talked about how fulfilling multiple roles of professional, mother, and wife made each separate role more enjoyable. Several respondents commented on the relief of returning to work part-time after their maternity leaves ended. For example, Angie Jacobson remarked:

> When I was home, I didn't actually think I was that great of a stay at home mom. I didn't really like it that much. I'm not that patient or that great with my kids. I love them, but I love them better when I work three days.

Cindy Kroeger echoed:

> My baby was definitely on my mind, but at the same time, I was getting bored being home all day, every day taking care of him. As much as I loved him ... I would sort of work Tuesday, Wednesday and Thursday, and then I would have four days with him, and by the end of four days, I was ready for adult company and to have more freedom.

Similarly, Frances Swing noted:

> It is a really positive thing in my life to have an intellectually engaging and challenging job, to have children and to have a strong

partnership at home. Anything I can do to keep one makes me better at the other two ... It is not just an economic issue. It is part of my personality to keep them all going.

She is finding it impossible "to keep them all going" on a full-time schedule but hopes that this balance will be achievable if she can convince her company to let her keep her job part-time.[15]

Setting a limit on hours spent at work also gave respondents time to connect with the broader community.[16] Family-committed mothers who were home full-time had more opportunity to be involved with community activities. But part-timers also discussed civic ties. For example, Jane Leiserson's schedule allows greater civic engagement than she had had as a full-time manager. She said, "I spend more time with the kids now, but I also do a million volunteer things. But they are all kid-related. I have two Girl Scout troops. And there's Sunday School." Jane seems satisfied with building a life atop the contradictions of work versus family devotion. She acknowledges that even though she has no chance of further advancement at work, she is happy with the terms she has set. After all, she reasons, "all people plateau at some point," and she insists that, "I have the best of both worlds."

Others were less sanguine about living within the tension of both devotion schemas. Angie Jacobson, who had complained of being a second-class citizen at work, also feels rejected by the at-home mothers of her children's friends.

The moms who did not work outside the home felt like, "well, she's not really a mother. She's basically like really a working mother, but yeah, she's around two days during the week" ... If they wanted to do something, it's so complicated. I have to get my calendar out to figure out whether I can do anything on a particular weekday. Usually I can't ... So it's always a conflict and stress and stuff, trying to do both.

Despite these problems, she hastens to add, "I am not complaining . . . I'm lucky that I'm able to do both at all."

Rachel Kahn agrees that "Doing both [working part-time and raising children] is hard. You never feel you are doing either one well." Nonetheless, she insists that balancing her part-time, freelance business and time to spend with her two daughters gives her "the best situation of anyone I know."

It is easier to live squarely within one set of social structures—according to one cultural model and supported by a consistent set of positive interactions and rewards—than to live in the ambiguous interstices between social structures. The part-time women I interviewed live as double heretics, refusing to commit all of themselves to work or to motherhood and not fully accepted by either full-time colleagues or the full-time mothers of their children's friends. But despite the challenges, they persist in living openly in *two* worlds and to display manifest commitments to both workplace and home.

Possibilities for Change

By publicly splitting their allegiance between work and home, part-time employees in the family-committed group are no longer considered true believers and risk being confined to a "part-time ghetto" of "second-class citizens" or risk losing their jobs altogether. These women withstood wrenching redefinitions of their internal and social identities in order to try to resolve their professional commitment with their desire to live up to the cultural expectations of a devoted mother. Cultural change often occurs as people struggle to reconcile different schemas, competing cultural models of a worthwhile and desirable life. Family-committed mothers are trying to create a new workplace culture, in which dedicated professionals are not penalized by their formal part-time status. They make heroic efforts to provide dedicated service and total availability, yet also place some limits on work demands so they can spend more time with their children.

This effort to redefine worthiness extends to other groups of professional women as well. For example, at the financial services firm Deloitte & Touche, men tended to assume that people working flexible or reduced hours were less committed to their jobs, while women generally believed that these people were more committed. The women reasoned that, given the challenges of negotiating flexible work schedules with family responsibilities, these employees must be extremely committed to their work. Otherwise, they would have simply quit their jobs (reported in Williams and Calvert, 2001). Some female attorneys in a study of Washington, D.C., law firms insisted that they could be just as intensely committed to a smaller number of clients on a reduced-hours basis as they had been to a larger clientele on a full-time basis. For example, one Washington lawyer asked: "Lawyers can balance three cases and not get stigmatized. Why can't they balance two cases and a kid?" (quoted in Williams and Calvert, 2001: 14).

The part-time women I interviewed are both revolutionary and traditional. This chapter has illustrated the continuing resonance of the work and family devotion schemas, despite the challenge to them that these women pose by striving to be openly committed to both careers and involved motherhood.

In the workplace, the part-timers are mavericks. They are defying long-established cultural meanings, challenging bosses and colleagues, and trying to create new structures that accommodate and reward the contributions of dedicated part-timers. At the moment, the proponents of work devotion seem to be winning. But over time, part-timers' efforts could help reduce the pressure on all high-level professionals to demonstrate work commitment with very long hours.

By not staying home full-time, respondents are in some ways flouting the family devotion schema's prescription for the ideal mother. Some believe their professional engagements make them *better* mothers. However, many also said that their family workload had grown heavier after they began working part-time. They traded in full-time jobs for more housework, despite their generous full-time incomes. By taking on more domestic work and by affirming mothers' unique cultural mandate to be concerned with and protective of their children's day-to-day well-being, they demonstrate the resilience and resonance of the family devotion schema.

4

REINVENTING SCHEMAS:
FAMILY LIFE AMONG
FULL-TIME EXECUTIVE WOMEN

This chapter considers the fifty-six women in the career-committed group, thirty-five of whom are childless.[1] By dedicating their lives to their careers, these women affirm the work devotion schema. By relinquishing childbearing, they also implicitly uphold the family devotion schema's definition of motherhood as requiring one's primary allegiance. Thus many childless women in the career-committed group largely agree with the family-committed group that children deserve a mother's intensive care.

Yet twenty-one career-committed respondents (38 percent) *do* have children, while continuing to pursue demanding, uninterrupted full-time careers.[2] An analysis of these women reveals that the family devotion schema is powerful but not static; the younger mothers in this group are stretching the family schema to accommodate their career commitment.

The women in the career-committed group vary widely in age. To analyze the interplay and conflict between the two devotion schemas over time, I divided the career-committed group into three birth cohorts: the World War II era, the early baby boom, and the mid–baby boom. Each cohort has achieved extraordinary professional success. Yet each has been forced to reckon with the competing forces of the devotion to work and devotion to family schemas. One outcome is that all cohorts have far lower childbearing rates than the national population for women of similar ages.

Older career-committed respondents were more likely to accept both devotion schemas' definitions of an irreconcilable conflict between work and family, prompting many to avoid marriage and childbearing or to sequence childrearing before launching their finance careers. But the youngest cohort (mid–baby boom) took advantage of newly emerging career opportunities and established themselves professionally before marrying and having children. By raising children while pursuing full-time, demanding careers, the youngest cohort challenges the family devotion schema's mandate that children are fragile and deserve a mother's time-intensive, absorbing care.[3]

Cultural schemas shape our action in part by defining what is possible or reasonable. People are able to seriously imagine an alternative to something like the family devotion schema's definition of motherhood only if they come into contact with alternative cultural models. These alternatives provide new ideological resources, here, new ways of thinking about marriage and motherhood. People also need sufficient material resources, such as income and prestige, to challenge older cultural models and to ensure others' cooperation as they live into new ones.

Unlike older cohorts, the youngest cohort launched finance careers a median of ten years before marrying. They thus brought important material and ideological resources with them into their marriages, including high incomes, their own work devotion, and an emerging sense of gender egalitarianism. These resources allowed them to craft more equal marriages and to begin to refashion the family devotion schema. They have begun to reinvent the role of wife and mother as a strong breadwinner who is often physically absent and delegates immediate caregiving responsibilities to paid caregivers. Nonetheless, the family devotion schema continues to haunt even the youngest cohort, enduring in its cognitive, moral, and emotional power.

Cohort Definitions

Historical events affect our structural opportunities and our ways of interpreting the world. Thus, different cohorts will have different opportunities and cultural understandings available to them (Whittier, 1995; Mannheim, 1952). The resurgence of the women's movement was a historical event that helped establish the enforcement of equal employment rights, fostered gender-egalitarian ideologies, and encouraged young women to enter male-dominated occupations (Shu and Marini, 1998; Jacobs, 1989). In the early 1970s, the contemporary women's movement erupted onto college campuses, attracted national media attention, and enjoyed exponential growth (Ferree and Hess, 1985; Klein, 1984). Under pressure of feminist lobbying groups and changing public opinion, feminists won unprecedented victories in Congress and the courts in the early 1970s, including several landmark triumphs for women's rights in education and the workplace (Klein, 1984).

Yet these legal changes did not begin to be implemented until a few years later. For example, women's employment rights had been enacted in Title VII of the Civil Rights Act of 1964 but were not enforced until the early to mid-1970s (Kessler-Harris, 1994). Title IX of the Education Amendment of 1972 prohibited gender discrimination in schools, yet it had little effect until 1976 (Reskin and Hartmann, 1986). Public opinion throughout the 1970s and 1980s grew more favorable toward egalitarian gender roles (Mason and Lu, 1988).

This literature suggests three periods for college-educated women entering the adult work world. Women finishing college before 1969 would have come of age in an era of traditional gender role attitudes (Mason, Czajka and Arber, 1976). In contrast, women graduating between 1969–1973 would have been in college or poised to enter the work world when feminism took off as a mass movement and an unprecedented number of legal challenges to employment discrimination were undertaken.

Women finishing college 1974–1980 joined the labor force after many of these legal changes had become more institutionalized in the public realm and egalitarian ideologies had grown more acceptable in public opinion. In short, the women's movement helped make new ideological and material resources available to women aspiring to prestigious, male-dominated careers. I expect that these new career opportunities affect finance executives' cultural understandings and actions regarding family.

Thus, I divided the career-committed group into three cohorts. The oldest cohort was born around the time of World War II and graduated from college between 1956 and 1968, before contemporary feminism was a mass movement (N = 21). The middle cohort, from the early baby boom, graduated from college between 1969 and 1973 when the feminist movement ignited (N = 15). The youngest cohort, from the mid–baby boom, finished college between 1974 and 1980 when workplace gains had become more securely established (N = 20).[4]

Shared Conflicts

For all three cohorts in the career-committed group, countless meetings, travel, "face time" at the office, and evenings and weekends spent entertaining clients add up to very long days. Although many respondents may have originally felt that the pressure to work long hours was coercively applied by employers, they have at least partially internalized this ethic and now, as senior managers, enforce it among their subordinates.

Career-committed women claimed that most of their male colleagues had unemployed wives who helped care for them at the end of the exhausting workday. In contrast, only one woman in my study had a husband, employed part-time, who was primarily oriented toward caring for the family.[5]

Almost two-thirds of the career-committed group responded to these work demands and the lack of a caregiving spouse by not having children. For example, Penny Smith, a youngest cohort partner in an accounting firm discussed how she and her husband had decided to remain childless:

> [The decision not to have kids] was difficult and it took us a long time . . . Someone needed to be available. Not that somebody needs to be home full time. We could certainly afford whatever kind of childcare we would want to have, so that wasn't an issue. But that somebody needed to have flexibility and availability in their schedule. And I wasn't willing to give that up in mine and he wasn't willing to give that up in his . . . So we got a dog (laughter).

Despite her laughter, she says that the decision to remain childless was "difficult" and took "a long time" to make. Jen Carpenter from the middle cohort remained childless by default: "I never really made a conscious decision not to have kids. It was circumstantial. It's never been the right time at work." Yet she acknowledges regret over this default decision: "I still have pangs when I hold a baby."

These women are similar to the "transitional," "ambivalent" women Ireland (1993: 41–42) identifies who, for professional or other reasons, delay childbearing until it is too late. Other women I interviewed seemed more intentionally childless, like Ireland's (1993) "transformative," "childfree" women. For both groups, childlessness is at least partly a response to the irreconcilable demands of the work and family devotion schemas.

We see further evidence of the contradiction between schemas in some interviewees' reluctance to rely professionally on women with children. Martha Ungvarsky, a childless chief financial officer, says she openly discriminates against mothers when she hires an outside accountant or lawyer: "I find myself choosing men here every day over a woman with a child. If I had kids, I might not have made the same commitment to my job." Martha also finds that motherhood hinders the careers of her own professional staff and explains why a senior vice president will not be promoted:

> My senior VP has kids. She handles it well. She's got her routine. She's very disciplined. She's unique. But she only works 45 hours a week, and she couldn't stay all night to finish a deal . . . There's a big time commitment for partners . . . If you don't have kids, you can do it. There is no glass ceiling. It is a matter of commitment and time.

Despite her competence, the senior vice president is regarded as unpromotable to the highest ranks because of a deficit in "commitment and time"; she lacks sufficient devotion to work.

Even women who are mothers can be impatient with the pull that childrearing exerts on coworkers. Elizabeth Gold, one of the two highest-ranking women in her firm, complained that female subordinates wanted to spend too much time with their children:

> First, you must have a live-in nanny. I spend $30.00 a day on cabs sending my kids to school. Yes, I spend more money than my male counterpart with a wife. But how can you be catapulted into senior levels if you are in the car pool every morning? You can't be a fabulous mom and a valuable senior member. You have to make tradeoffs.

We have seen that part-time employees are treated as lacking work commitment. Here we see the career-committed members treating even full-time colleagues as lacking work devotion if they work "only 45 hours a week," or can't "stay all night to finish a deal," or if they drive in their child's car pool. The conflict between being a "fabulous mom" and a "valuable senior member" of the firm is rooted in the contradiction between the family devotion and work devotion schemas.

Elizabeth Gold also complained about women taking their entire allotted three-month maternity leave, reasoning that if the firm could get along without them for three months, the firm did not need them at all. A female executive's pregnancy is problematic because it is a reminder of the work devotion schema's chief rival, the family devotion schema. Similarly, when another youngest cohort member, Catherine Hanke, told her boss she was pregnant, he warned her not to say anything but to allow him to "disseminate this information" so that he could "put a positive spin on it." Although she was not fired, she believes that her advancement will slow. The three cohorts draw on different ideal and material resources to interpret and reconcile the conflict between dedication to their careers and devotion to their families.

The Oldest Cohort

Members of the oldest cohort were born in the World War II era, finished college between 1956 and 1968, and were mostly in their fifties when I interviewed them. Table 4.1 illustrates that about two-thirds of the twenty-one oldest cohort members were married at the time of the interview. Yet almost a quarter never married, which is a rate much greater than that of the national population.[6] These women found the family devotion schema and their career plans irreconcilable and avoided conflict by not marrying.

For example, banker Betty Maus said: "But, no, I've never been married. I never really believed that there's a man important enough to make the compromises that you have to be married. And then quite frankly, you get to a point where you just don't have to." She found the "compromises" of subordinating herself to a man according to the family devotion schema were not worthwhile, especially when she had no need of a man's income. In a society in which marriage is normative, the rejection of marriage appears to be an innovative solution

Table 4.1 Family Status of First Sample *vs.* National Population by Age Cohort

Cohort	Sample Rates, % (N)	Ratio of Sample Rates/ All White Women Rates[++]
Oldest cohort World War II era (N)		
(b. 1937–1946, grad 1956–1968, interview age 48–60)		
Cohort N	21	
Percent never-married	24% (5)	3.8
Percent married[+] (9 1st + 5 remarriages)	67% (14)	0.9
Percent divorced[+]	10% (2)	0.7
Percent childless among 16 ever-married	44% (7)	5.2
Middle cohort early baby boom (N)		
(b. 1947–1951, grad 1969–1973, interview age 43–47)		
Cohort N	15	
Percent never-married	13% (2)	1.4
Percent married[+] (no remarriages)	33% (5)	0.4
Percent divorced[+]	53% (8)	3.8
Percent childless among 13 ever-married	77% (10)	6.4
Youngest cohort mid–baby boom (N)		
(b. 1952–1958, grad 1974–1980, interview age 35–42)		
Cohort N	20	
Percent never-married	10% (2)	0.7
Percent married[+] (13 1st + 1 remarriage)	70% (14)	0.9
Percent divorced[+]	20% (4)	1.8
Percent childless among 18 ever-married	50% (9)	3.8

+ Married means currently married or remarried; divorced is as of the interview date.

++ My sample ages differ from the national sample as follows: Oldest chohort: my sample is 48–60 years; national sample is 48–57. Middle cohort: my sample is 43–47 years; national sample is also 43–47. Youngest cohort: my sample is 35–42 years; national sample is 38–42.

Note: National sample marital status percentages are calculated from the U.S. Bureau of the Census (1992, 18, Table 1). Childlessness figures for the middle and youngest cohorts are from U.S. Department of Commerce (1992, 71, Table 94). Age ranges are taken from 1991 ages (45–54 for the oldest cohort; 40–44 for the middle cohort; 35–39 for the youngest cohort). National figures for marital status refer to white women living in a metropolitan area. The childlessness figure for the oldest cohort is weighted by the proportion in the sample from age group 45–49 in 1991 (71 percent of sample) which was 9.4 percent childless when aged 40–44 in 1986 (U.S. Department of Commerce 1988, 66, Table 95) and the age group 50–54 in 1991 (29 percent of sample), which was 5.9 percent childless when aged 40–44 years old in 1981 (U.S. Department of Commerce 1986, 61, Table 92). National childlessness figures are for ever-married white women.

to the conflict between work devotion and family devotion schemas. At the same time, this solution is an implicit acceptance of both schemas' demands.

In the oldest cohort, seven (44 percent) of the ever-married women have no children (a far greater rate than the national average; see Table 4.1). Like the always-single women in this cohort, these childless women circumvented the family devotion schema by avoiding family formation. This behavior implies an acceptance of the schema's claims "that career and motherhood are incompatible" (Gerson, 1985: 187).

Among the nine mothers, five did not work at full-time finance jobs until their children were in school. By sequencing childbearing before career launch, they fulfilled at least some of the responsibilities of a devoted mother before launching demanding new careers. This delay in launching finance careers until their children were in school was facilitated—or required—by the fact that women's access to finance positions was severely limited until the early to mid-1970s (Blair-Loy, 1999).

We have seen how resilient the family devotion schema's gendered division of labor is among part-time employees in the family-committed group. Despite their significant part-time jobs, family-committed women continued to regard their primary responsibility for household and children as inevitable. Similarly, many oldest cohort members in the career-committed sample tried to orient their employment around their primary duties defined by the family devotion schema. For instance, when Dee Dee Hengen's children entered school, she decided against a lucrative consulting job in a large public accounting firm. She explained: "My kids were young and my husband's job was demanding, and I couldn't do any business traveling." Instead, she took a job trading on the stock exchange so that she could be home afternoons when the children came home from school. Despite the allure of the consulting job, she preferred a job that would let her continue to fulfill her traditional role in the gendered division of labor. Of course, this preference was also shaped by her husband's work devotion and unavailability for afternoon childcare.

However, most oldest cohort members worked longer hours than Dee Dee Hengen. After they started their finance jobs, there was usually a painful period of negotiation during which the entire family became accustomed to the new demands on the woman's time.

For example, Marge Parsons was born in 1946, married an accountant in 1968, had children, and worked part-time in a nursery school. She discussed growing up in Alabama: "Women didn't do things other than traditional female jobs . . . And that's how I looked at work, as something you do until you get married and have children. But I also found staying home with children very grueling." After her children reached school age, she pursued a law degree. She tried to continue to fulfill her homemaking responsibilities by scheduling classes while her children were at school. But once she started practicing law, her husband resented her success. "And Jim resented it for a little bit, for a long time. It was threatening to him for awhile . . . When I first started out of law school, I moved up very rapidly in terms of salary. As I started getting closer to his salary, it became very threatening to him."

She also discussed a painful period in which her children struggled to adjust to the loss of their full-time mother. "We had a lot of problems with our kids during that period . . . I mean, my oldest kid got into drugs and he's fine now, but it was a hard time."

Marge continually used the term "difficult" to describe the transformation in her family's understanding of her role. Yet as Jim learned to accept her career commitment, she and he gradually forged a new understanding that incorporated egalitarian elements.

He used to be very proud of me for my homemaking skills. I mean, he would hold me up in front of everybody and talk about what a good cook I was. And at some point, he stopped talking about that and started talking about what a good lawyer I was.

I'm not really sure when that happened, and it clearly was well after I had been practicing law.

The Parsons' marriage survived the contested transformation of a hierarchical family into something that was closer to an egalitarian one.

As Marge Parsons illustrates, even the mothers who sequenced childbearing before launching careers could not completely escape the contradiction between the family devotion and work devotion schemas. One way to try to resolve this dilemma is to weave some egalitarian strands into traditional marriages. In this way, the Parsons and the other married oldest cohort couples with children were pioneers. In contrast, seven other oldest cohort members' marriages did not survive the contradiction between the wife's emerging career commitment and the family devotion schema with which she and her husband were raised.

The Middle Cohort

Middle cohort members were born in the early baby boom (1947–1951), finished college between 1969 and 1973, and were in their mid-forties when I interviewed them.

Marriage

The conflict between the wife's growing career dedication and the family devotion schema was even sharper for the middle cohort than it had been for the oldest cohort. Thirteen out of the fifteen middle cohort members married, but eight are now divorced. While five of the seven ever-divorced *oldest* cohort members later married new husbands who would accommodate their careers, only one of the eight divorced *middle* cohort members ever remarried, and this remarriage also ended in divorce (see Table 4.1).

Divorced middle cohort members seemed to reject marriage more decisively and bitterly than their ever-divorced counterparts in the oldest cohort. They experienced a fundamental contradiction between an independent career and the role of wife prescribed by the family devotion schema. I argue that this is due to the era in which they came of age and married and due to the timing of their marriages relative to career launch.

With the exception of one woman who delayed marriage until 1983, all of the thirteen ever-married middle cohort members married for the first time between 1968 and 1978 (with a median year of 1972). This was a period when the wider culture took the family devotion schema for granted. For example, in the mid-1970s, two-thirds of Americans agreed with the statement that "it is much better for everyone involved if the man is the achiever outside the home and the woman takes care of the home and family" (Farley, 1996). Gender-egalitarian understandings had yet to be institutionalized in the broader culture.

However, many middle cohort women attended college in the late 1960s and early 1970s. Many were exposed to feminist ideology in college and elsewhere and held contested family schemas that included both the old hierarchical and new egalitarian strands. Their husbands and boyfriends tended to believe more strongly than they did in the model of female roles ordained by the family devotion schema. For example, Marina Lugviel, a CFO of a large corporation, said that in the late 1960s and early 1970s, even relationships with politically radical men were stratified by gender.

Well for many of us, roles changed. Thank God. But when we first lived with someone or got married, we were expected to do everything at home. The man comes home, reads the newspaper, puts his feet up . . . And there was a lot of tension as the result of that . . . Women in the 1960s and '70s who were part of demonstrations or whatever or in Students for Democratic Society, women would do that stuff and still be submissive at home.

Middle cohort women entered adulthood with contradictory schemas and married their male peers who generally embraced the family devotion schema. The women entered these relationships with little income or other resources. Seven of the thirteen ever-married cohort members were married *before* they entered the finance labor market; five others married three or fewer years after their finance careers began.[7] Most began marriages without the income that might have given them bargaining power to insist that the couple adopt the embryonic cultural understanding of an egalitarian marriage.

The workplace was an important source of new schemas of egalitarian gender roles. In the early 1970s, middle cohort women could take advantage of newly gender-integrated business schools and management training programs (Blair-Loy, 1999). Once launched, their finance careers caused unanticipated changes in their marriage relationships.

Whether or not their marriages survived, middle cohort women's finance careers undermined the meaningfulness of the family devotion schema in their lives. Demanding and rewarding jobs, organized under the work devotion schema, left little time or energy for homemaking. Moreover, new resources of income, prestige, and emerging ideologies of workplace equality subverted the hierarchical relationship between husbands and wives.

Mary Woods illustrates how dedication to her work proved to be incompatible with the family devotion schema that she and her former husband had initially shared.

I loved the corporate environment . . . I didn't want my career stifled because I didn't have an MBA, that magic degree. I got it while I worked full-time. That was the start of the nail in the coffin of my marriage. I was divorced shortly afterward . . . We just grew apart. At one point we had talked about having a family. Those were his expectations. At some point I made an unconscious decision not to. It took me two and a half years to get my

MBA. I was just not around. I worked or I was at classes, evenings and weekends. I graduated, and I was like—I'm back now. But he'd filled that void . . . I shouldn't have expected him to be there.

Mary's devotion to her job created a de facto challenge to the family devotion schema and led her, perhaps unintentionally, to abandon her responsibilities under this schema. The couple was unable to adapt or create a new schema under which the marriage could be salvaged.

As another example, Sue Jeffers believes that the contradictions between the devotion to family schema and her new career dedication—coupled with her firm's demands for long hours and travel—were irreconcilable.

My breakup with my . . . husband was career exacerbated due to the fact that I wasn't the person he initially married . . . I used to be home at night to put dinner on the table. Once I had my MBA, I was home at 8 P.M. and would leave by 5 A.M. He thought I was getting big for my britches . . . But at some point, everyone he played cards with, their wives were home in the evening. He tried to be supportive.

But her husband was unable to accept her transformation into an independent professional. Sue sadly described an instance when she returned from a business trip and found her husband crying from loneliness. According to the family devotion schema, she had abandoned him.

In contrast to the women who emphasized a job's impact on a personal marital relationship, Mindy Stone cites societal understandings of marriage as a threat to career success and financial independence. She married during college, graduated in 1970, and she and her husband both began banking careers in 1972. She explains why her career accelerated after 1979. "When I divorced in 1979, my salary jumped 50 percent. We were making the same amount of money [before the divorce]. Either my employer was holding my salary close to his at his bank, or they now realized I was a free agent and they were at risk of losing me."

Twenty years later, she began cohabiting with a man in her luxurious house. She has no plans to remarry. She says:

> No, I won't get married again. Society strips women of too many rights . . . It angers me . . . People are always surprised that a single woman could buy such a big house.

Several other oldest and middle cohort women cohabit with men they met later in life and do not plan to marry. When marriage is fraught with connotations of subservience, it is not surprising that these now older, independent women reject it.

Most middle cohort marriages were ruptured by a painful conflict between the wife's emerging allegiance to work and the family devotion schema's complementary, hierarchical model of marriage. Due to a lack of material and ideological resources, most failed in their semi-deliberate attempts to transpose an egalitarian understanding onto married life. They were unable to bridge the gap between work and family devotion schemas with new cultural rules.

On the other hand, five middle cohort women have maintained intact marriages. At least two appear to have egalitarian and companionate relationships. The members of one couple both work in financial services and spent their last long vacation hiking together in the Himalayas. The other couple includes two bankers; the husband has geographically relocated twice to support the wife's career. Like the currently married oldest cohort couples, these stable middle cohort couples pioneered an emerging egalitarian marriage schema that would become more widely established among the youngest cohort.

Motherhood

The family devotion schema puts most of the childrearing burden on the mother. Even middle cohort members who struggled for egalitarian relationships with their husbands accepted the family devotion schema's definition of childhood. They took for granted that children are fragile and need a mother's tender and intensive care.

Given this assumption, it is not surprising that twelve of the fifteen middle cohort members (77 percent of the thirteen ever-married women) never became mothers. For example, Mindy Stone remarks: "I couldn't give up the financial independence . . . Raising kids is a big responsibility." Despite their desire for egalitarian relationships with men, most middle cohort members still believe in the durable cultural model of intensive motherhood, which would conflict sharply with their hard-earned career success and financial independence. Childlessness is their response to this dilemma. Some women I interviewed experienced it as a painful loss, a forced choice given the limited options available under the reigning devotion schemas (Ireland, 1993).

Choosing both work and motherhood was an option for only the three middle cohort members who foreshadowed a new definition of motherhood that became more common with the youngest cohort. In this new definition, mothers delegated much day-to-day childcare to other women yet defined themselves as "involved mothers" (Uttal, 1996: 308), despite their long work days and frequent business trips.

For example, Sarah Jacobs was recruited as a partner to an entrepreneurial law firm in 1976, the same year her son was born and shortly before her divorce. She hired a live-in nanny and put in very long hours. She says:

I knew before I was pregnant that there was never a way I was giving up my career and just sitting at home . . . I couldn't have done it. It wasn't my nature. It wasn't what moved me. This profession gives me, in a lot of ways a real piece of me . . . It's been enormously good for me, and not just financially.

Sarah says she found fulfillment in her career and not in spending all day holding her baby. She continually justified her adequacy as a mother during our interview. For instance, she bought a city condominium near her office and her son's private school rather than move out to the suburbs. Although Sarah does not practice the time-intensive mothering the family devotion schema prescribes, she insists she has been there for her son when it counted. She elaborates:

> I never missed a school play, ever . . . Never missed a parent-teacher conference. Never not read a paper before it went through. Even if I somehow had to figure out how to get it faxed to me on a business trip. Did I make milk and cookies? I have food in the house. Do all these women [who stay home] actually serve dinner? No I really didn't [cook dinner every night]. Do I think my kid is suffering for it? Not particularly . . . The fact is that I think I spend more time reading his papers and discussing his books with him and giving him my input on what he wrote and making sure he studied than a lot of mothers would who stay home.

Sarah Jacobs' justifications of herself as a good mother, perhaps even superior to "a lot of mothers who stay home," are implicitly a defense against the models and judgments of the family devotion schema. She implies that her son is a lot more resilient than the family devotion schema's model of the fragile child. She suggests that as long as there was "food in the house," her son did not need her to pamper him by making milk and cookies or by fixing dinner every night. Sarah is a cultural pioneer, who foreshadows a new, less time-intensive mothering ideology. She relies on nannies and fax machines to fashion a close relationship based on intellectual sharing rather than on spending lots of time together. She believes that her commitment to her child has paid off. She proudly told me that her son, a high school senior when I interviewed her, had been admitted into an elite college.

Because she is an apostate vis-à-vis the mothering ideology that was widely shared while her son was young, Sarah Jacobson's words have a defensive and at times sarcastic tone that is not audible in the words of the youngest cohort women who were also often away from home. By the mid-1980s to early 1990s, when youngest cohort women began having children, the notions of delegating the traditional mothering labor out to others and spending little time personally with one's children became more firmly established in the cultural repertoire.

The Youngest Cohort

The youngest cohort in the career-committed sample was born during the mid–baby boom (1952–1958), finished college between 1974 and 1980, and had reached the ages of 35 to 42 when I interviewed them. This cohort displays a resurgence of intact marriages and childbearing (see Table 4.1). Fourteen of the twenty youngest cohort members are married, nine are mothers, and two more are trying to conceive. Recall that only one woman from the middle cohort had both an intact marriage and a child. In contrast, seven youngest cohort members have both a stable marriage and a child. Despite demanding careers and their embrace of the work devotion schema, just over half the youngest cohort members are mothers or are trying to conceive. And most have intact marriages.[8]

Marriage

Among ever-married women, the context in which the middle and youngest cohort had their first marriages differed in at least two important ways. Compared to most middle cohort women, most youngest cohort women married at later dates. While a majority of middle cohort women married in the late 1960s and early 1970s, twelve of the eighteen ever-married youngest cohort members married in the 1980s or 1990s.[9] By that time, an emerging egalitarian schema of marriage, in which the spouses have equal power and similar-rather-than-complementary work and domestic roles, was one part of the cultural repertoire (Farley, 1996). An egalitarian schema of marriage was far from universally accepted, but the economically and educationally advantaged women in this cohort were well placed to adopt it.

A related difference is that youngest cohort members generally delayed marriage until after establishing themselves in their careers. These women married at later ages than the earlier cohorts partly because they enjoyed more career opportunities. By the time youngest cohort members finished college, women's access to and advancement in finance careers had become more institutionalized. While over half the members of earlier cohorts worked in nonfinance jobs before eventually entering finance, virtually all of the youngest cohort members specialized in finance during or immediately after college and moved quickly up job ladders (Blair-Loy, 1999).

The youngest cohort's delay in marriage not only added to the array of schemas they encountered but also augmented their material resources. Fourteen of the eighteen youngest cohort ever-married women were first married *after* they had already devoted between one to sixteen years (a median of ten years) to their finance careers.[10] In contrast, over half the oldest and middle cohort women married before or about the same time as starting finance careers. Youngest cohort members' work experience provided them with cultural models of gender egalitarianism and work devotion, and the financial resources to begin developing more egalitarian marriages.

For example, Debbie Havton, an entrepreneur, worked in finance for twelve years before marrying a much younger man in the late 1980s. She says: "I was making significantly more money when we got married . . . We handled the different incomes by having a formalized budget. Each of us has the same discretionary income. It has to do something to the male ego, but he never discussed it. We knew we were at different points in our careers." Similarly, Penny Smith married an artist in the mid-1980s after working in finance for nine years. She claims that by the time she met him, she was already a "workaholic."

So anybody who was gonna date me had to accommodate that, and he did. And I hadn't had terribly many relationships with men in part because my work came first and they came second . . . It just wasn't a big deal to him. He is very self-confident, has no self-esteem problem, very independent, has his own set of friends. So if I was available, fine, if I wasn't that was okay too. He does his own thing, he still does.

In contrast to middle cohort husbands like Mr. Jeffers, youngest cohort husbands like Penny Smith's spouse are more accustomed to getting along on their own. By the time youngest cohort members married, they and their partners took their career commitment for granted.

Motherhood

Youngest cohort members' adoption of the work devotion schema and an emerging egalitarian marriage model precluded them from fulfilling the traditionally feminine role in the domestic division of labor. Moreover, the youngest cohort wives and their husbands took her prior career dedication for granted. Their somewhat more egalitarian marriages put pressure on the motherhood role mandated by the family devotion schema. Recall that family-committed women, who left full-time work after childbearing, ultimately reinforced the family devotion schema. In contrast, youngest cohort members in the career-committed group are reformulating the family devotion schema into a model that incorporates the mother's frequent extended absences.

All youngest cohort mothers used full-time care. Two relied on regular childcare from their own mothers; the rest pay for a live-in nanny

or a full-time babysitter. Their marriages were not completely egalitarian. Like the family-committed women who worked part-time,
most career-committed mothers were responsible for hiring, scheduling, supervising, and—if necessary—firing their childcare workers.
Most of these caregivers were from racial and ethnic minority groups;
many were immigrants.[11]

Unlike the family-committed group, some of the women in the
career-committed sample have begun to redefine childhood such that
young children really just need custodial care (see also Uttal, 1996).
For example, one woman said: "infants and toddlers, as long as they
are getting quality care, it can be done by almost anyone." Later,
career-committed mothers rely on private schools to provide much of
the intellectual and moral development deemed necessary for older
children.

Anna Lampe, a real estate developer who earns three times the
salary of her professional husband, illustrates both a limited egalitarian schema of marriage and the schema of a mother who is often absent but who is supported by paid childcare. She reports that her
husband is "very good at being flexible. We have a sharing relationship in every sense of the word." Anna says they have been "fortunate"
to have the same nanny for three years, who cares for their preschool
children Pam and Joel. Anna takes the "early shift" at home before the
nanny arrives at 8:00 A.M. Her husband is home by the time the nanny
leaves at 6:30 P.M. Anna often works at the office until late. After dinner, her husband works past midnight in his home office. Another executive, Dorothy Green, hires a housekeeper to clean but relies on her
mother for childcare. She says, "I have the best possible situation. My
mother sits for my children . . . [My husband and I] both travel a lot.
If necessary, my mom stays overnight."

Dorothy Green and Anna Lampe both paint their family arrangements as "fortunate" or "the best possible situation," that is, as desirable and morally acceptable. Because egalitarian schemas had emerged
in the broader cultural repertoire and because of wives' resources of

incomes and professional identities, their attempt to transpose egalitarian schemas onto family life can partially succeed.[12]

A few pioneers in the earlier cohorts also model this emerging new model in which mothers delegate much of the day-to-day caregiving to others. The clearest example of this is oldest cohort member Harriet Simpson. She became a corporate lawyer eleven years before having a child in 1985. Now a managing partner in a large law firm, she works long hours and earns 95 percent of the family income. She is the only woman I interviewed whose husband (assisted by the nanny) is the primary caregiver for her child. This arrangement accommodates her intense work devotion. She said:

> I work long, hard hours now . . . I was never conflicted about a career. Once I decided to go to law school, I intended to do it full-time for the rest of my life. It never would have occurred to me to change my level of involvement.

This book documents a fundamental, gendered conflict between career and family devotion for professional women, so it may sound astounding that Harriet Simpson says she was "never conflicted about a career." She resembles the husbands of family-committed women who are so consumed by work devotion that it "never would have occurred" to them to become less intensely involved at work. Harriet's single-minded work devotion is only possible because she has a caregiving spouse at home (cf. Acker, 1990).

Like Sarah Jacobs (whose son faxes her his homework), Harriet Simpson's justifications of herself as a good mother are directed against the family devotion schema's definition of childhood. Harriet explicitly rejects this definition as an excuse for women to weaken their career commitment:

> As a mom who works full time, you can't believe that you are at all times the most significant person in your child's life . . . If you

secretly want your child to cling to you, that's what will happen. If you aren't completely convinced that you want to keep doing what you're doing, it's very easy for children to be the reason to lessen commitment. It's almost an excuse if you're afraid to go the distance.

We have seen that people in the family-committed group accuse mothers who pursue demanding, full-time careers as deluding themselves that their children are independent and resilient. Family-committed respondents believe that this view is empirically wrong, self-serving, and harmful to the children. Harriet Simpson turns this critique on its head. She accuses mothers who stay home of squashing autonomy and promoting an unhealthy dependence in their children in order to justify their own fears about career commitment. Yet at the same time, Harriet worries about her daughter, now in middle school. She told me that she is afraid her daughter is in fact not as independent and "tough minded" as she would like her to be. "We've also seen [my daughter] exhibit some victim behavior. That scares me the most. [My daughter] and I both know that I will never be a victim. You want your child to see herself the same way."

Harriet Simpson discusses both the privileges and the responsibilities of being the primary breadwinner. She enjoys not having to cook but worries about her financial responsibility to her family: "I feel the pressures when you're largely responsible, the pressures that men in the same position feel also . . . That they'll be taken care of if I die. I worry about the responsibility of amassing enough money." Harriet explains that she cares as deeply about her family as any intensive mother but expresses that care by being a good provider.

Yet embodying this new schema of mothering is not automatic or easy. Harriet Simpson's and Sarah Jacobs' elaborate justifications are hints of the ideological work mothers do in order to relinquish the family devotion schema's assumption of mothers' intensive and continual presence in their children's lives. Others speak directly about the difficulty of abandoning the family devotion schema. Youngest cohort member Anna Lampe, who had said how "fortunate" she was to have a long-term nanny, nevertheless feels conflicted over her work and family arrangements. "I often don't see my children one and a half hours every night . . . I want to participate in Pam's activities. I've missed her snack days. I can't even remember to find time to buy a few bottles of juice and bags of cookies. It's traumatic, for her and for me." By the last sentences, she had lost her professional demeanor and was close to tears. Providing for her daughter's snack day was one of the few mothering duties she personally performed, and thus it took on great symbolic weight. Forgetting that duty was an indictment against her worthiness as a mother. In her and in many executive mothers' minds, the work and family devotion schemas are painfully tangled in competing strands.

Catherine Hanke, a youngest cohort financial services executive, was strongly tempted to stay home full-time for a while after her baby was born. She explained:

When I had the baby, my very supportive husband, he really is, he does fully 50 percent of the housework and childcare. He said I had to decide what works best for me . . . if I should stay home for one to two years before going back. A piece of me thought that is what the really perfect mother would do . . . It was an internal battle, between wanting to perceive myself as a perfect mother but knowing I couldn't fit into it. It was my own role definition crisis. [But] I would have lost my sanity if I'd stayed home.

Cultural change often occurs as the outcome of a struggle between different ideologies, different models of a worthwhile and desirable life, enacted in the lives of people responding to social structural change. In the midst of cultural conflict, youngest cohort members are trying to create a new culture of motherhood. Yet their efforts are marked by ambivalence and pain as they struggle with the family images ordained by the family devotion schema.

From the perspective of youngest cohort executives in the career-committed group, much has changed. They can embrace the roles of marriage and motherhood rejected by many older cohort members because these roles have been somewhat transformed. Youngest cohort members have more or less successfully transposed a limited egalitarian schema onto their domestic roles. Like fathers, they are dedicated breadwinners, do little housework, and parent from a distance.

Yet this creation of a new culture is limited by the logic of the older family devotion model. It preserves the gendered and hierarchical logic of the devotion to family schema. Men are still breadwinners, largely buffered from day-to-day caregiving duties. It is women's responsibility to oversee the traditional mothering labor now often done by women who are from racial and ethnic minority groups or from lower social classes.[13]

Reinventing the Devotion Schemas

Although the devotion schemas are powerful and compelling, they are neither static nor omnipotent. Despite their strong influence on professional women's cognitive, emotional, and moral understandings, they can be reshaped by people equipped with alternative cultural schemas and sufficient resources. We have seen how family-committed women employed part-time challenged the work devotion schema's demand for single-minded allegiance. And this chapter shows how mid–baby boomers in the career-committed group, equipped with ideologies of gender egalitarianism and the material resources of high incomes before marriage, can reinterpret and refashion the family devotion schema into one allowing egalitarian marriages and breadwinner mothers who delegate most childcare and household maintenance to other women.

In practice, mothers in the career-committed youngest cohort probably do not spend their days very differently from the hardworking part-time employees in the family-committed group. But each group's interpretation of their lives is widely divergent. In the ways in which they understand their lives, family-committed mothers ultimately challenge the demands of work devotion and fulfill the mandates of family devotion, while career-committed mothers do the opposite.

Both groups do so in ways that preserve their self-understandings as good mothers. Family-committed mothers define their children as fragile and needful of their attentive care while accusing full-time employed mothers of selfish careerism. Most career-committed women agree with them and therefore forgo having children. But the career-committed women who do have children try to understand their children as autonomous and resilient. Some accuse women who stay home with their children as selfishly fostering an unhealthy dependence in their children.

At the same time, many mothers in both samples continue to feel haunted by the ghosts of the schema they have renounced. About half of the family-committed members grieve the full-time careers they have abandoned, while many career-committed mothers mourn the time they have lost with their young children.

We have seen that the possibility for social and cultural change depends on period effects that occur in historical time. The youngest cohort mothers in the career-committed group, equipped with new ideological and material resources, began to refashion the family devotion schema to accommodate their full-time careers. Next, we consider why similarly aged mothers in the *family-committed* sample did not do likewise. Why did the family devotion schema remain so much more tenacious and compelling for this group?

5

TURNING POINTS

Audrey Weyler is typical of the career-committed mothers from the youngest (mid–baby boom) cohort. After receiving her MBA from an elite business school, she quickly moved up the ranks of a firm that provides financial advisory services to corporations. Now in her late thirties, she is an executive vice president and managing director. She is in charge of the office in her city and is the highest-ranking woman in the corporation overall. Audrey is married and has two young children. She has always relied on full-time childcare. She loves her job but is increasingly worried about the frequent turnover among her childcare providers. She also notes that she knows almost no other female professional "counterparts" with young children:

> I used to have numerous professional friends—now they're all at home. Now I have virtually no counterparts working full-time. I'm almost alone among members [of the women executive's professional organization she belongs to]. Not many members are with kids this age. Most [professional women] have no kids or they're grown. If I didn't have a challenging career, it would be so easy to opt out.

Hearing stories like Audrey Weyler's from career-committed mothers prompted me to expand my study to include the women of the family-committed group, former full-time businesswomen who left their careers when they had children.

Now consider Christine Colarullo, a woman in her early forties who stays home full-time with her two preschoolers. Christine's early professional career is similar to Audrey's. After receiving her MBA, Christine moved up the corporate hierarchy in a bank before landing a job as the highest-ranking professional in a consulting firm. A few years later, she went into business for herself and was wildly successful. Now that she has two children, Christine plans to stay home with them full-time until they are in school and then hopes to restart her business on a part-time basis.

It is only within the last twenty years or so that a growing number of women have had access to the cultural and social structural resources for combining childbearing with executive careers. For the first time, women like Audrey Weyler and Christine Colarulla face a socially structured choice after motherhood between two dramatically different types of lives. Like Audrey and other youngest cohort members of the career-committed group, they may continue their demanding business careers while delegating most traditional mothering duties. Or, like Christine and the other family-committed group members, they may relinquish their full-time careers to become involved mothers.

As we have seen, age cohort differences within the career-committed group help explain these executive mothers' orientation toward the family devotion schema. But how do we account for the differences between mothers of roughly the same age in the career-committed group, like Audrey Weyler, and in the family-committed group, like Christine Colarullo?

This chapter explores these women's lives from the life course approach, a perspective that examines the intersections of people's work and family lives over time (for example, Blair-Loy and DeHart, forthcoming; Moen, 1992). The decision of family-committed women like Christine to leave full-time careers is a turning point, a short transition that redirects life paths from one pathway or trajectory to another (Abbott, 1997b; George, 1993; Sampson and Laub, 1993; Elder, 1985). In contrast, career-committed women like Audrey maintain one stable trajectory before, during, and after childbirth.

The decision about whether to turn away from full-time, demanding careers around the time of childbearing is not a purely personal, idiosyncratic matter. Rather, this decision is a social choice structured by career and family opportunities, demands, and cultural meanings, all of which change over historical time.[1] For example, unlike earlier cohorts in the career-committed group, the youngest cohort took advantage of newly opening opportunities for women and specialized immediately in business education and professional careers (Blair-Loy, 1999). This meant that they lacked an earlier stage of less-demanding, nonfinance work that could better accommodate childrearing. Career-committed women continued pursuing their careers, which were constructed by their firms and industries and their accompanying models of work devotion as uninterrupted, time-intensive, and demanding.

Given these constraints, the only way these women could give substantially more time to their families was to abandon their full-time jobs, which is the choice made by family-committed mothers. These women, whether at home full-time or employed part-time, have relinquished the career path that is socially organized by internal labor markets and employers' expectations and normatively defined by the work devotion schema to be full-time, single-minded, and all-encompassing. Furthermore, most of these women and their husbands subscribe to the family devotion schema's definition of the appropriate gender division of labor.

Thus, the decision about whether to turn away from full-time business careers is also structured by competing cultural understandings of what constitutes a meaningful and worthwhile life. Is a woman's talent, energy, and passion best oriented toward advancing her career or toward caring for her family?

This chapter tries to understand reasons why the family-committed women experienced a turning point onto new trajectories dedicated to family caregiving while mothers in the career-committed group did not. I first look at the long-term conditions of work and family life that might either support mothers' demanding careers or prompt them to leave their full-time careers to spend more time caring for family. I then examine contingencies, those unexpected discrete events such as firing a nanny or losing a job, that may motivate women's decisions to stay in or to leave their careers after childbirth. In the case of both long-term work and family conditions and most contingencies, I find that it is not the events per se but how women interpret them that is key to their power to trigger a turning point.

Finally, I look closely at six women whose lives were struck by multiple difficult contingent events, some of which occurred with the force of tragedy. I find that if extreme negative contingencies dictate the need for family nurturing beyond what paid caregivers can provide, even the most career-oriented, high-earning women may well abandon their careers to provide personal, intensive caregiving while their husbands continue working. But before presenting these results, we need to consider some of the difficulties inherent in analyzing turning points.

Methodological Considerations

Turning points require at least two points in time; we cannot identify them without looking backward to see that a new trajectory has been established (Abbott, 1997b). At time one (before childbearing), both groups were in demanding, full-time, business careers. At time two, the career-committed group remains in these full-time careers whereas the family-committed group has embarked on a new trajectory, that of highly involved motherhood.

However, analyzing retrospective data is perilous. People's present accounts of their pasts may be shaped as much by what is happening to them in the present as by what "really" happened in the past. People shape their past histories into followable narratives with a beginning, middle, and end that make sense in terms of the present problems with which they are grappling or identities they are trying to convey (Cohler, 1982; Ricoeur, 1977). Thus, people construct post hoc explanations that may or may not have been salient at the time the event to be explained occurred. Analysts can take different approaches to this dilemma. One approach is to treat the post hoc quality of narrative as random error and hope that factual errors in individuals' accounts of their behavior will at best cancel one another out or at worst not swamp the main effects one is studying. Unfortunately, there is no reason to suspect that factually inaccurate reinterpretations are randomly distributed across the group. Reinterpretations themselves may be patterned in complex ways, producing interaction effects rather than a random distribution of error terms (cf. Abbott, 1988).

Another approach is to define the retrospective accounts as the object of study rather than as indicators of something that "really happened" back when interviewees said it did for the reasons they attributed to it. This strategy can yield insights about the construction of discourses. But it does not get us closer to understanding the historical and life course factors that actually helped shape a person's trajectory as it unfolded.

I combine these two approaches. I am first interested in the actual work and family conditions and events of a person's adult life that helped shape her life course. I take respondents' information about the long-term conditions of work and parenting as accurate, straightforward data points. I examine these to see whether they are correlated with women's choices to maintain full-time careers after childbirth or turn onto a new trajectory of involved mothering. As a separate step in the analysis, I examine the women's interpretations of these conditions.

I also consider discrete work and family contingencies that impact the women I interviewed unexpectedly during their lives. I examine whether their presence or absence tends to be associated with the trajectories of women who relinquish their full-time business careers.

Unfortunately, the contingent events that the women I interviewed relayed in the course of telling their stories are not straightforward data points. "The personal narrative which is recounted at any point in the course of life represents the most internally consistent interpretation of presently understood past, experienced present, and anticipated future at that time" (Cohler, 1982: 207). Similar events may have been reported by some respondents, who interpreted them as important to a given transition, yet ignored by others, for whom they were not salient.

For example, two family-committed members, Naomi Schumacher and Linda Giovanni, had both begun careers at the same time at the same bank. I first interviewed Naomi, who told me irately that she and Linda were the only two members of their management trainee class who were passed over for a standard promotion in March of 1987. Naomi insisted that this was because she and Linda were both out on maternity leave at the time the promotion decision was made. She reported that both women were angry at the time and demanded an apology from their supervisors. The supervisor assured them that they were both valuable employees and would receive their promotions in June. Naomi explained:

Linda and I were *mad.* Everyone in our class was on the March list, except for Linda and me, who were on maternity leave. Does that sound suspicious? When I called my boss, he just said ya-da-da-da ya-da-da. We knew it was bogus. You get that ya-da-da ya-da-da from male bosses . . . It was humiliating . . . Looking back, we were very worried about what our classmates would think. We thought our careers were ruined. We weren't on the March list. We were both getting bonuses. The EVP [her boss's supervisor] called to reassure us of our value to the company. Blah blah, ya-da-da ya-da-da. He promised we would be on the next list [in June].

Naomi Schumacher was furious at this "second-class citizen" treatment. She cited that negative work experience plus the joy of caring for her new baby as the reasons she quit her job when her maternity leave ended. She offhandedly mentioned that her colleague, Linda Giovanni, "went back to work, and she got on the next list."

When I interviewed Linda Giovanni, I said nothing about the Naomi Schumacher interview because I wanted to see how two different people would portray a shared history. Linda duly reported the promotion in June of 1987 but *did not mention* that it was three months later than the promotion of the rest of the class. I expect that since Linda spent five years working part-time for the bank after her maternity leave, the March 1987 occurrence had receded in importance so far that she did not report it; she had probably not even thought about it for some time. In contrast, this occurrence was the last event in Naomi Schumacher's banking career and remained highly salient as one of her justifications for leaving finance.

This vignette illustrates how the reporting of contingent events may be selective. People may only remember or report occurrences that they currently understand as relevant to their subsequent actions. When I probed for reasons for career transitions or for leaving full-time careers, the women I interviewed reported a fairly limited set of work and family events.

Still, the problem of differing interpretations of certain situations remains. For example, respondents' definition of an event as a childcare crisis partly depends on their understanding of children as either resilient and independent or as vulnerable and deserving of intensive and time-consuming care. This assessment hinges on their stance toward the family devotion schema. Furthermore, discovering that a nanny ignores one's child may motivate one woman to fire her, which would create a childcare crisis that I would code as a negative family contingency. Another woman in the same situation might not consider this such a grave problem and would tolerate it until she could hire someone else. She would have no childcare crisis to report and thus no career transition prompted by the crisis, and I would have no negative family contingency to code.

The general methodological problem is that my data are not well suited to explaining why some women maintained business careers after childbirth while others in the same cohort did not. I chose the two groups on the basis of the choices the women had already made. I cannot know all the ways women may have self-selected into the two groups; the reasons they give for why they chose one or the other path are post hoc constructions.[2] To fully explain how similarly situated individuals make different socially and culturally structured choices, one would need to interview the members of a large group at the outset of their careers and then re-interview them at regular intervals for several years. With my retrospective data on two small groups that have already sorted themselves into the two dependent variables, I can offer only exploratory findings. It would be interesting to see whether they are confirmed by future research using a larger group of truly longitudinal data.[3]

Nonetheless, the data do provide a gold mine of information on an understudied group about many objective conditions and events as well as people's interpretations of them. The detailed information on work and family events and rich interview material allow us to begin to understand how long-term conditions, events, contingencies, and interpretations channel people's movements onto and off of socially and culturally constructed family and career trajectories.

Long-Term Conditions of Work and Family

Stable conditions of work and family life may be more or less supportive of a mother's full-time, demanding career. I examine whether conditions such as a respondent's age at marriage and the years of business experience she had before marrying, the amount of business travel she does, and the availability of her husband and extended family for childcare help explain the turning point in family-committed women's lives and its absence in the career-committed group.

Age and Years of Business Experience at Marriage

As we have seen, a relatively egalitarian marriage is a precondition for a career-committed woman to construct a motherhood that is compatible with a demanding career. Compared to earlier cohorts, youngest cohort members married at older ages and well after their finance careers were established. Thus, youngest cohort members in the career-committed group entered into marriage already commanding considerable financial resources and professional prestige, which gave them more marital power. The youngest cohort members and their husbands took the women's career commitment for granted and organized family life so that they could continue working.

I calculated whether the timing of marriage relative to career launch varies along the same lines between work-committed and family-committed mothers. My intergroup comparison of marriage timing only includes currently married mothers in the youngest age cohort, those mid–baby boomers born between 1952 and 1958. These restrictions are necessary because we found stark cohort differences in the career-committed group, and divorced mothers might be more financially compelled to work than married mothers.[4]

I found that among married mothers in the youngest cohort, family-committed women did not delay marriage as long as career-committed women did. Career-committed women married at a median age of thirty-three, compared to a median age of twenty-five in the family-committed group. Moreover, career-committed individuals in this analysis established their careers a median of eleven years before marrying, whereas family-committed members started business careers a median of only two years before marrying.

Thus, by the time they married, family-committed women had invested far less time in their careers and had accumulated fewer resources of income and prestige. Their shorter career tenure at marriage may have made them and their husbands less likely to view their careers as taken-for-granted commitments that the family would accommodate. The earlier marriages of family-committed women may have helped ensure that these women were less equipped to challenge the devotion to family schema's model of a breadwinner husband and a homemaker wife and were more likely to understand childbearing as naturally and appropriately triggering a turning point onto a life devoted to family caregiving. Another interpretation is that some family-committed respondents may have had an earlier and stronger interest in family rather than career from the beginning. Consistent with both explanations is the difficulty for mothers to maintain both an early marriage and a long-term devotion to a demanding, full-time career.

Other Long-Term Conditions of Work and Family Life

In addition to marriage timing, other aspects of work and family life may make it more difficult to combine full-time business careers with motherhood. I anticipated that if a job required a respondent or her husband to travel overnight frequently, she would be less likely to maintain her full-time business career after childbearing. I also expected that if her husband was rarely home or she did not live near extended family, she would lack the safety valve of childcare from relatives during an emergency and thus find it difficult to continue working. Finally, I expected that respondents whose own mothers had been full-time homemakers might be more likely to relinquish their full-time careers to provide their children the intensive attention and care they had received growing up.

In contrast to the last analysis, which was restricted to married mothers in the youngest age cohort, this analysis uses all mothers in each group (the twenty-one career-committed mothers and all twenty-five family-committed women). Table 5.1 presents the proportion of mothers in each group who experienced these conditions while they were maintaining full-time business careers.

In contrast to my expectations, the proportion of each group experiencing each condition is almost identical. About half of each group had jobs that required fairly frequent overnight travel. Similar proportions had husbands who traveled on business (50 percent of the career-committed group and 43 percent of family-committed group). Over 45 percent of each group had husbands who were rarely home; these men had avidly embraced the devotion to work schema and were generally unavailable for childcare. Two-thirds of each group had no extended family living nearby. Over three-quarters of each group had a mother who had been home full-time while respondents were growing up.

There was also no intergroup difference in interactions between these variables. Thirty-six percent of each group faced conditions in which either both spouses traveled or in which neither the husband nor extended family were available for childcare. One member of each group experienced all five long-term conditions.

Because the two groups were about equally likely to experience these long-term work and family conditions, they do not in and of

Table 5.1 Proportion of Mothers Who Experience Long-Term Conditions Hypothesized to Increase Work-Family Conflict

Sample (N)	Career-Committed (21)	Family-Committed (25)
Respondent's full-time job requires travel	0.52	0.50
Spouse's job requires travel	0.50	0.43
Spouse rarely home	0.48	0.47
No extended family in area	0.67	0.67
Respondent's mother was a homemaker	0.86	0.76

themselves explain why the career-committed group maintained their careers after childbearing and the family-committed group did not. However, the people in each group tend to interpret these conditions quite differently. Career-committed women who enjoyed the luxury of not traveling or the support of involved husbands or extended family were grateful. But if they lacked these resources, they and the children made do. However, people in the family-committed group often cited precisely these conditions as the reasons they left full-time business careers.

Career-committed mothers did not enjoy traveling overnight; but when it was necessary, they arranged for an adult to be home and telephoned their children before bedtime. It apparently did not occur to them that overnight travel would be a reason to relinquish their careers. For instance, one career-committed respondent reports:

> After I had my first child, I began to really hate the travel because it was terribly disruptive at home. I didn't like being away, but I didn't think about quitting. It wasn't so bad that I thought [as if addressing her husband], "I really hate this, honey. I really wanna stay home."

In contrast, family-committed mothers were more likely to say that a lot of overnight business travel was harmful to their children and to consider it a legitimate reason to leave a job. For example, Christine Colarullo, a former communication consultant, brought her baby and nanny with her when she had to go out of town and worked for only six hours a day. But she eventually decided that this schedule "wasn't fair to my son. I decided to retire until the kids are in school full time."

Table 5.1 shows that over three-quarters of each group had mothers who were full-time homemakers. Career-committed group members generally did not mention what their mothers did until I specifically asked about their parents' occupations. In contrast, family-committed respondents tended to bring this up on their own. They saw their mothers' homemaking vocations as more salient to their current lives. Although most family-committed women believed that women are biologically suited to childrearing, many also invoked their homemaking mothers as socializing and inspiring them to take on a similar vocation.

For example, Marsha Dickens explains why she felt it was necessary to leave her full-time attorney position at a law firm after having a baby:

> The reason that I feel this way is because it's something that was implanted in me at a very early age, it's my role as a parent, and it's never—some very fundamental concepts there have never changed . . . My mother was home full-time.

Growing up with a full-time mother helped her learn, "at a very early age" that her "role as a parent" was irreconcilable with a full-time legal career.

Susan Pflanz and I discussed her decision to stay home full-time while we joined her young son and his friend in constructing a Legos edifice on her kitchen table. She explains: "I feel like home should be a nice calm place, where the kids enjoy being, where they can come home and play. That's how I grew up." She elaborates: "A lot comes from role modeling. My mother was very involved. You think you should be that way too." Looking around her lovely, old house, I did sense the tranquility her presence established.

Nina Lombardi notes that her decision to quit her job and stay home with her children was partly due to "societal expectations." She argues that because "everyone grew up with a mother as a primary caretaker, [and] we all grew up with those values," society allows women the freedom "to feel what we feel about our kids . . ." She believes that what she assumes is a near-universal experience of having a homemaking mother creates a society in which women but not men are encouraged to love their children intensely and to stay home with them.

Rachel Kahn also speaks of socialization. She says that one reason she was more willing than her husband to give up her full-time career when they had children was that she was raised by a homemaking mother. She continues:

> And I suppose part of it is socialization. My mother didn't work outside the home. She was very skilled in the home arts. A part of me grew up with that expectation—that that's what mothers do with their kids. I try to create something that looks as much like that socialized image as possible. Although, I'm not anywhere near as good at it as my mother was.

Several people in the family-committed group spoke admiringly of their mothers' creativity and skill "in the home arts." Elizabeth Cruz noted: "My mom stayed home. She was very creative around the house, and she wrote and painted."

Family-committed respondents use the involved mothering they experienced from their own mothers as a template for their own devotion to their children. In contrast, career-committed women, who were even more likely to have been raised by homemaking mothers, scarcely alluded to their mothers in the interviews. If they did mention their mothers, it was either to express horror at their mothers' economic dependence or to emphasize how sharply their lives had diverged. For example, the director of corporate affairs for a Fortune 500 company said:

> My mother didn't work outside the home except before she got married . . . She has no clue what I do. She can't explain it. She says: "she's the assistant to the Chairman." It's easy for her to explain that my sister is a social worker.

Among career-committed women, their own mothers' homemaking lives represent something to avoid rather than emulate.

Long-term work and family conditions acquire significance only in the context of a particular cultural schema. From the perspective of the work devotion schema, business travel is at worst a necessary inconvenience. But from the perspective of the family devotion schema, overnight absences from home are unfair and perhaps damaging to one's children. Most members of each group have a homemaking mother available to emulate. Seen through the lens of the work devotion schema, that model is either irrelevant or appalling. Seen through the lens of the family devotion schema, the family-committed group invokes it as a crucial reason for veering off the full-time career path and onto the homemaking trajectory.

However, many people do not see the world through just one lens. Many women I interviewed feel conflicted, whether they sacrificed demanding careers for the sake of their children or renounced involved motherhood for the sake of their careers. Which model of a meaningful life springs into focus as the most compelling may be partly shaped by contingent work and family events.

Work and Family Contingencies

Long-term conditions of work and family sometimes become intolerable if they are combined with an unfortunate and unforeseen event. Work and family contingencies unexpectedly upset people's routines. Depending on the schemas individuals use to interpret them, contingencies may help throw people onto a new life trajectory. In the interviews, I uncovered three types of unexpected events: positive career contingencies; negative career contingencies; and negative family contingencies. A positive career contingency is something like an unexpectedly large promotion or work-related opportunity. Negative career contingencies are unexpected events that might challenge one's faith in the promised rewards of the work devotion schema. They include layoffs, acquiring a new unpleasant job or boss after a merger, or experiencing sexual harassment. Negative family contingencies include illnesses of the respondents and their close family members as well as the sudden loss of a nanny.

From the analyst's perspective, most contingencies are not uncommon, and they might even be predictable by an economic model of industry turbulence or a vacancy chain model of career movements.[5] But from the perspective of the people living their own lives, contingencies strike out of the blue, disrupting routines and creating stress.

Table 5.2 presents standardized percentages of mothers in each group who reported each type of contingent event.[6] It shows that both groups were about equally likely to describe a negative career contingency, controlling for age. However, family-committed women were over twice as likely to report a negative family contingency, while career-committed women were over twice as likely to recount a positive career contingency. This is what we would expect. Women who left full-time demanding careers when they had children were twice as likely to report that family crises had occurred, while women who maintained these careers after childbirth were more than twice as likely to describe unexpected positive occurrences at work. Of course, we cannot fully determine the extent to which these intergroup dif-

Table 5.2 Standardized* Percentages of Mothers Who Reported Contingent Events during Their Adult Lives

Sample (N)	Career-Committed (21)	Family-Committed (25)
Negative career contingency	15%	17%
Negative family contingency	8%	19%
Positive career contingency	15%	7%

*Percentages are standardized by dividing them by the total number of years in each group's sequences and multiplying by 1000.

ferences are based on empirical differences in the numbers of actual contingent events or are due to distinct interpretations of their lives based on the devotion schema through which they are interpreted.

Perhaps contingent events in the period surrounding childbirth are particularly potent for triggering a turning point for the family-committed group. This is the period in which the work devotion's requirements for single-minded career dedication most conflict with the family devotion schema's understanding of infants' and young children's needs for a mother's tender care. For example, mothers might especially resent an unexpected and extended business trip if their very young child is nursing or ill. Remember family-committed respondent Vicki Orlando's comment: a "sick kid tears at our heart, if you're open to that."

Moreover, perhaps positive career contingencies shortly before or after childbirth are particularly salient for nurturing the career dedication of career-committed women. For example, Anna Lampe was a senior vice president of a financial services company when her second child was born a few months before my interview with her. She told me that she had felt overwhelmed and had been considering asking for a four-day-a-week schedule. Then a sudden promotion to managing director made her feel newly appreciated and challenged by the company. She said that now she has delved into this new opportunity and "put all that thinking about part-time aside."

The interesting question is this: To what extent do the contingencies reported in Table 5.2 strike around the time of the potential turning point away from full-time business careers? The analysis here centers on the vulnerable segment of the life course where the turning point onto the involved mothering track potentially (for the career-committed group) or actually (for the family-committed group) took place. I define this segment as beginning five years before the birth of the first child for the career-committed group or five years before the departure from full-time careers for the family-committed group. I define this segment as ending two years after the birth of the first child for the career-committed group or two years after the departure from a full-time career for the family-committed group.[7]

During this vulnerable segment of the life course, only 5 to 10 percent of career-committed mothers but about 25 percent of family-committed respondents reported difficult career or family contingent events.[8] Thus, family-committed women were two and a half to five times more likely to have experienced negative contingencies during this segment of the life course that is most susceptible to a turning point occurring.

Moreover, almost all the family-committed respondents who reported any negative career or negative family contingencies at some point during their lives said they occurred during this crucial period leading up to their departure from full-time business careers. Specifically, 86 percent reporting some negative career contingency and 88 percent of those relating some negative family contingency experienced them during this vulnerable segment.

In contrast, the career-committed respondents experienced their reported contingent events more evenly throughout the adult life cycle. Only 14 percent of the career-committed women who reported difficult career contingencies said they occurred shortly before or after the birth of their first child, and just 50 percent of them relating negative family events said they occurred during this vulnerable segment.

In these data, we cannot tell whether this finding more closely represents differences in respondents' retrospective rewriting of their autobiographies or actual timing differences in contingent events for the two groups. On the one hand, the family-committed group sees the period shortly before and after childbirth as saturated with contingent events because it now interprets these contingencies as meaningful events that make their turning point comprehensible and perhaps even inevitable. It is possible that similar events may have been forgotten by the career-committed group, as it continues its stable trajectory. On the other hand, people in the family-committed group probably did see a real decline in negative family events, now that they are home, and a decline in negative work events, now that they have either left the labor force entirely or shifted to part-time work.

These results have been gleaned from observing the work and family sequences in a very small group using retrospective data. These findings need to be confirmed on a larger group that ideally would be truly longitudinal. Despite these data limitations, I have revealed some consistent patterns. A certain confluence of negative work and family contingencies may help predict respondents' turning points out of full-time, demanding business careers. Alternatively, a different constellation of positive work events may help encourage new mothers to maintain full-time careers.

However, there is no simple formula for predicting which events will either pull a woman out of her full-time career or inoculate her against this turning point. This is because work and family contingencies are viewed through the lenses of the different devotion schemas. Career-committed mothers, who likely already adhered more strongly to the work devotion schema, are likely to interpret negative work and family contingencies as less demoralizing to their career commitment and less damaging to their children than are family-committed women.

Extreme Negative Contingencies

To better understand this complex interaction between work and family events and women's interpretations of these events, let us consider a group of women who are extremely dedicated to work but have been hit by more than one negative event within a few years. While 40 percent of the women in my study reported at least one difficult work or family contingency, two career-committed mothers and four family-committed interviewees reported two or more negative events within a few years. We will see that the careers of these particularly unlucky women are significantly altered or derailed, despite their work devotion. Although these contingencies struck individual women randomly, their responses to these unexpected and unfortunate events are patterned by social institutions and cultural models. This analysis brings us back to my earlier argument: work and family decisions, which may feel like individual choices, are actually highly structured by cultural schemas and the institutions they define.

Negative Contingent Events for Career-Committed Respondents

The two women in the career-committed group suffering multiple contingencies both left their employers and conventional finance careers after the contingencies occurred. Dee Dee Hengen, then a trader for a brokerage firm, reported suffering two episodes of extreme sexual harassment on the male-dominated trading floor. Furthermore, an adversary organized other traders against her and used informal coercion and formal complaints to the Securities and Exchange Commission (SEC) to drive her off the exchange floor. Dee Dee then established an independent, entrepreneurial firm that does electronic trading from a remote location.[9]

Career-committed Myrna Cubley had initially relished being a public accountant. In the late 1980s, she became the first female partner in her department at a Big 6 public accounting firm. Partnership responsibilities and a recent merger magnified her workload. Then a stint of very long hours combined with family crises created an intolerable situation. Six weeks straight of solid work for an important client during a period in which her husband and brother both had cancer and in which she was helping care for her infirm mother drove Myrna out of her public accounting firm, spurred her rejection of an enticing executive job offer in another company, and encouraged her to abandon for-profit work altogether. This combination of bad luck, a period of extremely long hours deemed necessary by the work devotion schema, and the family devotion schema's assignment of family care to women made it impossible for her to continue her public accounting job or even accept the attractive proffered position. She now works much shorter hours as the chief financial officer for a non-profit organization.

For both women, the negative quality of these contingent events was magnified by their gender. Dee Dee Hengen probably would not have received so much hostility at work if she were male, and Myrna Cubley may not have had to provide so much family care if she were male. Because their children were older and these negative contingencies did not include threats to their children's well-being, Dee Dee and Myrna did not abandon their careers for the nursery. These multiple negative contingencies within the context of gendered expectations and inequalities helped produce a turning point not into homemaking but into nonmainstream careers: a risky independent venture for Dee Dee and a pay cut and professional backwater for Myrna.

Negative Contingent Events for Family-Committed Respondents

Gender, as refracted by the devotion schemas, also affects the family-committed group's response to multiple difficult contingencies. The four family-committed individuals reporting multiple grueling contingent events all had very young children. Elizabeth Cruz's agribusinesses financing firm suffered losses and foreclosures, which made it increasingly difficult to do business. Elizabeth went back to work shortly after her first child was born but tried to avoid overnight travel while she was nursing. One night she was almost stranded in Iowa, far from her new baby.

> It was stressful. Especially when I had to go out of town on business. I had to fly to Des Moines in a terrible snow storm. Later, I couldn't get out of town; the plane couldn't land. I had to get home. I missed my baby, and I needed to nurse her. And my husband was out of town and couldn't relieve the childcare person. Luckily, the last flight out left. And I got the only seat. God smiled on me.

Continuing business problems, the stress of traveling, and the desire to have another child combined to prompt her departure from the company.

Elizabeth Cruz abandoned a failing business. In contrast, the other three family-committed group members who suffered multiple contingencies—Yvonne Smith, Deborah Stein, and Jane Rowan—had been exceptionally successful businesswomen. They all had MBAs from elite schools and had invested eleven to twenty years in their careers. They all earned at least double their husbands' salaries. These women had relished their full-time work. After childbirth, they look just like the youngest cohort mothers in the career-committed group, who hired nannies and continued their careers with uninterrupted work devotion. Childbirth per se did not engineer a turning point out of full-time business careers.

We've heard the euphoria Yvonne Smith experienced as general manager and president of a small, highly successful company. Childbirth did not initially deter her from her career:

> I worked every day of my pregnancy. I flew through the 8th month . . . I worked the day before the child was born . . . 2 weeks later I took calls at home and started working at home. After the baby was 6 weeks, I was back in the office . . . I nursed for 5 months. I pumped my breasts on airplanes, between client visits. I froze my milk . . . I couldn't be gone. I had to travel. My clients needed me. I hired a full-time baby sitter.

She enthusiastically continued working until her son was fifteen months old. At that point, she was traumatized by having to leave on a business trip while her son was recovering from surgery. That experience prompted her to shift to a less-demanding, part-time job. Then Yvonne had a second child. She initially considered this part-time episode as temporary and planned to put her career back into "high gear again" as soon as her children were a bit older.

She worked as a part-time, freelance consultant for the next few years. After her children were ages three and six, she considered accepting a lucrative position with a prestigious consulting firm. But that year she had fired four babysitters and could not countenance introducing her children to a fifth. At the same time, her husband took a job requiring international travel, which further limited his availability for childcare. Around the time of our interview, she had decided to turn down the job offer.

> It is hard. I would love the work . . . It would have been more money than I would ever hope to make. I'm going to turn this down . . . I don't want the pressure, the conflict, of doing well at both jobs.

Yvonne finds it impossible simultaneously to fulfill the work devotion schema's requirements for one job, the consulting position, and to satisfy the family devotion schema's demands of the mothering vocation. Although she finds the job offer highly attractive, she will reject it to continue her focus on mothering and homemaking, even as her husband is spending increasing amounts of time away from home in his career pursuits.

Deborah Stein is another family-committed mother who did not leave her full-time career until she faced multiple contingencies. Her son was born in 1990. By 1992, she had worked her way up to chief operating officer of a medium-size health maintenance organization. Under Deborah's leadership, the organization tripled in size. The combined effects of the growing size, a merger, and a management shakeup made her job more stressful. Then in 1993 and 1994, she was hit with multiple family crises.

> There's been a lot of stresses in my life over the last two years. My father-in-law and his mother both died. My husband had open heart surgery. . . My younger brother had a nervous breakdown. I had to have him committed. And my older brother was diag-

nosed with colon cancer last year. Oh, and then my son's first caregiver it turned out that her husband or alleged husband was sexually molesting her daughters and she was aware of it and then that became really lousy, so we had to fire her. I think I'm missing something in this list. Anyway, there were a fair number of intervening issues in this time period in addition to normal job stress and my husband's job. And of course I had our son.

I have been like the Energizer Bunny [cartoon from a battery ad], just keep on chugging, keep on chugging. And my final straw was last spring, because my husband had a three-week trip to Japan. And while he travels huge amounts, it's usually Monday through Friday and then back for the weekend, but he's never done it three weeks in a row, solid, nonstop. I got to the middle of those three weeks and I said, this has got to stop [laughter]. It was just way over the edge, too much happening, too much going on, too much responsibility only on my shoulders, just plain too much.

Despite her tremendous "Energizer Bunny" work devotion, two deaths and three illnesses in the family, a childcare crisis, and her husband's prolonged absence made it impossible for Deborah Stein to continue her demanding job. Shortly before our interview, she shifted to part-time. As with other family-committed individuals who requested to work reduced hours, this move created its own set of problems. Her boss disapproves of her reduced hours, and she expects to have to look for another job soon.

The final family-committed woman who suffered multiple contingencies is Jane Rowan, a highly successful venture capitalist. After bearing two children, she continued to enjoy her work immensely and earned double her husband's banker salary.

Jane spent about twenty-five minutes telling me about a horrific event that occurred in 1988. Her then-kindergarten-aged daughter witnessed a woman spray an adjacent classroom with bullets, killing and injuring several children. This event severely disturbed the young girl. Jane intended to keep working and took her daughter with her on business trips. But the daughter continued to be traumatized and had to stay home to attend psychotherapy sessions. Even then, Jane did not quit her job but took an extended leave. It was not until her employer closed the venture capital division and terminated her with a large severance package in 1989 that she stopped working. When I interviewed her in 1994, Jane had just gone back into business as a full-time venture capitalist.

Yvonne Smith, Deborah Stein, and Jane Rowan were strongly committed business women at the pinnacle of their respective careers. They had substantially outearned their husbands while they were working full-time (and Yvonne and Deborah's part-time salaries were also higher than their husbands' full-time incomes). Childbirth per se did not weaken their embrace of the devotion to work schema. After their children were born, these women hired full-time nannies and, like their husbands, did much of their parenting from a distance.

But the new delegatory model of motherhood remains gendered and hierarchical. When a family's nurturing needs exceed what can be purchased, it remains the *woman's responsibility* to make sure the nurturing gets done. The exhausting emotional and practical labor of caring for the family through difficult times is still shouldered by even career-dedicated, high-earning women at the expense of their professional callings. Deborah Stein, Jane Rowan, Myrna Cubley, and to a lesser extent Yvonne Smith, were all hit with extreme contingencies that dictated the need for family nurturing beyond what paid caregivers could provide. They curtailed their careers to provide personal, intensive care while their husbands continued working and traveling unabated.

Deborah, Jane, and Yvonne became homemakers while they watched their husbands do the breadwinning less competently than they had. Deborah explained that her husband's earnings were "cyclical," although they had been on a low swing for some time. In the midst of a turbulent economy, Yvonne's and Jane's husbands both suffered job losses. Jane saw her generous severance payment disappear during her husband's year of unemployment in the early 1990s.

But, these women assured me, their husbands could never handle the career sacrifice, identity crisis, and tedium that staying home would entail. Yvonne Smith maintains that her husband "would find it would be very difficult . . . It would drive him crazy." Deborah Stein said, "the truth is, my husband, he loves his work." When I asked Jane Rowan if they had ever thought about her husband staying home with their troubled daughter, she had said that no, "he just wouldn't be able to not work."

As we have seen, some women invoked biology to explain their husbands' inability to be primary caretakers. For instance, recall Yvonne Smith's comment:

> This is typical of males versus females. Moms can put their own needs below others in the family. Most fathers are not as able. Some of it is the biological attachment between the child and the mother. How the child is born, the experience of nursing . . . It's impossible for me not to completely accept that commitment [of being the primary parent]. I can't look the other way.

Her belief that her husband is simply biologically unable to forgo his own career ambition for the sake of their children helps her defuse her anger at him and make sense of her own career sacrifice.

However, their belief in their own biological destiny did not buffer these women from the agony they faced in abandoning their full-time vocations. Yvonne Smith continues to grieve for her career. Deborah Stein described the decision to go part-time as a "terrible struggle":

> And I guess the truth is that it was a terrible struggle. It took me months to come to terms with it and to—I mean, I've worked full-time essentially since I was 22 years old . . . A big chunk of

my identity, not all of it, but a big chunk of it comes from my sense of self at work and this was very difficult.

Similarly, Jane Rowan also mourned the loss of the respected and glamorous person she had been while she was working:

> It was like I totally lost my identity. When I was working, everyone knew who I was. I was a senior partner in the firm. I had a glorious career. That defined me. I've got it all, I thought. Status, respect. It was a terrible shock to think, I'm nobody now. I'm somebody's mom.

Yvonne, Deborah, and Jane are among the ten women I categorized as discontented family-committed mothers. Because they had initially intended to continue their full-time careers while raising children, they are late and ambivalent converts to the family devotion schema's worldview. Yet they are converts nonetheless and use the family devotion schema to make sense of their new vocations as involved mothers.

For example, Deborah Stein "adores" walking her son to school every morning. Similarly, Jane Rowan decided that if she were going to be a full-time mother, she would be a great one. "I approached it [staying home] the same way I do everything. I barreled into it . . . I was even doing some freelance writing for *Parents Magazine!*"[10]

And as inspiration for her own intensive mothering, Yvonne Smith resurrected the image of her homemaking mother, who gave so much to her children:

> My mother was home full time. She would have been a fabulous career woman. She was really busy. She was involved with the PTA; she was a Cub Scout leader . . . I had a wonderful family background. That makes it harder for me not to invest in my kids. My parents have three very successful children . . . They are all achievers. They invested a lot in their kids . . . My father

traveled a lot . . . He was gone a lot. We were a typical, Midwest-
ern family, a very traditional family. We went camping as a
family.

This model also gives meaning to Yvonne's life now. Like her mother,
she is married to a man who is seldom home and spends her days "investing" in her children.

Ironically, Yvonne's icon of the family devotion schema, her own
mother, now believes she was duped by the schema and encourages
Yvonne to go back to work:

But my mother is the one who wants me to work. She thinks it's
unsatisfying to be home full-time. She lived through her kids
and was underappreciated. If she had had her kids now, she
would be a working mom.

Rachel Kahn, another ambivalent intensive mother, observes a similar irony. She wonders what the point is in giving up her own career
to heavily invest in her daughters' well-being, who, if they follow in
her shoes, will end up sacrificing their own careers as well:

I try to do the best I can [for my kids] . . . I have two girls, and I
want them to grow up to be anything they want. Yet, here I am. I
went to a good college, to Harvard Business School, I was president of a company at 32. And now I'm home with them.
    What's the point of raising kids to be astronauts if their career
only lasts until they have kids? . . . It's troubling to me, personally. What kind of role model am I providing, if I'm raising
them?

Rachel fears that her career sacrifice on behalf of her daughters provides them with a martyr for a role model and thus may sabotage
their own potential achievement.

*   *   *

Respondents' decisions about whether to turn away from executive careers after childbearing are patterned by career structures, constrained by the gendered division of labor, shaped by cultural schemas, and sometimes triggered by contingencies. The women I interviewed can either continue along a pathway oriented toward career advancement, or they can abandon that pathway for one oriented toward family care. It is very difficult to straddle both paths. Even the family-committed women who maintain part-time professional jobs find themselves defined by their employers as uncommitted and their advancement possibilities curtailed.

The extremely work-dedicated, high-earning women in the family-committed group who were hit with multiple negative contingencies initially strove to maintain their full-time vocations. Neither childbirth nor extreme contingencies could engineer their turning point without the context of the family devotion schema's model of gender roles. Even though these women did not personally adhere to the family devotion schema, it still made their decision to stay home almost inevitable when family crises exceeded the resources of hired care. It is the default master script for these women's lives. The family devotion schema's organization of gender roles ensures that their husbands, off dedicating themselves to their own careers, are unable to respond to family emergencies. The family devotion schema imparts meaning to the women's renunciation of their careers and absolves their husbands from making a similar sacrifice for the sake of their children. It both engineers and interprets an abrupt turn of fate.

In interviews, several family-committed women said they hoped to rebuild full-time careers someday. But at the time of my interviews, only Jane Rowan was attempting to do so. She and a male business partner were just getting ready to open a new venture capital firm. A beautiful woman of average size, Jane sipped a low-calorie meal-replacement shake during our lunchtime interview and discussed trying to lose a few pounds to help her project a stronger business image. She worries not only about her physical shape but also about whether

her social capital has grown too old to be useful in today's market: "A lot of people have left the business. People have made enough money and retired, so a lot of people that I knew are not involved anymore." Whether she can engineer a new turning point out of homemaking and back to the business career of her early adulthood remains to be seen.

6

IMPLICATIONS

This chapter answers three "so what?" questions. First, I discuss the contributions of my research to sociological theory on social and cultural structures, human agency, and gendered inequality. Next, I discuss the applicability of insights from this study to the predicaments of many working Americans. Finally, I explain why this study matters for employees, employers, and policy makers. I argue that, at least among professionals, the human resources ideology of "work-family balance" is a feeble competitor to the work devotion schema. Calls for policy changes to make workplaces more "family friendly" will continue to lack effectiveness without our coming to grips with the devotion schemas.

Implications for Sociological Theory on Structure, Agency, and Gender

As Americans, we tend to believe that our work and family problems are private and solvable by individual effort (cf. Kelly, 1999). This view is reinforced by the popular and business press.

Social scientists are trained to analyze how these individual struggles are shaped by social context as well as the ways institutions and cultural assumptions help determine how people conceive of and realize their priorities. However, much social scientific work-family research implicitly views people as autonomous actors considering options and incentives as they make strategic and economically rational choices. Much of this research does not fully consider the extent to which the available options and people's evaluation of those options are structured by social institutions, including their cultural definitions. Even work-family research that does consider culture tends to simplify it as a set of external norms, which impinge upon individuals otherwise presumed to be autonomous, or which individuals cognitively manipulate to serve rational ends. Moreover, many studies implicitly present work and family demands as external to people, like separate balls to be juggled.[1]

We see these assumptions in even the best scholarly research on this issue. For example, although Kathleen Gerson's (1985) classic book *Hard Choices* explicitly advocates a theory of women actively constructing their lives, the analysis actually relies on a thin, fairly passive conception of human agency. In her argument, most of the action resides offstage in general trends pushing women into and out of workplaces and homes. She portrays her respondents as surprisingly passive and overly calculating, largely limited to *rationally responding to* the given "options and incentives" they confront (p. 218; see also p. 42). A more active and interpretive conception of agency would better capture how people not only react to circumstances but also actively shape their lives. Furthermore, Gerson fails to analyze how deep-seated cultural structures shape and constrain women's responses as well as provide them with resources to creatively reformulate or reinterpret extant options.

Other good research efforts recognize that choices are socially structured but then unfortunately fall back on language imbued with strategic, individualistic, or reactive assumptions (for example, Clarkberg and Moen, 2001; Gerson and Jacobs, 2001; and Bond, Galinsky, and Swanberg, 1998). Even studies that acknowledge cultural norms, such as those supporting long work hours, assume that the norms are just another set of external constraints on workers' behavior rather than investigating the ways in which they may powerfully shape—and be shaped by—workers' own self-understandings (for example, Drago et al., 2001; Maume and Bellas, 2001; and Fried, 1998). Gerson's (2002) recent essay usefully examines the moral dimension of work-family conflict, but it falls back on charting voluntaristic, individual strategies to reconcile work and family. Moreover, she posits work as the domain for achieving autonomy rather than what I see as a site of an intense relationship competing with family in its demand for commitment. One book that transcends the limitations of most work-family research is Garey's (1999) study of how employed mothers use cultural models to understand and justify their action while at the same time expanding these models into new shapes.

Overall, research on organizations and careers has done perhaps a better job of documenting certain kinds of constraints on women's achievement. This literature includes research on how women in the securities industry continue to confront overt and subtle forms of gender discrimination in their firms (Blair-Loy, 2001b; Catalyst, 2001; Costen, 2001; Levin, 2001; Roth, 2001a, b). Moreover, senior finance-related jobs have become more competitive, demanding, and turbulent in recent decades (Blair-Loy, 1999; Stearns and Allan, 1996; Flynn, Leeth, and Levy, 1995). High-ranking professional women, like their male colleagues, face workplace cultures that assume elite employees will put in very long hours on an uninterrupted and full-time basis, even during their chief family formation years (Williams, 2000; Epstein et al., 1999; Fried, 1998; Epstein et al., 1995). Yet most women lack support from a spouse at home (Catalyst, 2001; Hochschild, 1997; Wajcman, 1996; but see Morris, 2002). Thus the ideal worker is assumed to be a male removed from processes of human reproduction and free of family responsibilities (Acker, 1990). Women striving to get ahead must conform to that ideal as best they can.

The work-family and organizations and careers literatures have taught us a great deal. However they have not sufficiently analyzed the cultural foundations of these external constraints nor the ways culture has shaped people's identities. That is this book's contribution.

The Impact of Culture

This book analyzes how deep-seated, taken-for-granted, powerfully compelling cultural schemas help shape these constraints and people's interpretations of them. It draws on Sewell's (1992: 27) abstract theoretical formulation of structure as composed of "mutually sustaining cultural schemas and sets of resources that empower and constrain social action and tend to be reproduced by that action" (see also Emirbayer and Mische, 1998; Alexander, 1988).[2] I combine this cultural theory with feminist theories of gender as an "institution" (Lorber, 1994) or "structure" (Risman, 1998) that creates distinctions and inequalities throughout society (see also Potuchek, 1997 and Wharton, 1991). My synthesis and extension of these theoretical ideas illuminate the power of gendered schemas to constrain and enable action in everyday life.

I support Risman's (1998) project of seeing gender as a structure at every level of analysis and understanding the relationships between structure and agency. I also agree with Gerson's (1985: 37) argument that analysts must study "how women themselves, as actors who respond to the social conditions they inherit, construct their lives out of the available raw materials." My research focuses on aspects of structure that Risman, Gerson, and others undertheorize: cultural schemas as institutionalized and partially internalized models for cognition, morality, and emotion. I argue that analysts cannot fully comprehend the pervasiveness of the gender structure or the complexity of human agency without understanding how schemas constrain and enable action.

In contrast to my usage, some scholars use the term "schema" more narrowly to denote a socially constructed, cognitive map in people's heads, which helps apprehend and organize information. For many cognitive psychologists, schemas are the "representations of knowledge and information-processing mechanisms" that provide shortcuts to simplify cognition (DiMaggio 1997: 269; see also Zerubavel, 1997). Similarly, Bem (1983: 603) defines a schema as an individual's "cognitive structure, a network of associations that organizes and guides an individual's perception." These gendered associations are made salient and functional by the culture. Risman (1998: 27) also emphasizes culture's role of structuring cognition; she defines "the cultural aspect of the social structure" as "the taken-for-granted or *cognitive* image rules that belong to the situational context" (emphasis added). Bem, Risman, and West and Zimmerman (1987) all share a concern with normative rules and situations of moral accountability in which individuals feel compelled to appropriately present themselves as men or as women. Yet these analysts primarily treat these rules as another set of *cognitive* constraints rather than as aspects of a *moral* universe analyzable in its own right.

Bem's more recent formulation of the "gender lens" is closer to my framework. For Bem (1993: 2–3), gender lenses are assumptions that "shape how people perceive, conceive, and discuss social reality" and thus shape material reality. But while Bem (1993: 153–155) notes that one's thoughts, feelings, and normative self-definitions are shaped by the gender lens, she does not fully develop the emotional and normative dimensions of this lens. Moreover, because she posits the gender lens as universal, her framework has limited utility for explaining agency and change in particular historical settings.

In contrast, I argue that culture provides powerful moral evaluations and evokes intense emotions in addition to ordering cognition. I locate this aspect of culture in schemas of devotion, which are particularly gripping, cultural models that orient us toward where we devote our time, energy, and passion. In a historical time and place, they tell us what to care about and how to care about it. I use the term "devotion" rather than "commitment" or "interest" to emphasize that these schemas define more than just cognitive maps or rational interests. Devotion schemas specify that which we are invited or compelled to devote ourselves to, body and soul. Like articles of faith, they promise to provide meaning to life and a secure connection to something outside ourselves. Thus, I envision a more powerful and invasive role of culture than that seen by Risman (1998: 29), who examines how "interactional pressures and institutional design create gender and the resultant inequality *even in the absence* of individual desires" (emphasis added). In contrast, I argue that devotion schemas also help *create* those individual desires, induce appropriate emotions (cf. Hochschild, 1979), and thus powerfully reinforce interactional and institutional patterns.

Toward a "Moral Turn"

This book then, mounts a broader critique of the "cognitive turn" in sociology. This cognitive turn has been fueled by neo-institutional research, which studies how new practices and rules become adopted and established in organizations, institutions, and environmental fields (DiMaggio and Powell, 1991; Friedland and Alford, 1991). Neo-institutionalism has critiqued earlier formulations of culture as oversimplified, uncontested values (DiMaggio and Powell, 1991). Explicitly rejecting the old institutionalists' moral framework, neo-institutionalists see culture as a set of taken-for-granted routines or as a set of cognitive schemas that classify information. "Normative obligations . . . enter in social life primarily as facts that must be taken into account by actors" (Meyer and Rowan, 1977: 341) rather than as moral definitions of ultimate ends.

Yet this book and research done by Amy Wharton, Jerry Goodstein, and myself argue that the neo-institutionalist version of culture is ill suited to the job of understanding the problem of work-family conflict. In contrast to the neo-institutionalists' anemic, amoral understanding of culture, we argue that work-family conflict cannot be understood empirically without fully acknowledging and analyzing the moral dimension of this conflict. We argue that work-family conflict is fundamentally a conflict between emotionally salient, moral definitions of what it is to be a good worker and a good parent.[3] Within individuals, work-family conflict cuts to the heart of what it means to be fully human. Within institutions, these normative definitions influence corporate ideologies, work scheduling, evaluation standards, and promotion patterns at work and shape the gender division of labor at home.

Wharton, Goodstein, and I argue that this clash of normative definitions affects individuals in powerful ways. These include "moral distress," in which employees feel unable to fulfill what they believe is the right thing to do for their families due to constraints imposed by employers. Or this clash may create "moral dilemmas," in which adults feel torn by two compelling but incompatible models of right action (Kelly, 1998; Emirbayer and Mische, 1998: 1012–1113; cf. Jameton, 1993). Many employees live and work within an emotional tug-of-war, in which their identity and integrity are under siege. Moral distress and moral dilemmas are understudied factors that may underlie common research findings, including the employee reluctance to use certain work-family policies, work-family "spillover," the motherhood wage gap, and the relatively high turnover among employed mothers. For example, part-time or flextime arrangements may give employees more time at home but may also damage their moral reputation as committed workers, shred their network ties, and violate their professional identities. "Work-family balance" may entail not the equilibrated fulfillment of multiple tasks but the compromise of valued goals and the neglect of cherished relationships with family or colleagues.

Much of what is empirically important about work-family conflict will escape sociologists unless we recognize that it is not an individual problem, not primarily a cognitive problem, and not just an interesting study in how taken-for-granted scripts do or do not get established in organizations. The analysis of work-family conflict and any cultural solutions to it must also explicitly focus on the issue's moral dimension.[4]

Devotion Schemas, Conformers, and Mavericks

This book analyzes the power and the limits of the competing cultural schemas of work devotion and family devotion.[5] I show that even highly resourceful women must constantly grapple with them, as they create meaning through them, defy them, or try to reconcile them. These devotion schemas ordain relationships, roles, and identities that are emotionally and normatively charged.[6] Whatever her particular response to these cultural models, every woman I interviewed was passionate on these issues. No one was neutral.

Among the upper-middle and upper-class families in my study, the devotion schemas each demand total allegiance to a social institution (firm or family). Each dictates a moral prescription for a meaningful and rewarding life. Each schema invites one into a calling, the life task for which one feels particularly suited for and by which one is fulfilled (Weber, 1958a, 1958b).

Each cultural model is reinforced by patterns of social relationships and ideologies. For example, the work devotion schema is sustained by the boss and community of coworkers, by the flow of firm resources to those expressing the most dedication to the company, and by the ideology of being a good provider. The family devotion schema is buttressed by a definition of children as vulnerable and by an ideology that women are biologically suited for family caregiving, while men are not. It is further reinforced by a community of mothers who have given up full-time employment for a vocation of involved motherhood.

Each cultural model pledges financial stability as well as tremendous intrinsic rewards. The family devotion schema promises fulfillment, creativity, intimacy, and a community with other mothers. The work devotion schema promises status, collegiality, intense and engaging work, and even transcendence. Both pledge to provide a moral and fulfilling life, a life worth living.

Together, the work and family devotion schemas create an interdependent system that reproduces gendered inequality. Traditionally, they each model a hierarchical relationship between, on the one hand, the traditionally male, elite worker and his employer, and on the other hand, the economically dependent wife and her husband. Financial rewards allow the devoted worker to support a wife, who is not employed full-time, and children. The wife is able to embody the family devotion schema and care for the children, household, and the husband's personal needs, thus enabling his long hours and work commitment. The husband is consumed by work and professional advancement so that he can continue to support the family financially and increase his status and income. As the husband becomes increasingly unavailable for childcare and household duties, the wife finds the responsibilities for children and household weighing heavier on her shoulders. As long as men obeyed the dictates of the work devotion schema while women fulfilled the family devotion schema's mandate, conflict between the institutions of work and family was minimized.[7] This gendered cultural system reinforces the power of the capitalist employer over the family and the patriarchal power of the husband over the wife.

This is the abstract, cultural model, socially constructed in the nineteenth century and flowering in the post World War II era. But reality is more complex. People respond to these cultural models in a variety of ways.

First, most women today are not full-time homemakers. While 67 percent of American families conformed to the male breadwinner–female homemaker model in 1952, only 27 percent did in 1999 (Stebbins, 2001). Unlike many of my respondents, many women must work to support the family financially. Despite being employed, many middle-class and working-class women continue to understand their children as fragile and deserving of a mother's care, to define themselves as intensive mothers, and to try to fulfill as much of the traditional mothering role as they can (Garey, 1999; Hays, 1996). Their allegiance to the family devotion schema despite their employment is a testament to the schema's continued resonance in their lives.

A second empirical variation is that sometimes the institutions of work and of family do not live up to the devotion schemas' promises to provide a rewarding and meaningful life to their disciples. About half of the women in my career-committed group (who maintained demanding full-time careers) have soured on work devotion. And about half the women in my family-committed group (who left full-time careers after childbearing) live out the family devotion schema's demands with grim resignation. Both groups are composed of highly resourceful women, who presumably have other options for their lives. The willingness of both groups to continue to dedicate themselves to their respective vocations, despite disappointment and even betrayal, demonstrates the power of both schemas.

Before the early to mid-1970s, the gendered division of labor between intensive, professional work and intensive mothering, as defined by the devotion schemas, minimized the contradictions between the institutions of the firm and the family. Yet in the past two decades, substantial numbers of *women* have had opportunities to become elite workers.[8] This book is about what happens when the ideal worker, the devoted executive, is female. It explains how the elite women I interviewed live out the often-painful contradictions between work and family devotion in their own lives in complex, yet patterned ways.

Each group contains a subgroup of conformists who uphold one schema by choosing *either* work devotion *or* family devotion. And each group contains a subgroup of innovators, who strive to recast the cultural system by *combining* demanding careers with motherhood.

The conformists in each group try to circumvent the contradiction between the devotion schemas by implicitly obeying both. Thirty-five women in the career-committed group do not have children and honor the work devotion schema by dedicating most of their waking hours to their careers. At the same time, they obey the family devotion schema by forgoing childbearing.[9] And 10 women in the family-committed group abandoned their careers after childbearing despite their professional educations and high incomes. They succumbed to the work devotion schema's definition of themselves as unworthy elite workers. They fulfill the family devotion schema's demands and enable their husbands' embrace of the work devotion schema.

We have seen that the devotion schemas are taken-for-granted frameworks for defining and evaluating what we know as reality. These schemas define and are reinforced by important social institutions.[10] So how is it possible for people to challenge them?

Emirbayer and Mische (1998) analytically distinguish between three types of agency: habitual or iterative (actors' selective reactivation of past patterns of thought and action); practical-evaluative (actors' practical and normative judgments and actions among present alternatives and dilemmas); and projective (actors' imaginative and creative reconfiguration of received structures to generate possible future trajectories of action).[11] Often, people practice habitual agency and thereby more or less unreflectively reproduce social structures. Yet when actors find themselves at the intersection of contradictory or multivalent sets of social structures, they may have enhanced opportunities for practical-evaluative or even projective agency because they can reinterpret a given set of structures differently according to competing cultural schemas. Practical-evaluative agency and especially projective agency occur when people extend, transpose, or analogize schemas onto new situations, thus changing the definition of the situation and their power within it (Emirbayer and Mische,

1998; Clemens, 1997; Sewell, 1992). This allows them to reinterpret and even recast social structures.

We see this beginning to happen among the two maverick subgroups, who openly defy one or the other of these cultural models of a worthwhile life. Part-time workers in the family-committed group are challenging the work devotion schema's commandment of single-minded allegiance to one's career. And mothers in the career-committed group, especially the mid–baby boomers in the youngest cohort, had children while continuing their demanding, full-time careers and thus defy the family devotion schema's edict of intensive motherhood. Both groups are engaging in practical-evaluative action to address present dilemmas and projective action to envision and create new ways of combining work and family.[12]

The fact that some women in the family-committed group work part-time is unremarkable, as about 25 percent of employed women in the United States have part-time jobs. However, most part-time jobs are limited in terms of pay, benefits, and responsibility (Kalleberg et al., 2000; Blossfeld and Hakim, 1997; Drobnic and Wittig, 1997). My employed family-committed respondents are theoretically important because they are highly educated and experienced women working in demanding and responsible positions in male-dominated firms. In contrast to most part-time employed mothers, the part-timers I interviewed have the resources of education and high-status professional experience to ask to be treated like elite workers. Yet they also believe in the family devotion schema's prescription for a mother's biologically ordained, intimate care for her children. Their belief in the family devotion schema gives them the cognitive, moral, and emotional vantage point from which to challenge the work devotion schema's mandate that executives must be full-time. In sum, they use the resources of elite occupational status and their commitment to an alternative schema, the family devotion schema, to try to expand the work devotion schema into a new cultural model that accommodates and rewards dedicated part-time elite workers.

The part-timers I interviewed are trying to imaginatively redefine what is possible. They work hard to justify themselves as efficient, dedicated professionals, despite their family commitments (see also Meiksins and Whalley, 2002). It may be economically profitable for firms to support the careers of part-time professionals. But so far, the part-timers in my study are viewed as apostates, unworthy of advancement into the firm's celestial ranks. This hostility and the women's elaborate justifications of their deviant status both demonstrate the work devotion schema's resilience in their firms and in their lives.

The other maverick subgroup is composed of the career-committed mothers, who continued full-time, uninterrupted business careers after childbearing. These women are exemplars of the work devotion schema. The wide age range of the career-committed group allows us to see how the societal changes wrought by the 1970s women's movement helped make available new resources and schemas to the youngest women in this group, the mid–baby boomers in the youngest cohort.

The family devotion schema had to be modified before respondents could build demanding careers while raising children. But women in the career-committed group could not alter this schema without certain ideological and material resources, which the older cohorts lack. The youngest cohort finished college at an age in which societal changes wrought by the 1970s women's movement had begun to be institutionalized. Unlike their older colleagues, they could embark upon career tracks that were, at least formally, gender-blind. They married relatively late, after amassing the high incomes that gave them power in family decisions and after men had begun to share in the cultural idea of gender-egalitarianism.

The youngest cohort thus had access to the material and ideological resources that allowed them to successfully transpose the egalitarian schema from the workplace onto their family lives and alter their families' definitions of marriage and motherhood. They evolved a definition of motherhood as more delegatory than intensive and a definition of children as more independent than vulnerable. This recasting of the family devotion schema enabled the youngest career-committed women to combine motherhood with demanding executive careers. Thus, these pioneers are finding "new and creative ways of fusing, extending, and transforming these received schemas, as they experiment with practical strategies to confront the emergent challenges of historically changing circumstances" (Emirbayer and Mische, 1998: 1009).

Despite these redefinitions, the logic of the family devotion schema remains gendered and hierarchical. Women continue to do the day-to-day domestic labor. Respondents retain ultimate responsibility for their children's care, even if they delegate it to other women, who are often members of subordinated class and minority racial/ethnic groups.

Moreover, mothers in the career-committed group, who continued to work a demanding full-time schedule, elaborately justified their worth and involvement as mothers. Their spirited defense of their value as mothers, on the one hand, and their regret over lack of time with their children, on the other, demonstrate the tenacious grip of the family devotion schema on their hearts and minds.

In sum, the devotion schemas are useful analytic tools in understanding change and stability in executive women's work and family lives across historically specific time periods. These schemas elucidate how people can simultaneously conform to and challenge gendered social structures.

This analysis, then, adds context, complexity, and nuance to the standard view of adults as autonomous individuals making personal and strategic choices about separate and competing workplace and family demands. It provides a more multidimensional understanding of people's actions and decisions than is implied in much work-family research. In several ways, it shows how, among the women I interviewed, human agency is both more limited and more creative than this research generally represents.

First, human action is not purely idiosyncratic, thinly strategic, or largely reactive. The people in my study routinely defied the dictates of narrow economic rationality. For example, couples frequently decided that the higher-earning wife, rather than the lower-earning husband, should give up her full-time job for family care. And despite high turnover costs, some employers were loath to hold onto richly experienced managers and professionals on a part-time basis. Even businesspeople, accustomed to reading profit and loss statements, filter their economic decisions through the lenses of the devotion schemas.

Second, cultural definitions of the conceivable, the moral, and the desirable, embodied in institutions and personalities, shape human agency. Cultural schemas delineate what is possible—and impossible—by shaping the expectations, demands, and resource-allocating mechanisms of social institutions. Further, they mold the fundamental identities of hardworking adults. Indeed, cultural schemas may continue to shape action even when they no longer fit new demographic or institutional realities.

Third, agency is expanded when people attain access to new resources or when their lives straddle competing cultural schemas. Under these circumstances, they gain the capacity to defy or transform these schemas.

Fourth, this analysis shows how cultural schemas can constrain action, even among highly resourceful and privileged people. Specifically, it portrays the tenacity of gender as expressed in both devotion schemas, even among these beneficiaries of the women's movement. Whatever my respondents' personal responses to the work and family devotion schemas, this gendered cultural system defines and limits their actions. The work devotion schema pressures female executives to delay or sacrifice childbearing. At the same time, the family devotion schema pressures respondents with children to cut back on work commitment or to stay home, as their husbands, devoured by work devotion, are unable or unwilling to focus on the day-to-day requirements of childcare and household maintenance.

When some highly career oriented respondents faced family emergencies greater than could be solved by paid caregivers, these respondents left their full-time jobs while their lower-earning husbands continued to work unabated. And many career-committed mothers remain haunted by the normative image of what Catherine Hanke calls the "perfect mother," the ghost of the family devotion schema. Even among these resourceful and privileged executives, gender as expressed in the family devotion schema maintains a tenacious grip on women's hearts and minds.

Gender remains a "master status" that executive women continue to feel and do in older ways, despite emerging opportunities in the professional workplace.[13] As refracted in the devotion schemas, gender continues to structure institutions, define possible career paths, order interactions, organize cognition, and limit advancement. Through devotion schemas, it powerfully and personally defines the life worth living.

Schemas and Institutions

I have presented the devotion schemas in the form of ideal types, abstract, cultural models constructed by the researcher to simplify and make sense of a complex set of socially constructed understandings. I have argued that these schemas have a supra-individual, empirical presence as the symbolic dimension of social structure, the cultural definitions that people use to interpret and make sense of their lives. But how coherent are these schemas at the level of the individual?

Recently, sociologists of culture have argued that people hold onto more cultural information than they can use and believe logically incompatible things simultaneously (Swidler, 2001; DiMaggio, 1997). For example, the mothers in the career-committed group and the family-committed women with part-time jobs simultaneously partake of elements of both the work devotion and the family devotion schema.

Although culture may be fragmented and inconsistent at the level of individual thought and assumption, researchers argue that culture is given coherence by institutions (Swidler, 2001; DiMaggio, 1997; Friedland and Alford, 1991). These institutions, such as capitalist firms or nuclear families, help people switch to and organize the cultural information most relevant for relating successfully with other human beings (spouses, children, bosses, coworkers) within these institutions.[14]

However, the meaning of the phrase "culture is given coherence by institutions" depends on the researcher's definition of "institution." Ronald Jepperson's definition is widely cited: institutions are "those social patterns that, when chronically reproduced, owe their survival to relatively self-activating social processes," which use socially constructed rewards and sanctions to resist deviation from the patterns (Jepperson, 1991: 145). Swidler (2001: 202) adopts Jepperson's definition and argues that institutions set the problems for people to solve. People use culture to construct strategies of action that try to solve the dilemmas institutions pose. Swidler maintains that the institution of marriage poses two problems: how people decide whom to marry; and how people stay married. People use and elaborate the culture of mythic-romantic love to solve the first dilemma and the culture of prosaic love to solve the second one. Consistencies in people's cultural models are due to similarities in the institutional problems they are trying to solve.

A shortcoming of Swidler's analysis is that it posits a seemingly acultural institution (a self-replicating social process) as the causal principle that organizes culture. But it does not analytically address the fact that institutions are themselves cultural constructions. After all, the self-replicating activity alone is, for half of all American couples, marriage-and-divorce.[15] Instead, I prefer Friedland and Alford's (1991) definition, in which institutions are simultaneously symbolic and material; they are self-reproducing symbolic systems that create meaning at the same time that they maintain patterns of human activity and material subsistence.[16] This definition allows us to theorize the institution of marriage as including not only patterned activity and materiality but also the cultural and normative definition of a lasting commitment.

It might be fruitful to analytically bisect the symbolic dimension from the more material dimension of patterned human activity in order to sort out the historical story of how an institution emerged. When and how a set of patterned activity came to be defined by a particular symbol system or schema, and which dimension has more causal force in a given circumstance, are empirical questions. Sorting out the processes by which the late twentieth–early twenty-first-century American capitalistic firm and upper-middle-class, nuclear family came to be defined, in part, by the schema of work devotion and family devotion would require a historical analysis beyond the scope of this book. But my argument that the devotion schemas developed in concert with nineteenth- and twentieth-century capitalism but have since become semiautonomous from economic factors and developed their own normative force is consistent with other scholars' historical research (Wuthnow, 1996; Schor, 1991; Hunnicutt, 1988). Today, the cultural definition of work devotion is tightly interwoven with the patterned relationships and resources of evaluation, compensation, and advancement. This is illustrated by my finding that respondents at the highest levels are generally the most ardent disciples of work devotion. Firm resources flow to those with the most devotion, and their devotion is reinforced by the firm's faithfulness. The important point here is that for managers and professionals today, the institutions of firm and family in the United States require the symbolic system of the work devotion schema and the family devotion schema for their contemporary meaning.

The work devotion and family devotion schemas are durable even though they in some ways do not fit well with the changing demographics of the American family and firm. In vivid contrast to Swidler's (2001) view of culture working reciprocally with institutions to provide solutions to the problems institutions pose, I argue that the devotion schemas help solve some problems (for example, the employer's problem of how to motivate workers) but *exacerbate* the problems of how people can support themselves financially, care for their families, and do meaningful work. In a society in which work hours are lengthening, growing numbers of mothers are employed, and divorce rates are high, the devotion schemas create more dilemmas than they solve. They create work-family conflict. Their tenacity in people's lives—despite their lack of institutional fit—bespeaks the independent power of the devotion schemas to continue to organize the means and ends of action.[17]

I see the same situation in Swidler's (2001) empirical case. In contrast to her argument, I propose that the cultures of romantic love and prosaic love are both oriented toward the cultural end of a lasting marriage. I suggest that a loving, permanent marriage is part of the cultural definition or schema of marriage. And this schema persists *despite* the fact that it no longer fits the demographic reality that half of all recently contracted marriages will end in divorce. This schema continues to inspire belief in a loving, enduring marriage as people marry a first, second, or third time. While the patterned activity of people marrying may have historically helped generate the culture of love, it no longer shapes the culture of love in a direct, causal fashion. Today it is the culture of love itself, not the self-replicating pattern of marriage-and-divorce, that shapes people's commitment and actions toward maintaining an enduring marriage. This cultural definition or schema persists despite the fact that it encourages some action, such as the interruption in women's paid work, which exacerbates rather than solves the problems posed by the patterned activity of marriage-and-divorce.

In sum, I view institutions as components of social structure. Like social structure, institutions contain two dimensions: the symbolic and the material. The incoherent and contradictory bits of culture people hold are organized and activated by the cultural dimension of institutions, including the schemas of work devotion and family devotion. These schemas are durable but not deterministic. As the mavericks in my study illustrate, people who are invested in different institutions with competing logics can use the cultural schema defining one institution to try to transform the definition of another institution.[18]

Other Populations

This study has gleaned these cultural models from the experiences of extreme cases: unusually successful, predominantly white women in finance-related fields. The women I interviewed represent an extreme end of the distribution of employed women, the success stories of liberal feminism. They have attained extraordinary financial and professional success in male-dominated occupations, achieving parity with comparable men and indeed surpassing many men in similar occupations. This extreme case is important precisely because it includes people with ample resources—professional educations, elite jobs, and high incomes—as they negotiate tremendous social and cultural constraints. These constraints include overt and subtle gender discrimination in the macho, turbulent, competitive, and work-intensive world of the finance industry.

Human agency is highlighted and thus easier for us to discern when we study people with high resources confronting substantial constraints. Many societal constraints are so taken for granted as to be almost invisible to the analyst. Thus, this research usefully presents exaggerated constraints confronted head-on by people with extraordinary resources. An important question for future research is the extent to which the patterns identified here characterize the work and family lives of more typical Americans, perhaps in a more diluted form.[19]

Findings from studies of other professional and managerial groups of women are broadly consistent with my findings (Epstein et al.,

1999; Fried, 1998; Wajcman, 1996; Bailyn, 1993; Epstein, 1993). More-over, the cultural models of white professionals are more influential than the numbers of workers in these categories would suggest. Their cultural models influence general expectations around work and family in society more broadly (Garey, 1999). And as employers and super-visors, these workers can impose their cultural understandings on other workers (cf. Hochschild, 1997).

In contrast to many employed women, my respondents have the privileges of choice. They can pursue elite jobs or they can stay home with their children. Garey's (1999, 1995) research on women in nonelite, female-dominated jobs suggests that these occupations may engender or allow different constellations of work and family cultural models. Women confront cultural norms of motherhood "from vary-ing social locations, and they respond by adopting, modifying, or reinterpreting them" (Garey, 1995: 416). Yet family devotion remains paramount, as Garey's middle- and working-class subjects persist in doing the practical and symbolic work to define themselves as inten-sive mothers, despite their employment obligations (see also Hays, 1996). For example, night-shift nurses sacrificed sleep in order to de-fine themselves as "at-home" mothers and stay up with their children during the day. In contrast to my career-committed respondents who face more consuming work demands, these nurses do not experience work devotion as a serious threat to the "force and tenacity of the cul-tural ideal of the 'at-home' mother" (Garey, 1995: 434).

Results from Clarkberg and Moen's (2001) large, nationally repre-sentative sample of dual-earner couples are broadly consistent with my findings. Clarkberg and Moen find that preferences for work hours are gendered along lines my research would predict: wives are far more likely than husbands to say they prefer part-time work. Moreover, finding realistic and desirable part-time jobs is difficult. The researchers conclude that available options for work hours are largely structured and limited by "organizational policies and em-ployer expectations" to the "all-or-nothing breadwinner/homemaker cultural template" (Clarkberg and Moen, 2001: 1133).

I studied a group of predominantly white women. A question for further study is if and how women in other racial and ethnic groups are embedded in similar cultural systems of work and family. Previous research suggests that the ideology of motherhood among women in racial and ethnic minority groups is often constructed differently than among white women (Glenn et al., 1994). For example, African-American women are more likely than white women to see motherhood and employment as complementary rather than contradictory responsibilities (Collins, 1994). Studies of African-American professional women suggest that female attorneys experience work-family conflict life in ways similar but not identical to white professional women (Blair-Loy and DeHart, forthcoming; Epstein, 1973).

Another important question, which I am currently studying, concerns the ways in which men are embedded in cultural models of work devotion and their stance on family devotion. The scholarly literature suggests that more typical populations of men are shaped by older cultural definitions of men's roles at the same time these cultural understandings are changing (Coltrane and Adams, 2001; Coltrane, 1996; Gerson, 1993). Previous research suggests that the emotional, normative, and cognitive dimensions of men's work and family commitments would be fruitful areas of further investigation. One study has emphasized the emotional and sexual tenor of male managers' work lives (Roper, 1994). And other research has explicitly delineated some of the cultural structures—the moral and cognitive maps—with which men interpret and construct their lives. These cultural maps vary according to nationality, occupational status, and race (Lamont, 2000, 1992; Jackall, 1988).

This book found a correlation between executive women's work devotion and their position in their firm's hierarchy. Similarly, the grip that work devotion has on men's psyches might vary according to their occupational position. In a group of 519 professionals in a global financial services firm, Amy Wharton and I found that employees at the very top of the organizational hierarchy (15 percent of the group) look like the model devoted executive (Blair-Loy and

Wharton, 2002b). These employees are predominantly male. They tend to work long hours in line management jobs, have significant supervisory responsibility and high seniority, earn very high incomes, have homemaking spouses, and express no interest in corporate flextime or flexplace benefits. In contrast, the mid-level and lower-level managers and professionals are composed of roughly equal numbers of men and women. At these levels, both sexes tend to lack a homemaking spouse, are wracked by work-family conflict, and express interest in using their company's work-family benefits. This study lends support to this book's argument that greater resources flow to those who can approximate the ideal worker. This study also suggests that some gender differences may dissolve when comparing men and women who lack a homemaking spouse. At the middle and lower managerial ranks in this group, both men and women faced somewhat similar pressures to live up to the devoted worker ideal while fulfilling domestic responsibilities.

I speculate that there are many occupations that are built on the template of some form or other of the work devotion schema. These jobs require long hours and commitment, offer significant rewards (intrinsic and/or extrinsic), and can be conceptualized as a calling. These jobs can be seductive: they can impart so much meaning and identity to those that fill them that people may not be aware of how much time and energy they demand. They can also be coercive. Failing to fulfill the demands for total allegiance and fidelity can jeopardize one's chances of advancement or even employment. To the extent that these jobs require single-minded dedication, they are likely to be filled with people who lack significant family responsibilities or to engender profound work-family conflict for those who do.

Yet the analytical concept of work and family devotion schemas may also be useful in very different populations. For example, Judith Hennessy (2000) studied women at the other end of the continuum from my study. Hennessy's extreme case was a group of low-income, single mothers who had cycled in and out of welfare. She found that her respondents defined themselves by schemas broadly consistent with my work devotion and family devotion schemas. These low-income mothers invoked a moral commitment to both the "work ethic" and the ethos of "family values" as they struggled to balance breadwinning, caregiving, and their belief in the American Dream of upward mobility.

Future studies could fruitfully investigate both the power of devotion schemas and the ways in which they are changing over time. Research should analyze the relationships between the material dimension of structure, such as a firm or industry's material resources and patterned relationships, and the type of work devotion schema it espouses. For instance, how does work devotion affect, and how is it affected by, changes in firms wrought by globalization (cf. DiMaggio, 2001; Fraser, 2001; Frenkel et al., 1999)?

Another benefit of this line of research is its attention to links between macro social structures, meso firm-level and family-level interactions, and social-psychological processes of identity formation and change. It situates all of these processes within cultural definitions of meaning, constraint, and possibility.[20]

Implications for Workers and Employers

Employees, policymakers, and scholars are increasingly concerned about American workers' struggles to balance work and their family and personal lives (Parcel and Cornfield, 2000; Glass and Estes, 1997). Work-life conflict may be escalating in recent years, as more mothers are employed outside the home and as work hours have grown longer for managers and professionals (Clarkberg and Moen, 2001; Jacobs and Gerson, 2001, forthcoming). Thus, books on work-family conflict routinely end with a set of policy recommendations. These prescriptions are usually well crafted but of questionable influence on anyone with policy-setting power.

I echo concerns raised by other scholars that work-family conflict is exacerbated in the United States by our individualistic and laissez-faire culture, which views family rearing and workplace policies as fundamentally private matters. Compared to Western Europe, the United States provides much less governmental support for employed parents in terms of family-friendly workplace legislation or quality child care sites (Gornick, Meyers, and Ross, 1998). Thus, many work-family studies call for policy changes to make workplace culture more "family-friendly." These new policies may be worthwhile but will result in largely cosmetic change absent a thorough understanding of the devotion schemas. This book argues that, at least among professionals, long work hours are embedded in a cultural model of work devotion that celebrates work dedication and views professional part-time employees with hostility. This workplace culture may be more tenacious and systemic than is generally realized.

Many firms use long hours to measure an employee's economic value to the firm and to assess the employee's moral worth, whether or not long hours constitute an economically rational yardstick (cf. Fried, 1998; Hochschild, 1997). Even if individual employees do not personally subscribe to the work devotion schema, it is likely that their supervisors do. Moreover, this cultural model structures firm hierarchies, coordinates work flow and evaluations (such as organizing work and performance evaluation by "billable hours," the number of hours a professional can bill the client), organizes reward systems, and fosters gendered assumptions about the ideal worker.

Some human resource professionals, policy makers, and scholars have championed corporate work-family policies as the solution to a coercive culture of work devotion. Many employers do not offer generous work-family benefits (Kelly, 1999). But even if they do, taking advantage of these benefits is still a problem. The use of work-family programs, such as flextime, flexplace, parental leaves, and the use of sick days to care for dependents, directly contradicts the mandates of the work devotion schema and its accompanying crushing workload.

Not surprisingly, many professional employees are reluctant to use these policies out of fear for their career advancement (Blair-Loy and Wharton, 2002a, b; Fried, 1998; Hochschild, 1997; Rapoport and Bailyn, 1996). On average, women are more likely than men to need and to use work-family corporate policies, and so they are more likely to pay for using these policies—and for violating the work devotion schema—in terms of curtailed promotion opportunities (cf. Glass, 2002).

Erin Kelly (1999) has studied why the use of work-family benefits is so contested in American companies. Human resource professionals and policy makers have advocated the "business case" for these corporate policies, citing research that they increase productivity and profitability. Despite these claims, work-family policies are still not widely used in most American corporations. Kelly (1999) maintains that the ideology of "family-friendly" policies conflicts head-on with deeply seated, gendered cultural models of work and family, which are broadly consistent with those presented in this book (see also Rapoport and Bailyn, 1996). Moreover, the fundamental assumption that work-family balance is an individual and private problem undercuts any serious efforts at institutional and corporate change.

Simply introducing new work-family corporate policies is largely futile. Any serious effort to reduce work and family conflict among professional workers must be based on a recognition that this is a social structural dilemma founded on powerful, taken-for-granted cultural models of how women and men should spend their waking hours.

These cultural models are durable but not completely unyielding. Over time, they can be changed. A glimmer of hope shines in organized groups of critical constituencies, those employees who most need and want a workplace that enables work-family balance without undue career sacrifice (Blair-Loy and Wharton, 2001a; Goodstein, 1994). These critical constituencies need to pressure powerful actors at the top of corporations to radically rethink and reengineer how work is done (cf. Gerstel and Clawson, 2001; DiMaggio 1988). This will not be easy, as most organizational leaders reached the pinnacle of their firms precisely by embracing the work devotion schema. Critical constituents may be most effective if they, like the mavericks in this study, are senior enough to have legitimacy yet sufficiently marginal to be immersed in alternative schemas or alternative definitions of the situation.[21] These challengers must inspire powerful actors to implement a whole new way of evaluating workers that is not based on the automatic equation of long work hours with professional value and with personal morality.

The schema of devotion to work—the virtual dimension of structure—shapes and is shaped by the material dimension of structure, the material resources, and patterns of relationships in particular firms and industries. For most of my respondents, the work devotion schema is buttressed by the exigencies of attracting and holding the business of professional clients.[22] They are competing to serve clients, who themselves face competitive and turbulent conditions in a global economy.

Rosemary Daszkiewicz, a corporate attorney struggling to balance work and family, writes about this challenge in a recent trade publication:

> Those who climb the highest rungs are able to put client needs first, no matter how demanding and unyielding—business trips on a moment's notice; dinners, sports or cultural events several times a week; weekends golfing or skiing with clients—not to mention the long hours of work demanded by the economic model we have created. None of this is possible without someone who is available to tend to the children, accommodate their schedules, see to the needs of the extended family, and keep the home in order. (Daszkiewicz, 2002: 13)

Yet some workers are explicitly trying to challenge the taken-for-granted cultural equation of long work hours and constant availability to clients with professional value and personal worthiness. For example, Rosemary Daszkiewicz works a reduced schedule in exchange for somewhat lower status and pay than she would have achieved as a full-time partner. Yet she maintains a leadership role, as a principal in charge of a practice group, and struggles to gain respect from her colleagues despite her part-time practice. Her trade publication article appeals to her coworkers to accept alternative definitions of success or, in my language, alternative conceptions of work devotion.

> Just because you got where you are seeing your children only on weekends doesn't mean that this is the only way to succeed professionally. This is not a fraternity. Hazing rituals are not necessary to create a bond. (Daszkiewicz, 2002: 14)

A new cultural definition of work devotion would then empower attorneys to join together in limiting the voracious demands of clients on their time. Daszkiewicz continues:

> [W]e must remind our clients that there are limits to the scope of our jobs. Yes, I know how hard that is. But we all have to be willing to draw reasonable lines and stick to them, for ourselves as well as for the sake of our colleagues who have no option. (Daszkiewicz, 2002: 14)

Daszkiewicz realizes that until large numbers of attorneys embrace these new cultural definitions and set limits, clients can just go elsewhere to find the unlimited service to which they are accustomed.

As part of a broader change in the cultural definition of work devotion, new firm-level structures of work organization and compensation may also help mitigate client demands. In research on four brokerage firms, stockbrokers faced the challenge of serving clients invested in 24-hour financial markets (Blair-Loy and Jacobs, 2003; Blair-Loy and DeHart, 2003). Yet firm-level decisions about technology support, staffing, and compensation arrangements buffered brokers from clients' seemingly insatiable demands. In three of the firms studied, brokers are commission-based entrepreneurs dedicated to their personal stable of clients. In contrast, in the one discount firm studied, brokers are salaried and share their client base with a large group of other brokers. This client-service arrangement allows the brokers to work in shifts. Moreover, the discount firm has been the most aggressive in providing 24-hour electronic resources and call centers to provide customer support, financial advice, and transactions around the clock. Compared to the other three commission-based firms, male and female brokers in the discount firm were the most positive about their work-family balance and the least beleaguered by the rapid changes in the securities industry. An emerging 24-hour economy may prompt other firms to buffer client demands by organizing team-based client service, supplemented by electronic and call-center resources.

The challenge to the work devotion schema will take different forms in different organizations and industries but must confront root assumptions about how tasks are organized, productivity is assessed, and workers' value is measured and rewarded. Over time, the efforts of challengers, such as the mavericks studied here and like Rosemary Daszkiewicz and the discount brokers, could help reduce the pressure on professionals to demonstrate work commitment with very long hours. Future research should more closely investigate these processes of structural change. At what point do the innovations of mavericks make enough of a cumulative impact on these schemas and the resources they mobilize to create a real transformation?

Expect resistance to these challenges and changes, however. They would upset the route to power of the traditionally male executive with a homemaking wife who, in one respondent's words, is "bleeding" and "dying" for the firm. These changes would reduce men's advantage over the female competition at work. They would weaken the power of husbands over wives. Most of all, they strike at the heart of morally laden, emotionally charged, cherished understandings of who we are as men and women.

APPENDIX

NOTES

REFERENCES

ACKNOWLEDGMENTS

INDEX

APPENDIX: METHODS AND DATA

This book compares two groups: a group of executive women in finance-related fields (N = 56) and a group of women who left full-time business careers when they had children (N = 25).[1] The career-committed group comes from a professional networking organization, which only admits senior women in major firms with finance-related jobs. The family-committed group is a snowball sample of women who had relinquished their demanding full-time careers after child-bearing. I conducted interviews in 1994 and 1995. All names of individuals and firms are pseudonyms.

I chose this population for theoretical purposes. I wanted to understand the social construction of gender in the lives of successful, high-earning women who have, on the surface, escaped traditional forms of gendered inequality.

Elites are challenging for sociologists to study. They are extremely busy, travel frequently, and are insulated behind layers of receptionists, secretaries, and security guards. Yet they are vitally important for understanding the construction and reproduction of dominant structural and cultural models in our society. Executive women are particularly understudied in sociology.

This qualitative, comparative case study relies on a reciprocal process of inductive insights and deductive analysis (Glaser and Strauss, 1967). Data collection, the generation of conceptual categories, and the generation and verification of hypotheses were interactive steps in an ongoing process.

Although case-based approaches cannot make general statements of empirical regularity about large populations, they can uncover and interpret constellations of forces that change or reproduce social processes (Ragin, 1987). Qualitative methods are also useful in staking out new theoretical and empirical ground, particularly when the researcher is investigating multifaceted, context-dependent, nonlinear processes that violate the simplifying assumptions of most quantitative models (cf. Abbott, 1988).

In contrast to studies of representative or typical samples, I pursue the strategy of the extreme case. Human agency is shaped by at least two axes: the amount of resources and the level of social and cultural constraints (Sewell, 1992). Agency may be most visible to the analyst in cases in which highly resourceful agents face pronounced structural and cultural constraints (Blair-Loy, 1999). My case is high on both axes: respondents have ample resources and face formidable structural constraints, including conflicting schemas of what constitutes a life worth living. My findings are not statistically generalizable but may be hypothesized to occur in similarly situated cases and may illuminate similar processes in less extreme cases. Chapter 6 discusses the extent to which the findings from this extreme case may apply to other populations. For other studies using an extreme case strategy, see Hochschild (1983); Risman (1998); and Perry-Jenkins, Repetti, and Crouter (2000).

My research has a four-part design. These are: (1) questionnaire pretests and pilot interviews, (2) life history questionnaires, (3) in-depth interviews, and (4) observation.

I first conducted background interviews with four acquaintances in finance in order to become familiar with the general contours of the work. I developed and pretested evolving versions of my life history questionnaire on ten pretesters.

Next I mailed out the life history questionnaire to my survey recipients. This questionnaire is a multidimensional time line organized as a grid. Each row of the grid represents a year in the respondent's life from age seventeen to the present. Each column asks about a different facet of her life, including education, geography, work history, family formation, and participation in professional organizations. Separate questions at the end ask about income. This questionnaire provides the information I used to study career and family patterns and turning points.

Ideally, the respondent mailed the completed questionnaire back to me before my scheduled interview with that respondent. Sometimes, she returned the questionnaire to me when we met. These interviews were semistructured, in depth, and lasted between thirty minutes and several hours. I interviewed every woman once; some I talked with more than once. The interviews used the life history questionnaire to evoke chronological stories about their adult lives. I asked about the self-understandings and interpretations surrounding their careers, family, transitions, triumphs, and regrets. If the information had not been relayed by the end of the interview, I asked each respondent several questions: what were her parents' and spouse's occupations; what did she expect to be doing five, ten, and twenty years onward; whether looking back on her life with 20–20 hindsight, she ever wished she had done anything differently; and whether she was either directly or indirectly influenced by the women's movement. If she had children, I also included questions about the domestic division of labor, her and her spouse's work and travel schedule, and childcare arrangements.

I tape-recorded and transcribed about three-quarters of the interviews. For the remainder, I took notes and transcribed them as soon as possible after the interview. I used the qualitative data coding software NUDIST for coding and analysis.

Finally, I sought out opportunities for observation. Whenever possible, I spent time with respondents at work, in professional meetings, and at home.

Although the groups are small and nonrandom, the design provides detailed data on a theoretically important group that has been understudied by social science. It is appropriate for an exploratory case study that unravels some of the complex mechanisms shaping professional and executive women's life courses and generating change and stability in women's lives.

I call my two groups the career-committed group and the family-committed group. These terms are brief descriptors to distinguish the two groups. Of course, the career-committed group also cares about their families, and the family-committed group is also immersed in paid work or volunteer activities. These terms imply no valorization or indictment. I am not claiming or implying that one or the other group made the "right" or the "wrong" choice. Instead, I am analyzing how these cultural schemas and the institutions they define limit and shape women's choices and their evaluations of them.

Career-Committed Group

The universe for the career-committed group is the membership of a professional organization of top female executives in finance-related fields in a large city in the United States. The organization's mission is to enhance the professional development of women with major financial responsibilities. It has strict membership criteria, limiting involvement to the most senior financial women in major organizations. I let membership in this organization define my sample criterion of successful women who have reached senior levels. I also allowed this professional organization to define the boundaries of finance-related fields.

The professional organization supported my research by allowing me to introduce my study at their business meeting and solicit participation. The organization also gave me a directory of members, to whom I mailed my questionnaire, and they included a cover letter encouraging members to fill out the survey. In no way did the professional organization try to influence the study design or findings. The organization had a membership of 129. By consulting attendance sheets of past meetings, I determined that about two-thirds, or 84 members, were active.

Studying these elites proved to be challenging. Despite the organization's endorsement, it was difficult to get the members to fill out and return the questionnaire. I remailed the questionnaire and made at least three follow-up calls to nonrespondents. I cultivated their secretaries, who were crucial gatekeepers. Finally, sixty-four women returned the questionnaire, roughly 76 percent of the active membership and 50 percent of the organization as a whole. All but five respondents agreed to be interviewed. This book relies on the 56 female executives from whom I had the most complete information.

Characteristics

Career-committed respondents have all reached senior levels in their firms, and their job titles include senior vice president, chief financial officer, managing director, partner, managing partner, and chief executive officer. Most (forty-seven) work in firms that provide financial services (including investment banks, commercial banks, public accounting firms, consulting firms, brokerages, venture capital firms, and corporate law firms). The remainder (nine) have finance-related jobs (for example, treasurer, chief financial officer) in companies that use the services of financial services firms. This definition of finance-related fields is broader than that used by some studies that specifically study the securities industry (for example, Catalyst, 2001; Roth, 2001a, b; Blair-Loy and Jacobs, 2003).

Since launching finance careers, no career-committed group members have ever stopped working for pay and only two have ever worked part-time. In 1994, they ranged in age from thirty-six to sixty. All have bachelor's degrees, and most (86 percent) have graduate degrees. Twenty-one respondents (38 percent) are mothers, and these women have a median of two children. Forty-seven women (84 percent) were married at least once.[2] Of these, 20 had gone through a divorce, but six have remarried. In 1993 annual compensation for the for-profit employees ranged from $125,000 to $1,000,000, with a median of $250,000. Four women, who were in nonprofit firms or who

APPENDIX

had just started new businesses, earned between $75,000 and $125,000 in 1993. In past years, some women made additional millions selling stock. With the exception of one African American, all respondents are white. The findings are thus limited in terms of racial generalizations.

Interviews and Observations

Interviewing these finance executives required much persistence. Any time they spent with me detracted from the time they could be working. They frequently rescheduled our appointment. Sometimes I arrived at a respondent's office, only to be told that she had suddenly been called out of town or into an emergency meeting. Sometimes my promised one-hour time slot was whittled down to thirty minutes by the time the woman finally met with me. I was usually able to convince her to continue the interview at another time. Some respondents became so involved in the stories they were telling me that they postponed other meetings or invited me to return later so they could continue the conversation. Once the interview got going, most were eager to talk frankly. Most ended our meeting with promises of availability, should I need to see them in the future. When I did have an occasion to contact a few of them again, they were graciously helpful.

The fullest, most relaxed interviews happened when we left the office building for a meal or an after-work drink. Otherwise, the interview was closely bounded in time by inflexible appointments and phone calls as well as more closely bounded in content to material in keeping with the respondent's professional persona. Six women invited me to their homes on the evenings or weekends. Those interviews were the longest and richest.

I had originally hoped to supplement my interviews with formal observation of several hours of respondents' working days. Only one respondent agreed to have me watch her work for several hours. This time together allowed me to see that her contacts with clients were warm and personal as well as professional. I also noticed that she was the only female partner in her organization. Even at the junior professional levels, only a minority were women. Only one of the professional women I saw at the firm appeared pregnant. In contrast, I saw that several of the clerical employees were pregnant. They seemed at ease with their large bellies and enjoyed camaraderie with the other clerical workers. I gleaned my first hint that pregnancy may be natural and celebrated for secretaries but problematic for finance professionals.

I primarily relied on the glimpses of respondents' offices and the workplace interactions I saw before and during the interview. The office buildings were lush. The interiors ranged from overstuffed chairs and heavy desks surrounded by dark paneling and marble busts to bright windowed spaces sparsely filled with streamlined furniture. I was frequently served coffee in a ceramic cup and saucer and was treated with great courtesy by the respondent's staff. Respondents sometimes gave me a tour of the office building. Several met me in nice restaurants, where they picked up the tab. Two women invited me to their private clubs. Six met me in their homes.

I also attended five different meetings of the women finance professionals' organization. At the last two, I gave formal presentations on the research in progress. The business meetings were preceded by a cocktail hour and dinner. I shared taxi cabs home with some of the women and listened to them complain about their housekeepers. Because my academic world was so different from their world, I initially found it a challenge to make informal conversation. But by the last two meetings I attended, I was well enough acquainted with some of the women that social interaction had become easier. After the last meeting, a group of eight women invited me to go out drinking with them. We drank chardonnay in a nearby bar until it closed.

I collected additional observation data by attending four meetings of a bimonthly women's forum that was organized by a large law firm. This forum was a looser and more inclusive organization than the finance organization. The meeting began with a cocktail and networking hour followed by a formal presentation from a panel of experts. The presentations covered topics such as business development, planning for a financial future, communication, and self-presentation. The forums gave me a chance to be a quiet participant rather than a publicly designated researcher.

Finance executives live in an extravagant world. They spend small fortunes on wardrobes and personal grooming. At the professional meetings and forums, the caterer and bartender bills must be enormous. Some of the conference rooms that women had reserved for the interviews proffered the two of us enough soft drinks, cookies, coffee, and tea to serve twenty.

From the finance executives' perspectives, these expenses are not wasteful. The conference rooms generally host valuable clients rather than modest-earning social scientists. The luxurious and tasteful décor inspires confidence. Respondents told me that their wardrobes had paid for themselves several times over. Finance executives need to appear comfortable with wealth and competent in handling money. They need to exude trustworthiness and respectability.

In these interviews, I began to notice patterns. The majority of women in this group did not have children. But those who did—especially the mothers of young children—repeatedly told me that they were unusual and that there were virtually no other women they knew in their positions with young children. They told me that their female friends and colleagues in business had all left full-time careers once they had children.

I realized that if executive mothers were the exception, I should interview the rule: women who left full-time finance careers when they had children. This is an example of what Glaser and Strauss (1967) call theoretical sampling. Guided by the grounded theory approach, my data collection, empirical understanding, and theory building were reciprocal processes.

Family-Committed Group

I tried to find family-committed group members who resembled the career-committed group's initial investment and trajectory in business careers. The women I interviewed often referred to these as having held "high-powered" careers. I lacked the immediate access to a large population that I had in the career-committed group. The only way to find a sizable number of formerly successful businesswomen who left full-time careers to raise children was to conduct a snowball study, in which I relied on the few contacts I had to introduce me to similar women. Moreover, I had to broaden the group professionally to include not only managers in a finance-related field but also attorneys with corporate practices, communication consultants, and senior managers in health care and marketing. Nineteen of the twenty-five women in this group formerly or currently sold financial or other professional services to clients, while the others were senior staff members in firms that bought these services. These women filled out the same life history questionnaire and conducted similar interviews as the work-committed group.

Snowball sampling is a useful research technique for studying hard-to-reach populations. Of course, this data collection method does not provide random probability samples and does not allow the researchers to generalize their findings to larger groups. A snowball sample may not adequately represent the target population because individuals who differ from respondents and other referring individuals may be excluded from the sampling frame (Atkinson and Flint, 2001; Biernacki and Waldorf, 1981).

To avoid limiting the family-committed group to acquaintances of the first group alone, only my first of six snowball clusters was formed through a contact in the career-committed group. This contact, Yvonne Smith, had been a member of the finance executive's professional organization but had relinquished her full-time career. She introduced me to three similar women, whom she knew through her child's preschool. I also used five unrelated contacts to form five additional snowball clusters. These five contacts included an acquaintance from my university, a former colleague of my attorney husband's, and three acquaintances I knew through two Episcopal parishes.

Characteristics

The family-committed group includes twenty-five women who had all left full-time business careers after a median of nine years of work. I interviewed them in 1994 and 1995. Twenty-four had last worked full-time between 1986 and 1992, while one was actively trying to shift from a full- to a part-time executive position. Their full-time incomes had ranged from $35,000 to $350,000, with a median of $70,000 (not constant dollars). Sixteen women (64 percent) had had full-time incomes that were greater than or equal to their husbands'.

Thirteen family-committed respondents had attained ranks as high as those reached by career-committed group members; the other twelve were well up the ladder but had not reached executive levels before leaving their full-time positions. The fact that almost half the family-committed group had not attained top positions before abandoning full-time careers limits the strict comparability of the two groups. For example, my finding of a correlation between work devotion and job level in the work-committed group (Chapter 1) suggests that those family-committed group members who had left relatively lower-ranked jobs may have had lower levels of work devotion to begin with than the average work-committed group member. Nonetheless, this comparison group highlighted characteristics of the career-committed group that otherwise would have remained in the background.

At the interview date, ten family-committed women were home full-time, fourteen worked part-time, and one was actively trying to move to a reduced-hours schedule. All have bachelor's degrees; twenty-one (84 percent) have professional degrees. Twenty are married to their first husbands, four are remarried, and one is currently divorced. They have a median of two children. All are white. Thus, the group does not represent divorced women or women of color.

The career-committed and family-committed group members resemble each other on several dimensions. They are equally likely to have earned professional degrees, most of which are granted by elite schools. Married career-committed group members earned a median of half the family income, as did married family-committed group members when they last worked full-time. Among the mothers, both groups have a median of two children. Each group represents an extreme case of women with high levels of education and a current or former promising high-powered career track in an elite, male-dominated business or professional field.

There are also distinctions. By design, the career-committed group members continued their full-time executive career trajectories, while the second group's members cut back to part-time or left the workplace completely to become involved mothers. This design has demographic implications. The family-committed group includes only mothers who are on average younger because that group, by definition, included women who had relatively recently left full-time careers due to childbearing. Moreover, the fact that almost half the family-committed group had not reached the peak of their careers before leaving them or cutting back reduces the strict comparability of the two groups.

Each group meets the requirements of proving an extreme case to help me uncover and interpret constellations of factors that reinforce or change or reproduce social structures. Each group questioned and thus revealed taken-for-granted and cherished assumptions made by the other group.

Interviews and Observations

All the women I initially contacted as part of my snowball cluster agreed to be interviewed. This high participation rate is probably due to several factors: I was approaching them through personal network ties; I was studying a topic of great personal relevance to them; and the at-home mothers were probably eager for adult company. I interviewed them in a place of their convenience. This was generally in their home or in a café or diner either near their home or, for the part-time employees, near their offices.

I tried to combine my interviews with opportunities to watch family-committed group mothers doing the work of caring for their children. This was difficult because most respondents protected their time with their children and would only agree to be interviewed when their children were in school, asleep, or with a babysitter or husband. In five cases, I was present in the women's homes while the children were there. The houses were generally large and comfortable in affluent, suburban neighborhoods.

When the children were home, all the mothers gave them a great deal of attention. Most mothers played or conversed with their children in a relaxed manner. In contrast, one mother grilled her young son intensely about what had happened in school that day. She seemed to have high expectations of his ability to recall detailed events and communicate them to her.

Interview Style

My approach to interviews with both groups was to act as a sympathetic, discreet confidante. About three-quarters of the respondents were willing to respond with the reciprocal role. The remainder treated me like a junior person needing instruction. In those cases, I played the role of the naive listener.

I initially worried that, because many of my transcripts seemed cliché-laden, I was not getting good data. Career-committed group respondents listed "personal objectives" and glowed about being "challenged by new opportunities at work." Family-committed group members discussed having to "cut overhead" when they stopped working. They referred to their children as "happy little campers" thriving on "TLC" (tender loving care). I finally decided that many respondents actually understood the world in these terms.

Many women, particularly in the career-committed group, were unreflective. When I asked whether, looking back on their lives, they ever wished they had done anything differently, one woman pondered for several moments and then solemnly said she wished she had gotten a particular financial credential. Another woman confided to me that she wished she had specialized in ferrous metals as an investment area.

Two women explicitly announced that they avoided looking back on their lives. A partner in a public accounting firm remarked:

> I don't [look back] . . . I'm always looking forward. And my children and my husband are all runners, and they always say the race is in front of you, not behind you (laughter). Whenever you see a runner looking back, you know they're in trouble. 'Cause they're worried about someone coming up behind them.

Similarly, a chief financial officer in a brokerage firm said:

> I try to think forward, not backward. My sister has childhood memories. I don't remember much of what happened during my childhood.

In their line of work, reflection and soul-searching are not practical. Far more useful skills are quick decision making, good judgment about business deals, the ability to cultivate business relationships, and technical competence (see Blair-Loy, 2001a).

The women who struck me as the most reflective were those who had held an alternative worldview (or set of schemas) before adopting their current one. This previous experience gave them a sense of detachment and reflexivity about their current situations. These women tended to be extremely insightful. A few had come from blue-collar backgrounds and had to learn to pass as upper middle class. On average, the family-committed group was more reflective than the career-committed, but mothers in both groups agonized over conflicting work and family responsibilities before finally deciding to privilege one or the other. My most reflective respondents include a woman who had worked in the Peace Corps and then as a community organizer, one who had worked for a battered woman's shelter, and one who had been a teenage mother and waitress before eventually going to college and business school. Their perspectives were a little broader; pieces of them were still strangers in the business world (Simmel, [1908] 1971).

Turning Points: Details of Coding Contingent Events

Chapter 5 compares the mothers in the career-committed group to the family-committed group. This analysis required coding contingent events.

Long-term conditions of work and family may become unbearable if they coincide with an unexpected contingency. Depending on the schemas individuals use to interpret them, contingencies may help move people onto a new trajectory. I uncovered three types of unexpected events: positive career contingencies, negative career contingencies, and negative family contingencies.

These events were reported only if my interviewees thought to mention them. I probed for them only if they preceded something that the woman had already identified as a transition in her life history questionnaire or interview.

To chart the locations of these contingencies in the life course, I created two digit codes representing work and family events for each year of each respondent's life. The first digit codes the type of full-time jobs, part-time jobs, and homemaking. The second digit codes family formation (including marital and parenthood status). I assembled these codes into sequences representing each woman's life from age 22 to the present. I inserted the contingent events into the sequences at the year they occurred.

I then calculated the proportion of women in each group who experienced at least one instance of each kind of contingency.[3] Age increases the risk of having experienced a contingency. Therefore, I standardized these proportions by dividing them by the total number of years in each group's sequences, which run from age 22 to the interview date. (To make the figures easier to read, I then multiplied them by 1000.) In Chapter 5, Table 5.2 presents standardized percentages of mothers in each group who reported each type of contingent event.

Conclusion

The multipart design and multiple methods permit me to integrate inductive and deductive insights. The grounded theory approach to interviewing and sampling allowed concepts and changes over time in the meaning of concepts to emerge from the data. Concurrently, the life history questionnaire elicited systematic data on the particular steps of career and family formation that previous research had suggested in advance were relevant.

The observations let me see respondents in action (at work, in professional gatherings, or at home). In contrast, the interviews focused on each respondent's post hoc reconstruction of her life course. In the comparison between women who maintained full-time business careers and those who left them to care for their children, each group questioned and thus made visible taken-for-granted assumptions held by the other group. Because the different methods reveal complementary and consistent findings, we can have more confidence in the results than if they were discovered by one method alone.

NOTES

Introduction

1. Congress passed legislation protecting women's employment rights in the 1960s, but these laws were not enforced until the early to mid-1970s (Kessler-Harris, 1994; Mills, 1994; Costain and Costain, 1987; Cancian, 1981). In 1972, Congress passed the Equal Rights Amendment as well as Title IX of the Higher Education Act, which prohibited sexual discrimination in school admissions. There was a concurrent surge in female enrollment in business and law schools that prepared the way for women's subsequent movement into high-paying, male-dominated business and professional occupations (Shu and Marini, 1998; Cancian, 1981). The dismantling of explicit, legal barriers impeding women's access to male-dominated professional schools and occupations was a major victory of the feminist movement (Ferree and Hess, 1985). Among the work-committed group of women studied here, those entering finance careers in the 1970s enjoyed much easier career entry and faster advancement, on average, than women entering these careers in the 1960s (Blair-Loy, 1999). Yet these women still face more subtle forms of discrimination. There is an extensive literature on historic and current direct and indirect discrimination against women in male-dominated, elite occupations (for example, Wajcman, 1996; Epstein et al., 1995; Epstein, 1993; Cole and Zuckerman, 1991; Walsh, 1977). For evidence of ongoing discrimination against women in financial services, see Roth, 2001a; 2001b; Costen, 2001; Catalyst, 2001; Blair-Loy, 2001a; and Reed, 2001. On the macho culture of the financial services industry, see Levin, 2001 and Lewis, 1989.

2. I use the term "professionals" the way it is used in the business world. In my usage, the term includes managers and senior exempt employees as well as members of the classic professions, such as lawyers.

3. Throughout the book, I use the term "work" as a shorthand for paid work, even though other activities (housework, volunteer work) can also be described as work. On longer work hours among professionals, see Jacobs and Gerson (forthcoming). On the ideology that children are fragile and that motherhood is time- and emotion-intensive, see Hays, 1996.

4. Hochschild (1989, 1983, 1979) discusses the ways that particular social structural situations (including white collar jobs and middle-class family life) put a premium on the individual's capacity to do emotion work, to induce or suppress feelings to make them appropriate to the situation.

5. Some employers in Silicon Valley describe employees who have non-work obligations as having a "drag coefficient" (Hochschild, 2000: xix).

6. This individualistic formulation of work-family conflict is dependent on the historical and cultural construction of the individual as a voluntary, free, and rational person (cf. Kelly, 1999; Friedland and Alford, 1991).

7. Chapter 6 discusses some of this work-family literature.

8. Schemas are the virtual dimension of social structure (Sewell, 1992). I define a cultural schema as an ordered, socially constructed and taken-for-granted framework for understanding the world. Schemas organize cognition, norms, and affect. My usage contrasts with that of some scholars, who use "schema" or a similar term more narrowly to denote a person's socially constructed, cognitive map (Risman, 1998; DiMaggio, 1997; Bem, 1983). Chapter 6 discusses my use of and contribution to this cultural theory.

9. Other schemas of devotion that might emerge in other populations include the devotion to social movements, politics, religion, or art.

10. This is Max Weber's usage of the term "ideal type" (Gerth and Mills, 1958: 58–60).

11. The family devotion schema has roots in the nineteenth century and flowered after World War II. As an ideal type, the family devotion schema presumes a stable, interdependent, heterosexual marriage, in which wives are dependent on husbands for livelihood and social status, while husbands rely on wives for care of themselves and their children (cf. Williams, 2000; Skolnick, 1991; Stacey, 1990; D'Emelio and Freedman, 1989). Normative models

of motherhood may be understood differently in working class and minority communities. For example, African-American women are more likely than white women to see motherhood and employment as complementary rather than competing responsibilities (Collins, 1987, but see Blair-Loy and De-Hart, forthcoming). However, cultural models of white professionals influence general expectations around work and family (Garey, 1999), and are imposed on other workers.

12. This cultural understanding of children as vulnerable and sacred did not emerge until the eighteenth and early nineteenth centuries (Aries, 1962; Zelizer, 1985; Hays, 1996).

13. As an ideal type, the work devotion schema is a middle-class, masculine, twentieth-century model of dedication to a managerial or professional career that helps shape managers' commitments and employers' expectations (Hochschild, 1997; Potuchek, 1997; Jackall, 1988; Coser, 1974; cf. Whyte, 1956). This schema traditionally calls men to all-consuming, professional careers while their wives provide domestic care. Work devotion does not compete with family commitments for men's souls, as being a good provider is believed to satisfy an individual's family obligations (Coltrane, 1996).

14. Unlike their male colleagues, executive women are highly unlikely to have a homemaking spouse to care for them and for the children (Wajcman, 1996; Hochschild, 1989).

15. Hochschild (1983) provides another example of a study based on extreme cases. Findings from an extreme case are not statistically generalizable but may be hypothesized to occur in other similarly situated cases (Blair-Loy, 1999; Risman, 1998). These findings may not characterize minority or working-class women (Garey, 1999; Collins, 1987; Weiner, 1985). Chapter 6 addresses the issues of the applicability of findings from this extreme case to other populations.

16. Members of the career-committed group belong to the financial services industry, broadly defined by the women themselves and by the professional group in which I found them. This definition of finance-related fields is broader than that used by some studies that specifically examine the securities industry (for example, Blair-Loy and Jacobs, 2003; Blair-Loy and De-Hart, 2003; Catalyst, 2001; Roth 2001a, b).

17. Coser (1974) also argues that this demand for exclusive loyalty is functional for the institutions, as it allows them to hold a monopoly on people's time, talent, and creativity. I argue that the work devotion and family devotion schemas persist despite the fact that in some ways they are not functional for firms or for families.

18. These findings also cast doubt on the Cosers' argument that the demand for exclusive loyalty is functional for the "greedy institutions." Here, the family and the firm might arguably be better served if each relented its demands and accepted the talent and experience of a part-time family caregiver or a part-time executive.

19. Swidler (2001) argues that institutions shape culture, which shapes strategies of action. In contrast, I argue that institutions themselves are already cultural, as well as material, systems (Friedland and Alford, 1991). In contrast to Swidler's emphasis on culture shaping the means of action, I argue that culture shapes the means and the ends of action. I discuss these issues further in Chapter 6.

1. The Devotion to Work Schema

1. On long work hours among powerful and senior employees, see Hochschild, 1997; Wajcman, 1996; and Kanter, 1977. Some work-family research has acknowledged the importance of culture by explicitly discussing workplace norms that enforce the lengthening workday (Drago et al., 2001; Maume and Bellas, 2001; Epstein et al., 1999; Fried, 1998). However, this literature has spent little time analyzing these norms as important and complex cultural phenomena per se. These norms are generally assumed to be just another set of external constraints on workers' actions; the ways in which they may powerfully shape—and are shaped by—workers' own self-understandings have not been investigated. An exception is Hochschild's (1997) nuanced account of this process in one firm.

2. My ongoing research investigates work devotion in male executives.

3. The growth of fringe benefits as a percentage of wages and salaries, and the structure of employer's contributions to social security, unemployment insurance, and other taxes add further incentives for employers to require ex-

isting employees to work longer hours rather than to hire additional workers (Schor, 1991: 66–67). Yet these incentives would presumably affect all workers, not just professionals. According to Jacobs and Gerson (forthcoming), it is mainly managers and professionals who have seen their hours increased markedly since the 1970s.

4. Similarly, the Catalyst organization's study of 838 finance professionals found that the "advancement strategy" cited by the largest proportion of the sample (91 percent) was their "perceived strength of commitment to work" (Catalyst, 2001: 9).

5. To some extent, these corporatist work rewards have also been documented by others (McDuff and Mueller, 2000; Wallace, 1995a; Lincoln and Kalleberg, 1990). What is newly revealed here is, at least among female executives, the intense connection to and interdependence with one's colleagues and clients that can lead to a sense of transcendence.

6. Four career-committed sample respondents, who were in nonprofit firms or who just started their own businesses, had lower salaries: they earned between $75,000 and $125,000 in 1993.

7. The "ideal worker," usually male, is generally supported by family members' domestic labor (for example, Williams, 2000; Wajcman, 1996; Acker, 1990; Hochschild, 1989). For example, in a study of a large corporation, Hochschild (1989: 255) found that among top executives, two-thirds of the men (and none of the women) were married to full-time homemakers.

8. Retrospective data must be interpreted with caution. People's present accounts of their pasts may be shaped as much by what is happening to them in the present as by what "really" happened in the past. People shape their past histories into logical narratives with a beginning, middle, and an end that make sense in terms of present problems they are grappling with or identities they are trying to convey (Ricoeur, 1984; Cohler, 1982).

9. On competition, volatility, and consolidation in the finance industry, see note 2.

10. For a factually similar case that was litigated in the Supreme Court, see *Price Waterhouse v. Hopkins* (1989).

11. The appendix discusses the common lack of introspection among career-committed members. Introspection is not a useful skill or attribute for their jobs.

12. The job level analysis excludes seven long-term entrepreneurs, reducing the sample size to forty-three. In this group, twenty-three women still fully embraced the schema, fifteen felt ambivalently toward it, and five had rejected it completely. Among the eighteen women at the very highest levels, twelve (67 percent) had fully intact schema, five (28 percent) were ambivalent, and only one person had abandoned the schema. Compared to their highest-achieving colleagues, the twenty-five respondents who had not reached the very top levels were less likely to embrace the schema and more likely to view it with ambivalence or repudiation. Specifically, only eleven of them (44 percent) had fully embraced the schema, ten viewed it with ambivalence (40 percent), and four respondents (16 percent) rejected it entirely. Presenting the same cross-tab results from a different angle, among the twenty-three true believers in the schema, twelve (52 percent) were those who reached the very highest levels. In contrast, the twenty skeptics were in relatively lower positions. Specifically, among the fifteen ambivalent women, only five (33 percent) had reached the very highest levels, and among the five rejecters of the schema, only one (25 percent) had reached the very top level.

13. Whether declining promotion opportunities and layoffs undermine the implicit postwar contract (Edwards, 1979) between firms and managerial employees is disputed in the literature (Grunberg, Anderson-Connolly, and Greenberg, 2000; Capelli, 1999; Jacoby, 1999; Kunda and Van Maanen, 1999; Osterman, 1996; Heckscher, 1995).

2. The Devotion to Family Schema

1. In spite of the trend that some analysts identify toward companionate, egalitarian marriages (Barnett and Rivers, 1996; Goldscheider and Waite, 1991; Hertz, 1986; Cancian, 1987), family responsibilities still are far more inconsistent with the career orientation of women than that of men. Only about one-third of married mothers are employed full-time (Risman, 1998; Hayghe and Bianchi, 1994), and those who are lag behind men in work achievement and earnings, in part due to their domestic responsibilities (Budig and England, 2001; Waldfogel, 1997; Spain and Bianchi, 1996). Moreover, professional women are less likely to be married and to have children

than are their male colleagues or other women (Deloitte and Touche, 1998; Wajcman, 1996; Korn/Ferry International, 1993) and far less likely to have a homemaking spouse (Hochschild, 1989).

2. One of the ten corporate employees, Frances Swing, was actually working full-time but trying to shift to part-time when I interviewed her. I wait to consider her case until the next chapter, which focuses on the challenge of working part-time in firms organized around full-time work devotion.

3. This model formed when production began shifting from family farms to factories, and distinctions appeared between men's wage labor in the public sphere and women's domestic work in the private sphere (Cott, 1977). It flowered in the postwar baby boom era (Stacey, 1990). In 1950, three-fifths of American families were of the male breadwinner/female full-time homemaker variety (Skolnick, 1991). Women from the working class and minority and immigrant groups have always been likely to work for wages in addition to taking care of the home (Glenn et al., 1994; Collins, 1987; Weiner, 1985).

4. Hochschild (1989) reveals the durability of the "second shift" for married women, even among feminists. Brines (1994) argues that female responsibility for and male avoidance of housework are stably rooted in the symbolic expression and maintenance of gender, broadly consistent with what I call the family devotion schema.

5. Before leaving their full-time jobs, eight women in the family-committed sample (32 percent) had earned full-time incomes greater than their husbands', and another eight had earned full-time incomes roughly equal to their husbands' salaries. All of the women had last worked full-time between 1986 and 1992, when they had earned a median of $70,000 (not in constant dollars).

6. The family-committed sample, by design, includes women who no longer work full-time. They are married to professional men with demanding jobs. Other studies, designed to study couples with a more egalitarian division of labor, have documented how the family devotion schema's role designations are questioned and challenged in some couples (for example, Risman, 1998; Schwartz, 1994; Hertz, 1986).

7. The fourteen part-time workers in the family-committed sample currently earn between 10 and 84 percent of the family income. In 1993, the me-

dian salary was $66,000, which was a median of 36 percent of the family income. Of course, the wealth and investments accumulated during all family-committed sample members' full-time careers continue to provide economic support to the family.

8. See England and Kilbourne (1990) and Folbre (2001) for discussions of income and power in family relationships.

9. Susan Pflanz's five-year-old son overheard this and piped up nervously, "Mom, are you going to get a job?" She said in a voice meant to be reassuring but with an anxious edge, "only part-time, Tim, and not until you go to school." "When I go to first grade or to kindergarten?" "Not 'til you're in first grade." "Good!" he said and resumed playing, reassured.

10. My characterization of family-committed sample members as either contented or discontented is my best effort, based on one or two in-depth interviews with each respondent, to interpret a complicated emotional picture. I tried to take into account the tendency many people have of presenting their lives in the best possible light for the interviewer and to acknowledge the possibility that some might have just been having a bad day when I talked with them. The thirteen discontented mothers generally first presented their situation favorably and then much later confided a more negative assessment of their lives, ranging from ambivalence to deep anguish.

11. Respondents' priority of spending time with their children was revealed as I tried to schedule interviews. They clearly privileged their family's needs over spending time talking to me. If they had children of school age, respondents generally agreed to be interviewed only before 3:00 P.M. on weekdays. (If I was still there when the children returned, I was sometimes invited to remain.) If the children were younger, the women were only available during naptime or at night after the children's bedtime. Children sometimes awakened early from naps, which required me to continue the interview at a subsequent naptime. In contrast to career-committed group members, who sometimes canceled appointments at the last minute if a client or boss needed them, women in the family-committed group would abruptly cancel interviews if a child refused to go down for a nap or if a husband unexpectedly returned home from a business trip.

12. Garey (1995) provides a similar account of how employed women (nurses on the night shift) nonetheless construct themselves as intensive mothers.

13. I lack complete data on my respondents' psychological views and rationalizations. But the best I can tell is that these contrasting definitions of childhood are not just "techniques of neutralization" or post-hoc psychological justifications to protect the individual from self-blame for acts she knows are wrong (Sykes and Matza, 1957). It is true that each set of proponents has to justify its actions in the face of oppositional practices by other women they know. But each side is thoroughly convinced of its own moral authority. Proponents of each definition feel justified. They do not have to protect themselves from self-blame, although they do condemn the other side for brandishing their definition of childhood to do just that.

14. This gendered division of household labor is a common finding in social scientific research (for example, Coltrane, 2000; Spain and Bianchi, 1996; Brines, 1994; Blair and Lichter, 1991; Hochschild, 1989).

15. Similarly, Epstein et al. (1999) find that part-time female attorneys claim that their husbands expect them to do the majority of domestic work.

16. These findings should be verified in a larger sample of women who out-earn their husbands. Interestingly, in a sample of dual-career doctors, Lundgren, Fleischer-Cooperman, Schneider, and Fitzgerald (2001) find that wives are more likely to shift to part-time status than their husbands, even when the wives have more stable career tracks.

17. I discuss "emotion work" (Hochschild, 1983, 1979) later in the chapter.

18. My family-committed sample is homogenous by design. All the women had left promising full-time careers to focus on family caregiving. Within this small and homogenous sample, I found no correlation between the respondents' level of discontent and their current status as homemaker, part-time freelancer, or part-time corporate employee. I also found no correlation between discontent and respondents' former career success. These correlations may exist in a larger, more diverse sample of women. I note that a few discontented family-committed women—including Deborah Stein, Jane Rowan, and Yvonne Smith—had attained phenomenal career success and only very reluctantly left full-time careers after being hit with multiple negative contingencies.

19. For discussions of the social construction of gender and gendered definitions of social responsibilities, see Coltrane, 2000, 1988; Risman, 1998, 1987; McMahon, 1995; Glenn, 1994; Lorber, 1994; Bem, 1993; Coltrane, 1989; Epstein, 1988; and Connell, 1987. For a contrasting viewpoint emphasizing the

importance of biological sex differences, see Rossi, 1985. Many social scientists argue that the cultural construction of gender serves the interests of powerful men and subordinates many women. Ignoring the social construction of gender masks the ways in which powerful men and their organizations benefit from women's caregiving. Moreover, assuming that women's nurturing care is "only natural" devalues the great skill that competent mothers and caregivers have developed.

20. Studies of involved fathers, especially single fathers, show that men can learn from the experience of taking care of children to be as nurturing as "mothers" (Coltrane, 1989; Risman, 1987).

21. The term "biological" implies a construction of reality grounded in the body, while the term "natural" points to a construction of reality grounded in the socially taken for granted. While these two processes are analytically distinct, my respondents conflate them empirically. They use their beliefs about biological determinism of male and female roles to support their understanding of these roles as natural and taken for granted.

22. These discussions suggest a nascent construction of men as biologically self-centered and, unlike women, inherently unable to put their "own needs below others in the family." This construction is a symbolic boundary that categorizes women morally superior, while also rendering men blameless for their own inferiority, because they are believed to be biologically programmed.

23. However, studies of samples of managers suggest that senior male managers are likely to have wives at home (Blair-Loy and Wharton, 2002b; Wajcman, 1996; Hochschild, 1989).

3.   Creating Part-Time Careers

1. On one hand, Hochschild's (1997) qualitative study of one large company concludes that most workers have no desire to cut down on work hours, ignore company policies that would allow them to do so, and prefer time at work over time at home. Similarly, a qualitative case study of four securities firms finds that many stockbrokers work longer hours than their supervisors actually require (Blair-Loy and DeHart, forthcoming). On the other hand,

quantitative studies of national survey data find that most parents and
people with long workweeks would prefer to work fewer hours, and that the
average professional would like to reduce work hours by 8 hours a week or
more (Clarkberg and Moen, 2001; Galinsky and Swanberg, 2000; Jacobs and
Gerson, 1998).

2. More generally, most part-time jobs in the United States are devalued;
they tend to be filled by women and offer low pay and few or no benefits
(Wenger, 2001; Williams, 2000; Tilly, 1992).

3. Estimates to replace a second-year legal associate in a law firm range
from $200,000 to $500,000 (Williams and Calvert, 2001). The average cost of
replacing each skilled worker who left the firm studied by Hochschild (1997)
is $40,000. Other studies place the cost of replacing a skilled worker at .75 to
1.5 times the worker's annual salary (Williams, 2000). The skill levels and
high salaries of my respondents would likely place their replacement costs on
the top end of these estimates.

4. Economic considerations also play a role. Benefit costs can be expensive for employers if part-time workers receive full benefits (Tilly, 1992;
Schor, 1991). I did not collect data on benefits and do not know how many
respondents had full versus prorated benefits.

5. Catalyst (1993) and Kropf (2001) also find that professionals working
part-time are viewed as uncommitted by their full-time coworkers in corporations. This deeply held assumption that only full-time workers are
completely committed and fully worthy is one of several ways in which organizations and institutions are gendered, in other words, are imbued with
assumptions and practices that uphold distinctions and inequalities between
men and women (see, for example, Risman, 1998; Lorber, 1994; Acker, 1990).

6. The figures for family-committed women's last full-time incomes are
not in constant dollars.

7. The fourteen part-timers (who worked either for a corporation or freelance) earned a median of $66,000 in 1993 (which constituted a median of
36% of their families' income).

8. Unfortunately, I lack consistent data on the number of hours worked
by part-time employed respondents. The data I do have suggest that the
hours are variable, depending on clients' and employers' demands. Part-time
respondents need to be flexible and available; thus, most have full-time child-

care. Their work hours are generally less than the 60 or more hours a week demanded of full-time employees in similar positions. (Although some respondents have to work a full-time schedule on occasion, when their employer or client requires it.) Their regular hours often exceed 20 hours a week.

9. Epstein et al. (1999) also found that part-time lawyers claim they are more committed than many other attorneys because they insist on working although they have children.

10. For more on symbolic boundaries, see Blair-Loy, 2001a; Epstein, 1992; and Lamont, 1992.

11. The negative effect of part-time work on advancement in law firms and in business firms is a common research finding (Williams and Calvert, 2001; Hull and Nelson, 2000; Women's Bar Association of Massachusetts, 2000; Epstein et al., 1995; Hagan and Kay, 1995; Kalleberg, 1995; Tilly, 1992). One study reports that the advancement prospects for part-time lawyers have improved somewhat since 1996 (Women's Bar Association of Massachusetts, 2000).

12. The mothers I interviewed challenge the gendered assumption in organizations that elite workers are somehow disembodied and severed from the process of human reproduction (Acker, 1990).

13. In Emirbayer and Mische's (1998) terms, I am referring to the practical-evaluative and especially the projective orientations of agency. I discuss this further in Chapter 6.

14. Women generally spend far more time than men personally caring for family members, and thus their work lives are often curtailed by family obligations (for example, Spain and Bianchi, 1996; Gerson, 1985; Hertz, 1986). Hochschild (1989) calls the extra work women do at home, on top of their paid employment, the "second shift."

15. Other research has found that combining work and family responsibilities can be energizing rather than depleting for women, especially when the work and family roles are both experienced as rewarding (Barnett, 1999).

16. Increased demands at work and the rise of dual-earner couples are among the factors that have contributed to a decline of civic engagement and social capital over the last two decades (Putnam, 2000). Part-time employees, especially well-educated women who work part-time by choice, have high

levels of volunteering. Thus, a shorter workday and increased opportunities for professionals and managers to work part-time would likely lead to an increase in civic participation (Putnam, 2000; Schor, 1991).

4. Family Life among Full-Time Executive Women

1. The findings in this chapter are drawn in part from my article entitled "Cultural Constructions of Family Schemas: The Case of Women Executives." *Gender & Society* 15:687–709 (2001).

2. Only two career-committed sample women had spent time at part-time status since their professional careers began.

3. Of course, large proportions of working-class women and minority women have always worked in addition to raising children, and most mothers are employed today.

4. Limitations of the cohort comparison include: (1) the greater opportunity for selective attrition in the older cohorts; and (2) the possibility of future attrition of married mothers from the youngest cohort.

5. Morris (2002) offers a journalistic account of the small numbers of executive women married to men who are primarily responsible for family caregiving.

6. I did not ask about sexual orientation, considering this question intrusive. No one identified herself as a lesbian.

7. Middle cohort members contracted their first marriages between nine years before and six years after starting finance careers, with a median of being married for one year before career launch.

8. Table 4.1 gives a snapshot picture, not a representation of these rates over the lifetime. Heuristic extrapolations of the likelihood of divorce over time by cohort suggest that the middle cohort members' higher incidence of divorce is not due to differing lengths of marriage. Similarly, middle cohort members' lower incidence of childbearing than the other cohorts is not due to differing lengths of marriage. Detailed calculations are available from the author.

9. The youngest cohort's first marriages occurred between 1974 and 1993, with a median of 1982.

10. Youngest cohort first marriages were contracted between one year prior to and sixteen years after beginning finance careers, with a median of starting the career five years before marrying.

11. Unfortunately, time constraints in the interviews prevented me from garnering detailed information on the relationships between respondents and their nannies. Wrigley's (1995) research suggests these relationships are often complex and can be fraught with problems.

12. Recall that several family-committed sample members who work part-time also painted their situation as the best of all possible worlds. It is impossible to know the extent to which this self-presentation by some members of both samples as living in "the best possible situation" is motivated by the wish to present oneself as socially desirable to the interviewer. Of course, members of both samples have also revealed deep unhappiness with their work or family lives.

13. Rothman (1989) argues that the hiring of minority and working-class caregivers by middle-class white women extends to the middle-class white women some of the privileges of patriarchy at a cost to other women.

5. Turning Points

1. Examples of studies of the impact of historical time on people's life trajectories include Blair-Loy and DeHart, forthcoming; Blair-Loy, 1999; Whittier, 1995; Elder, 1974; and Mannheim, 1952.

2. Moreover, the fact that almost half the family-committed group had left promising full-time careers but not yet reached top positions limits the strict comparability of the two groups. For example, the finding I reported earlier of a correlation between work devotion and job level in the work-committed group suggests that those family-committed group members who had left somewhat less advanced positions may have had lower levels of work devotion to begin with than the average career-committed group member.

3. The quantitative calculations in this chapter are based on a small, nonrandom group. The quantitative results should not be reified. Instead, they should be viewed as heuristic ways of summarizing the data to help us better understand patterns and interpretations, which might one day be tested on a larger and ideally longitudinal group.

4. Restricting this analysis to married mothers in the youngest cohort leaves us with a group size of eight career-committed and twenty family-committed respondents. Youngest cohort, married mothers in the career-committed group had a median age of forty at the interview date, while youngest cohort, married mothers in the family-committed group had a median age of thirty-eight.

5. For a discussion of the impact of industry turbulence on careers, see Blair-Loy, 1999. For a study of vacancy chain models of careers, see White, 1970.

6. The methodological appendix provides more details on my coding of the contingent events.

7. Family-committed respondents left full-time careers from zero to seven years after the birth of the first child.

8. These are raw, not standardized, percentages.

9. On the macho culture of a trading floor, see Levin, 2001.

10. Sharon Hays (1996) has documented how the ideology of intensive motherhood encourages women to consult childcare experts to help them to become the most competent mothers they can be. Not content with simply reading the childcare experts, Jane Rowan has become an expert herself.

6. Implications

1. Similarly, other scholars have argued that atomistic and economic presuppositions about human behavior mar much sociological research (for example, Emirbayer, 1997; Simpson 1989; Abbott, 1997a, 1988). This individualistic formulation of work-family conflict is dependent on the historical and cultural construction of the individual as a voluntary, free, choosing, and rational person (cf. Kelly, 1999; Friedland and Alford, 1991).

2. In contrast to my definition of schema, Sewell (1992: 7–8) explicitly defines the term schema more broadly. Nevertheless, his empirical examples of particular schemas (for example, apostolic succession, the American constitutional system, and capitalism [pp. 22–26)]) actually correspond to my use of the term to describe particular, coherent chunks of a society's overarching cultural system. My use of the term "schema" also resembles what Hays (1996: 21) describes as a "cultural model," a historically constructed, more-or-less logically coherent and elaborated model for thinking and acting.

3. "Affectively hot" schemas, like devotion to work or devotion to families, may be more salient and powerful than emotionally neutral schemas (cf. DiMaggio, 1997).

4. Other research empirically examining work and/or family issues as moral phenomena includes Jackall, 1988; Wuthnow, 1996; Lamont, 2000, 1992; and Gerson, 2002.

5. The devotion to work and the devotion to family schemas were the most salient to the group I studied. Other devotion schemas may be discerned in the study of other populations.

6. Hochschild (1979: 566) draws on Goffman, Durkheim, and Geertz to criticize the construction of ideology as a "flatly constructed cognitive framework, lacking systematic implications for how we manage feelings, or, indeed, for how we feel."

7. However, in even the ideal typical situation in which the disciples of the two devotion schemas are gender-segregated, some work-family conflict remained. Kanter's (1977) study of one firm in the 1970s found that managers' homemaking wives sometimes resented employers' demands on their husbands' time.

8. See Introduction, note 1, for more information on this process.

9. Relative to the work devotion schema and the long hours and rigid career trajectories of their male colleagues, these employed mothers are conformists (Blair-Loy, 1999). But women's adoption of this traditionally male schema can also be seen as an innovation and an outcome of the 1970s women's movement.

10. Other social institutions explicitly or implicitly reinforce the work and family devotion schemas. These include churches and other faith-based organizations (Edgell, forthcoming; Stolzenberg, Blair-Loy, and Waite, 1995), much of the body of American law relating to family and gender (Freeman, 1989), and the structure of contemporary American welfare capitalism, which finds it cheaper in terms of salary and benefits to hire fewer exempt workers to each work longer hours than to hire more exempt workers to each work fewer hours (Kalleberg et al., 2000; Jacobs and Gerson, 1998; Schor, 1991). Later in the chapter, I explicitly address the relationship of schemas and institutions.

11. Emirbayer and Mische (1998) refer to these three as "agentic orientations" and emphasize that they are analytical distinctions. Empirical human action often combines all three, although one type may predominate.

12. Ann Mische points out that the schemas of devotion each require the coordination of different temporal frames. The long-term project of building a successful and meaningful career and the long-term project of raising children into a happy and productive adulthood each involve day-to-day, practical juggling of competing immediate demands (personal communication May 25, 2002).

13. For the "master status" concept, see Hughes, 1945 and West and Zimmerman, 1987.

14. Social movement scholars have studied the ways that external cultural cues can act as "frames" to evoke and organize mental structures, such as values and beliefs of movement activists (Gamson, 1992; Schudson, 1989; Snow et al., 1986). Because there is wide disagreement in the literature about the definition of frames, the level of analysis at which they operate, what they do, and how consciously they can be manipulated (Fisher, 1997), I have chosen not to introduce that additional theoretical language here. Future research should empirically investigate and theorize the relationships between frames and devotion schemas.

15. Fields and Kreider (2000) estimate that about 50 percent of first marriages for men under age 45 and between 45–50 percent of first marriages for similarly aged women will eventually end in divorce.

16. Institutions are "supraorganizational patterns of human activity by which individuals and organizations produce and reproduce their material subsistence and organize time and space. They are also symbolic systems, ways of ordering reality, and thereby rendering experience of time and space meaningful" (Friedland and Alford, 1991: 243). Friedland and Alford's insistence that institutions empirically have both a symbolic and a material dimension parallels Sewell's (1992) insistence that social structures are dual, combining both material resources and the virtual schema that interpret those resources. I maintain that institutions (as defined by Friedland and Alford) are a component of social structures (as defined by Sewell).

17. Swidler's insistence that culture provides the means rather than the ends of action is misleading. Distinguishing between the means and ends of action can be empirically difficult and of questionable analytic utility. In Swidler's empirical case, she argues that people use and elaborate the prosaic culture of love to help them develop the *means*—communication and compromise skills—that help them maintain their marriages. Yet she fails to ana-

lyze the overriding *end* of action, which the culture of love *also* defines: an enduring marriage. In the case of the devotion schemas analyzed in this book, the means and ends of action constitute one another simultaneously. People use various strategies to enact their devotion to their careers or their families (means). But they enact this devotion because they believe this is necessary for ensuring the survival and well-being of that to which they are devoted: their careers or their families (ends). See also Friedland and Alford's (1991: 251) and Emirbayer and Mische's (1998) critiques of social scientists' creation of a dualism between means and ends.

18. My analysis of how women's access to heterogeneous and conflicting devotion schemas can generate the possibility for change is consistent with Friedland and Alford's (1991) focus on contradictions between potentially transposable institutional logics. The potential contradiction in the institutional logics of the nuclear family and the capitalist firm "make multiple logics available to individuals and organizations. Individuals and organizations transform the institutional relations of society by exploiting these contradictions" (Friedland and Alford, 1991: 232). My analysis is also consistent with Clemens' (1997) historical study of "organizational forms," defined as "templates, scripts, recipes, or models for social interaction" (p. 49). She argues that the "potential for innovation lies in the fact that individuals can master more than one form; they can cultivate an organizational repertoire that will offer alternative scripts for action" (Clemens, 1997: 48).

19. Hochschild (1983) provides another example of an extreme-case methodology. By elucidating the processes of emotional labor in the extreme case of flight attendants and bill collectors, she enabled other analysts (for example, Pierce, 1995; Leidner, 1993) to see emotional labor as a job requirement in other occupations.

20. For a similar call for research that better explains how adults give meaning to and construct their work and family roles, see Perry-Jenkins, Repetti, and Crouter, 2000.

21. As Clemens argues (1997: 63), "to produce institutional change, challengers are likely to be marginal, but not too marginal. Change requires that other political actors adopt new models or accept new political actors; to the extent that such demands are too extreme, challengers are likely to be trivialized, marginalized, or suppressed."

22. Forty-seven of the fifty-six work-committed women direct or work in firms that sell financial services, and nineteen of the twenty-five family-committed women formerly or currently sold financial or other professional services to clients.

Appendix

1. To familiarize myself with the world of financial services, I conducted four preliminary interviews with acquaintances in this industry. I also conducted interviews with thirteen men in order to get the perspective of the dominant gender in this industry. I use these two sets of interviews purely for background and context.

2. I did not ask about sexual orientation because I considered such questions too intrusive. No one mentioned being a lesbian.

3. From these raw counts, I calculated that negative career contingencies were reported by 32 percent of the career-committed sample and 28 percent of the family-committed sample. Negative family contingencies were reported by 18 percent of the career-committed and 32 percent of the family-committed sample. One third of the career-committed sample and 12 percent of the family-committed sample recounted positive career contingencies.

REFERENCES

Abbott, Andrew. 1988. "Transcending General Linear Reality." *Sociological Theory* 6:169–186.

———. 1997a. "Of Time and Space: The Contemporary Relevance of the Chicago School." *Social Forces* 75:1149–1182.

———. 1997b. "On the Concept of Turning Point." *Comparative Social Research* 16:85–105.

Acker, Joan. 1990. "Hierarchies, Jobs, Bodies: A Theory of Gendered Organizations." *Gender & Society* 4:139–158.

———. 1992. "Gendered Institutions." *Contemporary Sociology* 21(5): 565–568.

Alexander, Jeffrey C. 1988. "Action and Its Environments." In *Action and Its Environments: Toward a New Synthesis,* by J. C. Alexander. New York: Columbia University Press.

Altman, Edward I., ed. 1987. *Handbook of Financial Markets and Institutions.* New York: John Wiley and Sons.

Aries, Philippe. 1962. *Centuries of Childhood: A Social History of Family Life.* New York: Vintage Books.

Ashenfelter, Orley, and Timothy Hannon. 1986. "Sex Discrimination and Product Market Competition: The Case of the Banking Industry." *The Quarterly Journal of Economics* 10:149–173.

Atkinson, Rowland, and John Flint. 2001. "Accessing Hidden and Hard-to-Reach Populations: Snowball Research Strategies. *Social Research Update* 33(Summer), http://www.soc.surrey.ac.uk/sru/SRU33.html.

Bailyn, Lotte. 1993. *Breaking the Mold: Women, Men, and Time in the New Corporate World.* New York: Free Press.

Barley, Stephen R., and Gideon Kunda. 1992. "Design and Devotion: Surges of Rational and Normative Ideologies of Control in Managerial Discourse." *Administrative Science Quarterly* 37: 363–399.

Barnett, Rosalind C. 1999. "A New Work-Life Model for the Twenty-first Century." *Annals of the American Academy of Political and Social Science* 562:143–158.

Barnett, Rosalind C., and Caryl Rivers. 1996. *She Works/He Works: How Two-Income Families Are Happier, Healthier, and Better Off.* San Francisco: HarperCollins.

Barnett, Rosalind C., and Douglas Hall. 2001. "How to Use Reduced Hours to Win the War for Talent." *Organizational Dynamics* 29(3):192–210.

Becker, Gary S. 1981. *A Treatise on the Family.* Cambridge, Mass.: Harvard University Press.

Becker, Penny E., and Phyllis Moen. 1999. "Scaling Back: Dual-Earner Couples' Work-Family Strategies." *Journal of Marriage and the Family* 61:995–1007.

Bem, Sandra L. 1983. "Gender Schema Theory and Its Implications for Child Development: Raising Gender-Aschematic Children in a Gender-Schematic Society." *Signs* 8:598–616.

———. 1993. *The Lenses of Gender: Transforming the Debate on Sexual Inequality.* New Haven, Conn.: Yale University Press.

Bianchi, Suzanne M. 1995. "Changing Economic Roles of Women and Men." In Reynolds Farley, ed. *State of the Union. America in the 1990s.* Volume 1: *Economic Trends.* New York: Russell Sage Foundation.

Biernacki, Patrick, and Dan Waldorf. 1981. "Problems and Techniques of Chain Referral Sampling." *Sociological Methods and Research* 10:141–163.

Blair, Sampson L., and Daniel Lichter. 1991. "Measuring the Division of Household Labor: Gender Segregation of Housework." *Journal of Family Issues* 12:91–113.

Blair-Loy, Mary. 1999. "Career Patterns of Executive Women in Finance: An Optimal Matching Analysis." *American Journal of Sociology* 104:1346–1397.

———. 2001a. "It's Not Just What You Know, It's Who You Know: Technical Knowledge, Rainmaking, and Gender among Finance Executives." *Research in the Sociology of Work* 10:51–83.

————. 2001b. "Cultural Constructions of Family Schemas: The Case of Women Executives." *Gender & Society* 15:687–709.

Blair-Loy, Mary, and Gretchen DeHart. Forthcoming. "Family and Career Trajectories among African American Female Attorneys." Forthcoming, *Journal of Family Issues.*

————. 2003. "Benefit or Liability? Workplace Flexibility and Work-Family Balance among Stockbrokers." Unpublished paper, Washington State University, Pullman, Wash.

Blair-Loy, Mary, and Jerry A. Jacobs. 2003. "Globalization, Work Hours, and the Care Deficit among Stockbrokers." *Gender & Society* (17:230–249).

Blair-Loy, Mary, and Amy S. Wharton. 2002a. "Employees' Use of Work-Familiy Policies and the Workplace Social Context." *Social Forces* 80:813–845.

————. 2002b. "Globalization, Commitment, and Constraints: Corporate Flexibility Policies among Managerial and Professional Workers. Unpublished paper, Washington State University, Pullman, Wash.

Blau, Francine D., and Ronald G. Ehrenberg. 1997. "Introduction." In Francine D. Blau and Ronald G. Ehrenberg, eds. *Gender and Family Issues in the Workplace,* pp. 1–19. New York: Russell Sage Foundation.

Blossfeld, Hans-Peter, and Catherine Hakim. 1997. "Introduction: A Comparative Perspective on Part-Time Work." In Hans-Peter Blossfeld and Catherine Hakim, eds. *Between Equalization and Marginalization,* pp. 1–21. New York: Oxford University Press.

Bond, James T., Ellen Galinsky, and Jennifer E. Swanberg. 1998. *The 1997 National Study of the Changing Workforce.* New York: Families and Work Institute.

Brines, Julie. 1994. "Economic Dependency, Gender, and the Division of Labor at Home." *American Journal of Sociology* 100:652–688.

Britton, Dana. 2000. "The Epistemology of the Gendered Organization." *Gender & Society* 14(3):418–434.

Budig, Michelle, and Paula England. 2001. "The Wage Penalty for Motherhood." *American Sociological Review* 66:204–225.

Cancian, Francesca M. 1981. "Rapid Social Change: Women Students in Business Schools." *Sociology and Social Research* 66:169–183.

————. 1987. *Love in America: Gender and Self-Development.* Cambridge and New York: Cambridge University Press.

Cappelli, Peter. 1999. "Career Jobs are Dead." *California Management Review* 42:146–167.

Catalyst. 1993. *Flexible Work Arrangements: Succeeding with Part-time Arrangements.* New York: Catalyst.

————. 2001. *Women in Financial Services: The Word on the Street.* New York: Catalyst.

Cherlin, Andrew, and Pamela B. Walters. 1981. "Trends in United States: Men's and Women's Sex-role Attitudes: 1972 to 1978." *American Sociological Review* 46:453–460.

Clarkberg, Marin, and Phyllis Moen. 2001. "Understanding the Time-Squeeze: Married Couples' Preferred and Actual Work-Hour Strategies." *American Behavioral Scientist* 44(7):1115–1136.

Clemens, Elisabeth. 1997. *The People's Lobby: Organizational Innovation and the Rise of Interest Group Politics in the United States, 1890–1925.* Chicago and London: University of Chicago Press.

Cohler, Bertram J. 1982. "Personal Narrative and Life Course." *Life-Span Development and Behavior* 4:206–241.

Cole, Jonathan R., and Harriet Zuckerman. 1991. "Marriage, Motherhood, and Research Performance in Science." In Harriet Zuckerman, Jonathan R. Cole, and John T. Bruer, eds. *The Outer Circle: Women in the Scientific Community,* pp. 158–204. New York and London: W. W. Norton & Company.

Collins, Patricia H. 1987. "The Maternal Role: The Meaning of Mother in Black Culture and Black Mother/Daughter Relationships." *Sage: A Scholarly Journal on Black Women* 4:3–10.

————. 1994. "Shifting the Center: Race, Class and Feminist Theorizing about Motherhood." In Evelyn Nakano Glenn, Grace Chang, and Linda Rennie Forcey, eds. *Mothering: Ideology, Experience and Agency,* pp. 45–65. New York: Routledge.

Coltrane, Scott. 1988. "Father-Child Relationships and the Status of Women: A Cross-Cultural Study." *American Journal of Sociology* 93(5):1060–1095.

————. 1989. "Household Labor and the Routine Production of Gender." *Social Problems* 36(5):473–490.

————. 1996. *Family Man.* New York and Oxford: Oxford University Press.

————. 2000. "Research on Household Labor: Modeling and Measuring the Social Embeddedness of Routine Family Work." *Journal of Marriage and the Family* 62:1208–1233.

Coltrane, Scott, and Michele Adams. 2001. "Men's Family Work: Child-Centered Fathering and the Sharing of Domestic Labor." In Rosanna Hertz and Nancy L. Marshall, eds. *Working Families: The Transformation of the American Home,* pp. 72–99. Berkeley, Calif.: University of California Press.

Connell, Robert W. 1987. *Gender and Power: Society, the Person, and Sexual Politics.* Stanford, Calif.: Stanford University Press.

Coser, Lewis A. 1974. *Greedy Institutions.* New York: Free Press.

Coser, Lewis A., and Rose Laub Coser. 1974. "The Housewife and Her Greedy Family." In Lewis A. Coser, *Greedy Institutions,* pp. 89–100. New York: Free Press.

Costain, Anne N., and W. Douglas Costain, eds. 1987. *Strategy and Tactics of the Women's Movement in the United States.* Philadelphia: Temple University Press.

Costen, Wanda. 2001. "Where are the Women? Social Closure in the Financial Services Industry." Ph.D. dissertation, Washington State University, Pullman, Wash.

Cott, Nancy. 1977. *The Bonds of Womanhood: "Woman's Sphere" in New England, 1780–1835.* New Haven, Conn.: Yale University Press.

Crittenden, Ann. 2001. *The Price of Motherhood.* New York: Metropolitan Books.

Daszkiewicz, Rosemary. 2002. "The Corporate Spouse: A Necessary Ingredient to Business Success?" *Washington State Bar News* 56:13–14.

Davidoff, Lenore, and Catherine Hall. 1987. *Family Fortunes: Men and Women of the English Middle Class, 1780–1850.* Chicago, Ill.: University of Chicago Press.

Davis, James A., Tom W. Smith, and Peter Marsden. 1998. 1998 General Social Survey [computer file]. ICSPR version, National Opinion Research Center, University of Chicago. Ann Arbor, Mich.: Inter-university Consortium for Political and Social Research.

Deloitte and Touche. 1998. *The Top Rung. Working Our Way Up: The Choices We Make.* Seattle, Wash.: Deloitte and Touche LLP.

D'Emilio, John, and Estelle B. Freedman. 1989. *Intimate Matters: A History of Sexuality in America.* New York: Harper & Row.

Deutsch, Francine M. 1999. *Halving It All: How Equally Shared Parenting Works.* Cambridge and London: Harvard University Press.

DiMaggio, Paul. 1988. "Interest and Agency in Institutional Theory." In Lynne G. Zucker, ed. *Institutional Patterns and Organizations,* pp. 3–22. Cambridge, Mass.: Ballinger Publishing Company.

———. 1997. "Culture and Cognition." *Annual Review of Sociology* 23:263–287.

———. 2001. "Introduction: Making Sense of the Contemporary Firm and Prefiguring Its Future." In Paul DiMaggio, ed. *The Twenty-First Century Firm: Changing Economic Organization in International Perspective,* pp. 3–30. Princeton and Oxford: Princeton University Press.

DiMaggio, Paul J., and Walter W. Powell. 1991. "Introduction." In Walter W. Powell and Paul J. DiMaggio, eds. *The New Institutionalism in Organizational Analysis,* pp. 1–38. Chicago and London: University of Chicago Press.

Douglas, Mary. 1986. *How Institutions Think.* Syracuse, N.Y.: Syracuse University Press.

Drago, Robert, Ann C. Crouter, Mark Wardell, and Billie S. Willits. 2001. "Faculty & Families Project: Final Report to the Alfred P. Sloan Foundation." The Pennsylvania State University.

Drobnic, Sonja, and Immo Wittig. 1997. "Part-Time Work in the United States of America." In Hans-Peter Blossfeld and Catherine Hakim, eds. *Between Equalization and Marginalization,* pp. 289–314. Oxford: Oxford University Press.

Durkheim, Emile. 1965. *Elementary Forms of Religious Life.* New York: Free Press.

Edgell, Penny E. Forthcoming. "The Problem with Families Today." In *Religion and Family in a Changing Society: Transformation in Linked Institutions.* Press Series in Cultural Sociology, Paul DiMaggio, Michele Lamont, Robert Wuthrow, and Viviana Zelizer, eds. Princeton, N.J.: Princeton University Press.

Edwards, Richard. 1979. *Contested Terrain: The Transformation of the Workplace in the Twentieth Century.* New York: Basic Books.

Ehrensaft, Diane. 2001. "The Kindercult: The New Child Born to Conflict between Work and Family." In Rosanna Hertz and Nancy L. Marshall, eds. *Working Families: The Transformation of the American Home,* pp. 304–322. Berkeley, Calif.: University of California Press.

Elder, Glen H. 1974. *Children of the Great Depression: Social Change in Life Experiences.* Chicago, Ill.: University of Chicago Press.

———. 1985. "Perspectives on the Life Course." In Glen H. Elder, ed. *Life Course Dynamics,* pp. 23–49. Ithaca, N.Y.: Cornell University Press.

Emirbayer, Mustafa. 1997. "Manifesto for a Relational Sociology." *American Journal of Sociology* 103:281–317.

Emirbayer, Mustafa, and Ann Mische. 1998. "What Is Agency?" *American Journal of Sociology* 103:962–1023.

England, Paula, and Barbara S. Kilbourne. 1990. "Markets, Marriages, and Other Mates: The Problem of Power." In Roger Friedland and A. F. Robertson, eds. *Beyond the Marketplace: Rethinking Economy and Society,* pp. 163–188. New York: Aldine de Gruyter.

Epstein, Cynthia Fuchs. 1973. "Positive Effects of the Multiple Black Negative: Explaining the Success of Black Professional Women." *American Journal of Sociology* 78:912–935.

———. 1988. *Deceptive Distinctions: Sex, Gender, and the Social Order.* New Haven: Yale University Press; New York: Russell Sage Foundation.

———. 1992. "Tinkerbells and Pinups: The Construction and Reconstruction of Gender Boundaries at Work." In Michele Lamont and Michael Fournier, eds. *Cultivating Differences: Symbolic Boundaries and the Making of Inequality,* pp. 232–256. Chicago, Ill.: University of Chicago Press.

———. 1993. *Women in Law,* 2nd ed. Urbana and Chicago: University of Illinois Press.

Epstein, Cynthia F., with Robert Saute, Martha Gever, and Bonnie Oglensky. 1995. "Glass Ceilings and Open Doors: Women's Advancement in the Legal Profession." *Fordham Law Review* 64:291–449.

Epstein, Cynthia F., Carroll Seron, Bonnie Oglensky, and Robert Saute. 1999. *The Part-Time Paradox: Time Norms, Professional Lives, Family and Gender.* New York and London: Routledge.

Farley, Reynolds. 1996. *The New American Reality.* New York: Russell Sage Foundation.

Ferree, Myra M. 1990. "Beyond Separate Spheres: Feminism and Family Research." *Journal of Marriage and the Family* 52:866–884.

Ferree, Myra M., and Beth B. Hess. 1985. *Controversy and Coalition: The New Feminist Perspective.* Boston, Mass.: Twayne.

Fields, Jason S., and Rose Kreider. 2000. "Marriage and Divorce Rates in the U.S.: A Multistate Life Table Analysis, Fall 1996 SIPP." Presented at the annual meeting of the Southern Demographic Association, New Orleans, La.

Finnigan, Annie. 2001. "Tug of Work." *Working Mother Magazine.* Vol. 24 (October 2001): 52–62.

Fiorentine, Robert. 1987. "Men, Women, and the Premed Persistence Gap: A Normative Alternatives Approach." *American Journal of Sociology* 92:118–139.

Fisher, Kimberly. 1997. "Locating Frames in the Discursive Universe." *Sociological Research Online.* Vol. 2, no. 3, http://www.socresonline.org.uk/socresonline/2/3/4.html.

Flynn, Patricia M., John D. Leeth, and Elliott S. Levy. 1995. "Accounting Labor Markets in Transition." Final Report to the National Center on the Educational Quality of the Workforce at the University of Pennsylvania.

Folbre, Nancy. 2001. *The Invisible Heart: Economics and Family Values.* New York: New Press.

Fraser, Jill A. 2001. *White Collar Sweatshop: The Deterioration of Work and Its Rewards in Corporate America.* New York and London: W. W. Norton & Company.

Freeman, Jo. 1989. "The Legal Revolution." In Jo Freeman, ed. *Women: A Feminist Perspective,* pp. 371–394. Mountain View, Calif.: Mayfield Press.

Frenkel, Stephen J., Marek Korczynski, Karen A. Shire, and May Tam. 1999. *On the Front Line: Organization of Work in the Information Economy.* Ithaca, N.Y.: Cornell University Press.

Fried, Mindy. 1998. *Taking Time: Parental Leave Policy and Corporate Culture.* Philadelphia, Pa.: Temple University Press.

Friedland, Roger, and Robert R. Alford. 1991. "Bringing Society Back In: Symbols, Practices, and Institutional Contradictions." In Walter W. and Paul J. DiMaggio, eds. *The New Institutionalism in Organizational Analysis,* pp. 232–263. Chicago and London: University of Chicago Press.

Galinsky, Ellen, and James T. Bond. 1998. *The 1998 Business Work Life Study: A Sourcebook.* New York: Families and Work Institute.

Galinsky, Ellen, and Jennifer E. Swanberg. 2000. "Employed Mothers and Fathers in the United States." In Linda L. Haas, Philip Hwang, and Graeme Russell, eds. *Organizational Change and Gender Equity,* pp. 15–28. Thousand Oaks, Calif.: Sage.

Gamson, William A. 1992. *Talking Politics.* Boston, Mass.: Cambridge University Press.

Garey, Anita. 1995. "Constructing Motherhood on the Night Shift: 'Working Mothers' as 'Stay-at-Home Moms.'" *Qualitative Sociology* 18(4):415–437.

———. 1999. *Weaving Work and Motherhood.* Philadelphia, Pa.: Temple University Press.

Geertz, Clifford. 1973. *The Interpretation of Cultures: Selected Essays.* New York: Basic Books.

George, Linda K. 1993. "Sociological Perspectives on Life Transitions." *Annual Review of Sociology* 19:353–373.

Gerson, Kathleen. 1985. *Hard Choices: How Women Decide about Work, Career, and Motherhood.* Berkeley, Calif.: University of California Press.

———. 1993. *No Man's Land: Men's Changing Commitments to Family and Work.* New York: Basic Books.

———. 2002. "Moral Dilemmas, Moral Strategies, and the Transformation of Gender: Lessons from Two Generations of Work and Family Change." *Gender & Society* 16:8–28.

Gerson, Kathleen, and Jerry Jacobs. 2001. "Changing the Structure and Culture of Work: Work and Family Conflict, Work Flexibility, and Gender Equity in the Modern Workplace." In Rosanna Hertz and Nancy L. Marshall, eds. *Working Families: The Transformation of the American Home,* pp. 207–226. Berkeley, Calif.: University of California Press.

Gerstel, Naomi, and Dan Clawson. 2001. "Unions' Response to Family Concerns." *Social Problems* 48:227–298.

Gerth, H. H., and C. Wright Mills. 1958. "Intellectual Orientations." In H. H. Gerth and C. Wright Mills, eds. *From Max Weber: Essays in Sociology,* pp. 45–74. New York: Oxford University Press.

Giele, Janet Z. 1995. *Two Paths to Women's Equality: Temperance, Suffrage, and the Origins of Modern Feminism.* New York: Twayne Publishers.

Glaser, Barney G., and Anselm L. Strauss. 1967. *The Discovery of Grounded Theory: Strategies for Qualitative Research.* Chicago, Ill.: Aldine Press.

Glass, Jennifer L. 2002. "Blessing or Curse? Family Responsive Policies and Mother's Wage Growth Over Time." Unpublished paper, University of Iowa.

Glass, Jennifer L., and Sarah B. Estes. 1997. "The Family Responsive Work-place." *Annual Review of Sociology* 23:289–313.

Glenn, Evelyn N. 1994. "Social Constructions of Mothering: A Thematic Overview." In Evelyn Nakano Glenn, Grace Chang, and Linda Rennie Forcey, eds. *Mothering: Ideology, Experience and Agency,* pp. 1–29. New York: Routledge.

Glenn, Evelyn Nakano, Grace Chang, and Linda Rennie Forcey, eds. 1994. *Mothering: Ideology, Experience and Agency.* New York: Routledge.

Goldscheider, Frances, and Linda J. Waite. 1991. *New Families, No Families? The Transformation of the American Home.* Berkeley, Calif.: University of California Press.

Goodstein, Jerry. 1994. "Institutional Pressures and Strategic Responsive-ness: Employee Involvement in Work-Family Issues." *Academy of Management Journal* 37:350–382.

Gornick, Janet C., Marcia K. Meyers, and Katherin E. Ross. 1998. "Public Policies and the Employment of Mothers: A Cross-national Study. *Social Science Quarterly* 79:35–54.

Grunberg, Leon, Richard Anderson-Connolly, and Edward S. Greenberg. 2000. "Surviving Layoffs: The Effects on Organizational Commitment and Job Performance." *Work and Occupations* 27:7–31.

Hagan, John, and Fiona Kay. 1995. *Gender in Practice: A Study of Lawyers' Lives.* New York: Oxford University Press.

Hareven, Tamara K. 1982. *Family Time and Industrial Time: The Relation-ship between the Family and Work in a New England Industrial Commu-nity.* Cambridge, England: Cambridge University Press.

Hayghe, Howard. 1997. "Developments in Women's Labor Force Participa-tion." *Monthly Labor Review* 120(9): 41–46.

Hayghe, Howard, and Suzanne M. Bianchi. 1994. "Married Mothers' Work Patterns: The Job-Family Compromise." *Monthly Labor Review* 117:24–30.

Hays, Sharon. 1996. *The Cultural Contradictions of Motherhood*. New Haven and London: Yale University Press.

Heckscher, Charles. 1995. *White Collar Blues: Management Loyalties in an Age of Corporate Restructuring*. New York: Basic Books.

Heilbrun, Carolyn G. 2001. "Men Were the Only Models I Had." *The Chronicle Review, The Chronicle of Higher Education*, October 12, pp. B7–B11.

Hennessy, Judith. 2000. "Welfare to Work: Low-Income Single Mothers Navigate the Changing Landscape of Welfare Assistance." MA thesis. Washington State University, Pullman, Wash.

Hertz, Rosanna. 1986. *More Equal Than Others: Women and Men in Dual-Career Marriages*. Berkeley, Calif.: University of California Press.

Hewlett, Sylvia A. 2002. *Creating a Life: Professional Women and the Quest for Children*. New York: Talk Miramax Books.

Hochschild, Arlie Russell. 1979. "Emotion Work, Feeling Rules, and Social Structure." *American Journal of Sociology* 85:551–575.

———. 1983. *The Managed Heart: Commercialization of Human Feeling*. Berkeley, Calif.: University of California Press.

———. 1997. *The Time Bind: When Work Becomes Home and Home Becomes Work*. New York: Metropolitan Books.

———. 2000 [1997]. "Introduction." In *The Time Bind: When Work Becomes Home and Home Becomes Work*, 2nd ed. New York: Metropolitan Books.

———. 2001. "Eavesdropping Children, Adult Deals, and Cultures of Care." In Rosanna Hertz and Nancy L. Marshall, eds. *Working Families: The Transformation of the American Home*, pp. 341–353. Berkeley, Calif.: University of California Press.

Hochschild, Arlie R., with Anne Machung. 1989. *The Second Shift: Working Parents and the Revolution at Home*. New York: Viking.

Hughes, Everett C. 1945. "Dilemmas and Contradictions of Status." *American Journal of Sociology* 50(5):353–359.

Hull, K. E., and R. L. Nelson. 2000. "Assimilation, Choice or Constraint? Testing Theories of Gender Differences in the Careers of Lawyers." *Social Forces* 79:229–264.

Hunnicutt, Benjamin K. 1988. *Work Without End: Abandoning Shorter Hours for the Right to Work.* Philadelphia, Pa.: Temple University Press.

Ireland, Mardy S. 1993. *Reconceiving Women: Separating Motherhood from Female Identity.* New York: Guilford Press.

Jackall, Robert. 1988. *Moral Mazes: The World of Corporate Managers.* New York: Oxford University Press.

Jacobs, Jerry A. 1989. *Revolving Doors: Sex Segregation and Women's Careers.* Stanford, Calif.: Stanford University Press.

Jacobs, Jerry A., and Kathleen Gerson. 1998. "Toward a Family-Friendly, Gender-Equitable Work Week." *University of Pennsylvania Journal of Labor and Employment Law* 1:457–472.

———. 2001. "Overworked Individuals or Overworked Families: Explaining Trends in Work, Leisure and Family Time." *Work and Occupations* 28(1):40–63.

———. Forthcoming. *The Time Divide: Work, Family and Social Policy in Contemporary Society.* Cambridge, Mass.: Harvard University Press.

Jacoby, Sanford M. 1999. "Are Career Jobs Headed for Extinction?" *California Management Review* 42:123–145.

Jameton, Andrew. 1993. "Dilemmas of Moral Distress: Moral Responsibility and Nursing Practice." *Clinical Issues in Perinatal and Women's Health Nursing.* 4:542–551.

Jepperson, Ronald L. 1991. "Institutions, Institutional Effects, and Institutionalism." In Walter W. Powell and Paul J. DiMaggio, eds. *The New Institutionalism in Organizational Analysis,* pp. 143–163. Chicago: University of Chicago Press.

Kalleberg, Arne L. 1995. "Symposium: Part-time Work and Workers in the United States: Correlates and Policy Issues." *Washington and Lee Law Review* 52(3):771–798.

Kalleberg, Arne, Barbara F. Reskin, and Ken Hudson. 2000. "Bad Jobs in America: Standard and Nonstandard Employment Relations and Job Quality in the United States." *American Sociological Review* 65:256–278.

Kanter, Rosabeth M. 1977. *Men and Women of the Corporation.* New York: Basic Books.

Kay, Fiona M. 1997. "Balancing Acts: Career and Family among Lawyers."
    In Susan Boyd, ed. *Challenging the Public/Private Divide: Feminism
    Law and Public Policy,* pp. 195–224. Toronto, Canada: University of
    Toronto Press.
Kelly, Brighid. 1998. "Preserving Moral Integrity: A Follow-up Study with
    New Graduate Nurses." *Journal of Advanced Nursing* 28:1134–1145.
Kelly, Erin. 1999. "Theorizing Corporate Family Policies: How Advocates
    Built 'The Business Case' for 'Family-Friendly' Programs." *Research in
    the Sociology of Work* 7:169–202.
Kessler-Harris, Alice. 1982. *Out to Work: A History of Wage-Earning Women
    in the United States.* New York and Oxford: Oxford University Press.
———. 1994. "Feminism and Affirmative Action." In Nicolaus Mills, ed.
    *Debating Affirmative Action: Race, Gender, Ethnicity and the Politics of
    Inclusion,* pp. 68–82. New York: Dell Publishing Company.
Klein, Ethel. 1984. *Gender Politics.* Cambridge, Mass.: Harvard University
    Press.
Komter, Aafke. 1989. "Hidden Power in Marriage." *Gender & Society* 3:187–216.
Korn/Ferry International. 1993. *Decade of the Executive Woman.* Los Ange-
    les, Calif.: Korn/Ferry International.
Kropf, Marcia Brumit. 2001. "Part-Time Work Arrangements and the Cor-
    poration: A Dynamic Interaction." In Rosanna Hertz and Nancy L.
    Marshall, eds. *Working Families: The Transformation of the American
    Home,* pp. 152–167. Berkeley, Calif.: University of California Press.
Kunda, Gideon. 1992. *Engineering Culture: Control and Commitment in a
    High Tech Corporation.* Philadelphia, Pa.: Temple University Press.
Kunda, Gideon, and John Van Maanen. 1999. "Changing Scripts at Work:
    Managers and Professionals." *Annals of the American Academy of Politi-
    cal and Social Science* 561:64–80.
Lamont, Michele. 1992. *Money, Morals and Manners: The Culture of the
    French and American Upper-Middle Class.* Chicago, Ill.: University of
    Chicago Press.
———. 2000. *The Dignity of Working Men: Morality and the Boundaries of
    Race, Class and Immigration.* New York: Russell Sage Foundation and
    Cambridge and London: Harvard University Press.
———. 2001. "Symbolic Boundaries (General)." *International Encyclopedia
    of Social and Behavioral Sciences.* Amsterdam: Elsevier Science.

Lasch, Christopher. 1977. *Haven in a Heartless World: The Family Besieged.* New York: Basic Books.

Leidner, Robin. 1993. *Fast Food, Fast Talk: Service Work and the Routinization of Everyday Life.* Berkeley, Calif.: University of California Press.

Levin, Peter. 2001. "Gendering the Market: Temporality, Work, and Gender on a National Futures Exchange." *Work and Occupations* 29:112–130.

Levy, Frank. 1995. "Incomes and Income Inequality." In Reynolds Farley, ed. *The State of the Union: America in the 1990s.* Vol. 1: *Economic Trends,* pp. 1–57. New York: Russell Sage Foundation.

Lewis, Michael. 1989. *Liar's Poker: Rising through the Wreckage on Wall Street.* New York: Penguin Books.

Lincoln, James R., and Arne L. Kalleberg. 1990. *Culture, Control, and Commitment: A Study of Work Organization and Work Attitudes in the United States and Japan.* Cambridge: Cambridge University Press.

Litan, Robert E., and Anthony M. Santomero, eds. 2000. *Brookings-Wharton Papers on Financial Services.* Washington, D.C.: Brookings Institution Press.

Lorber, Judith. 1984. *Women Physicians: Careers, Status, and Power.* New York and London: Tavistock Publications.

————. 1994. *Paradoxes of Gender.* New Haven, Conn.: Yale University Press.

Lundgren, Lena M., Jennifer Fleischer-Cooperman, Robert Schneider, and Therese Fitzgerald. 2001. "Work Family and Gender in Medicine: How Do Dual-Earners Decide Who Should Work Less." In Rosanna Hertz and Nancy L. Marshall, eds. *Working Families: The Transformation of the American Home,* pp. 251–269. Berkeley, Calif.: University of California Press.

Mannheim, K. 1952. "The Problem of Generations." In Paul Kecskemeti, ed. *Essays on the Sociology of Knowledge,* pp. 276–322. London: Routledge and Kegan Paul.

Mason, Karen O., John L. Czajka, and Sara Arber. 1976. "Change in U.S. Women's Sex-role Attitudes, 1964–1974." *American Sociological Review* 41:573–596.

Mason, Karen O., and Yu-Hsia Lu. 1988. "Attitudes Toward Women's Familial Roles: Changes in the United States, 1977–1985." *Gender & Society* 2:39–57.

Maume, David J., Jr., and Marcia L. Bellas. 2001. "The Overworked American or the Time Bind? Assessing Competing Explanations for Time Spent in Paid Labor." *American Behavioral Scientist* 44:1137–1156.

McDuff, Elaine M., and Charles W. Mueller. 2000. "The Ministry as an Occupational Labor Market: Intentions to Leave an Employer (Church) Versus Intentions to Leave a Profession (Ministry). *Work and Occupations* 27:89–116.

McLanahan, Sara, and Lynne M.Casper. 1995. "Growing Diversity in the American Family." In Farley McReynolds, ed. *The State of the Union: America in the 1990s*, Vol. 2: *Social Trends*, pp. 1–45. New York: Russell Sage Foundation.

McKenna, Elizabeth P. 1997. *When Work Doesn't Work Anymore: Women, Work and Identity.* New York: Delacorte Press.

McMahon, Martha. 1995. *Engendering Motherhood: Identity and Self-Transformation in Women's Lives.* New York: Guilford Press.

Meiksins, Peter, and Peter Whalley. 2002. *Putting Work in Its Place: A Quiet Revolution.* Ithaca, N.Y.: Cornell University Press.

Meyer, John, and Brian Rowan. 1977. "Institutionalized Organizations: Formal Structure As Myth and Ceremony." *American Journal of Sociology* 83:340–363.

Mills, C. Wright. 1951. *White Collar: The American Middle Classes.* New York: Oxford University Press.

Mills, Nicolaus. 1994. "Introduction to Look Alike America." In Nicolaus Mills, ed. *Debating Affirmative Action: Race, Gender, Ethnicity and the Politics of Inclusion*, pp. 1–32. New York: Dell Publishing.

Mintz, Beth, and Michael Schwartz. 1985. *The Power Structure of American Business.* Chicago and London: University of Chicago Press.

Moen, Phyllis. 1992. *Women's Two Roles: A Contemporary Dilemma.* New York: Auburn House.

Morell, Carolyn M. 1994. *Unwomanly Conduct: The Challenges of Intentional Childlessness.* New York: Routledge.

Morgan, Hal, and Kerry Tucker. 1991. *Companies That Care: The Most Family-Friendly Companies in America—What They Offer and How They Got That Way.* New York: Fireside/Simon & Schuster.

Morris, Betsy. 2002. "Trophy Husbands." *Fortune Magazine.* October 14, 146(7):78–98.

National Survey of American Families. 1997. *Assessing the New Federalism.* Washington, D.C.: The Urban Institute.

Osterman, Paul. 1996. "Introduction." In Paul Osterman, ed. *Broken Ladders: Managerial Careers in the New Economy,* pp. 1–22. New York and Oxford: Oxford University Press.

Parcel, Toby. 1999. "Work and Family in the 21st Century: Its About Time." *Work and Occupations* 26:264–274.

Parcel, Toby, and Daniel Cornfield, eds. 2000. *Work and Family: Research Informing Policy.* Thousand Oaks, Calif.: Sage.

Perlow, Leslie A. 1997. *Finding Time: How Corporations, Individuals and Families Can Benefit from New Work Practices.* Ithaca and London: ILR Press.

Perry-Jenkins, Maureen, Rena L. Repetti, and Ann C. Crouter. 2000. "Work and Family in the 1990s." *Journal of Marriage and the Family* 62:981–998.

Pierce, Jennifer. 1995. *Gender Trials: Emotional Lives in Contemporary Law Firms.* Berkeley, Calif.: University of California Press.

Pleck Joseph H., Graham L. Staines, and Linda Lang. 1980. "Conflicts Between Work and Family Life." *Monthly Labor Review* 103(3):29–32.

Potuchek, Jean L. 1997. *Who Supports the Family? Gender and Breadwinning in Dual-Earner Families.* Stanford, Calif.: Stanford University Press.

Price Waterhouse v. Hopkins. 1989. 490 U.S. 228. http://laws.findlaw.com/us/490/228.html.

Pringle, Rosemary. 1988. *Secretaries Talk: Sexuality, Power and Work.* London and New York: Verso.

Putnam, Robert D. 2000. *Bowling Alone: The Collapse and Revival of American Community.* New York: Simon & Schuster.

Ragin, Charles. 1987. *The Comparative Method: Moving Beyond Qualitative and Quantitative Strategies.* Berkeley, Calif.: University of California Press.

Rapoport, Rhona, and Lotte Bailyn. 1996. *Relinking Life and Work: Toward a Better Future.* New York: Ford Foundation.

Reed, Susan E. 2001. "When a Workplace Dispute Goes Very Public." *New York Times.* Sunday, November 25, p. BU4.

Reskin, Barbara F., and Heidi I. Hartmann. 1986. *Women's Work, Men's Work: Sex Segregation on the Job.* Washington, D.C.: National Academy Press.

Ricoeur, Paul. 1977. "The Question of Proof in Freud's Psychoanalytic Writings." *Journal of the American Psychoanalytic Association* 25:835–872.

———. 1984. *Time and Narrative.* Chicago, Ill.: University of Chicago Press.

Risman, Barbara. 1987. "Intimate Relationships from a Microstructural Perspective: Mothering Men." *Gender & Society* 1(1):6–32.

———. 1998. *Gender Vertigo: American Families in Transition.* New Haven, Conn.: Yale University Press.

Roper, Michael. 1994. *Masculinity and the British Organization Man Since 1945.* New York: Oxford University Press.

Rose, Peter S. 1987. *The Changing Structure of American Banking.* New York: Columbia University Press.

Rossi, Alice. 1985. "Gender and Parenthood." In Alice Rossi, ed. *Gender and the Life Course,* pp. 161–191. Hawthorne, N.Y.: Aldine Publishing.

Roth, Louise M. 2001a. "Engendering Sex-Segregation: Queuing and Revolving Doors on Wall Street." Unpublished paper, University of Arizona, Tucson, Ariz.

———. 2001b. "Selling Women Short: A Research Note on Gender Differences in Compensation on Wall Street." Unpublished paper, University of Arizona, Tucson, Ariz.

Rothman, Barbara K. 1989. "Women As Fathers: Motherhood and Child Care under a Modified Patriarchy." *Gender & Society* 3:89–104.

Ryan, Mary P. 1981. *Cradle of the Middle Class: The Family in Oneida County, New York, 1790–1865.* Cambridge: Cambridge University Press.

Sampson, Robert J., and John H. Laub. 1993. *Crime in the Making: Pathways and Turning Points through Life.* Cambridge, Mass.: Harvard University Press.

Sawi, Beth. 2000. *Coming Up for Air: How to Build a Balanced Life in a Workaholic World.* New York: Hyperion.

Schneider, Beth. 1988. "Political Generations in the Contemporary Women's Movement." *Sociological Inquiry* 58:4–21.

Schor, Juliet. 1991. *The Overworked American: The Unexpected Decline of Leisure.* New York: Basic Books.

Schudson, Michael. 1989. "How Culture Works: Perspectives from Media Studies on the Efficacy of Symbols." *Theory and Society* (18)2:153–180.

Schwartz, Pepper. 1994. *Love Between Equals: How Peer Marriage Really Works.* New York: The Free Press.

Securities Industries Association. 1999. *The 1999 Securities Industries Factbook.* New York.

Sewell, William, H., Jr. 1992. "A Theory of Structure: Duality, Agency, and Transformation." *American Journal of Sociology* 98:1–29.

———. 1996. "Historical Events As Transformations of Structures: Inventing Revolution at the Bastille." *Theory and Society* 26:841–881.

Shu, Xiaoling, and Margaret Marini. 1998. Gender-related Change in Occupational Aspirations of Youth. *Sociology of Education* 71:43–68.

Simmel, Georg. [1908] 1971. "The Stranger." In Donald N. Levine, ed. *Georg Simmel on Individuality and Social Forms,* pp. 143–149. Chicago and London: University of Chicago Press.

Simpson, Ida H. 1989. "The Sociology of Work: Where Have All the Workers Gone?" *Social Forces* 67:563–581.

Skolnick, Arlene. 1991. *Embattled Paradise: The American Family in an Age of Uncertainty.* New York: Basic Books.

Snow, David A., E. Burke Rochford, Jr., Steven K. Worden, and Robert D. Benford. 1986. "Frame Alignment Processes, Micromobilization and Movement Participation." *American Sociological Review* 51(4):464–481.

Spain, Daphne, and Suzanne M. Bianchi. 1996. *Balancing Act: Motherhood and Employment among American Women.* New York: Russell Sage Foundation.

Stacey, Judith. 1990. *Brave New Families: Stories of Domestic Upheaval in Late Twentieth Century America.* New York: Basic Books.

Stearns, Linda B., and Kenneth D. Allan. 1996. "Economic Behavior in Institutional Environments: The Corporate Merger Wave of the 1980s." *American Sociological Review* 61:699–718.

Stebbins, Leslie F. 2001. *Work and Family in America: A Reference Handbook.* Santa Barbara, Calif.: ABC CLIO.

Stolzenberg, Ross, Mary Blair-Loy, and Linda Waite. 1995. "Religious Participation in Early Adulthood: Age and Family Life Cycle Effects on Church Membership." *American Sociological Review* 60:84–103.

Swidler, Ann. 1986. "Culture in Action: Symbols and Strategies." *American Sociological Review* 51:273–286.

REFERENCES **257**

———. 2001. *Talk of Love: How Culture Matters.* Chicago and London: University of Chicago Press.

Sykes, Gresham M., and David Matza. 1957. "Techniques of Rationalization: A Theory of Delinquency." *American Sociological Review* 22:664–670.

Taylor, Jeremy F. 1991. *The Keepers of Finance.* New York: Quorum Books.

Tilly, Chris. 1992. "Dualism in Part-time Employment." *Industrial Relations* 31:330–347.

United States Bureau of the Census. 1992. "Marital Status and Living Arrangements: March 1991. *Current Population Reports,* Series P-20, No. 461. Washington, D.C.: U.S. Government Printing Office.

———. 1998. *Statistical Abstract of the United States.* Washington, D.C.: U.S. Government Printing Office.

United States Department of Commerce. 1986. *Statistical Abstract of the United States 1986.* Washington, D.C.: U.S. Government Printing Office.

———. 1988. *Statistical Abstract of the United States 1988.* Washington, D.C.: U.S. Government Printing Office.

———. 1992. *Statistical Abstract of the United States 1992.* Washington, D.C.: U.S. Government Printing Office.

Uttal, Lynette. 1996. "Custodial Care, Surrogate Care and Coordinated Care: Employed Mothers and the Meaning of Child Care." *Gender & Society* 10:291–311.

Wajcman, Judy. 1996. "Women and Men Managers: Careers and Equal Opportunities." In R. Crompton, D. Gallie, and K. Purcell, eds. *Changing Forms of Employment: Organisations, Skills and Gender.* London: Routledge.

Waldfogel, Jane. 1997. The Effect of Children on Women's Wages. *American Sociological Review* 62:209–217.

Wallace, Jean E. 1995a. "Corporatist Control and Organizational Commitment among Professionals: The Case of Lawyers Working in Law Firms." *Social Forces* 73:811–840.

———. 1995b. "Organizational and Professional Commitment in Professional and Nonprofessional Organizations." *Administrative Science Quarterly* 40:228–255.

Walsh, Mary R. 1977. *Doctors Wanted: No Women Need Apply.* New Haven and London: Yale University Press.

Weber, Max. 1958a. "Science As a Vocation." In H. H. Gertz and C. Wright Mills, eds. *From Max Weber: Essays in Sociology,* pp. 129–156. New York: Oxford University Press.

————. 1958b. *The Protestant Ethic and the Spirit of Capitalism.* New York: Charles Scribner's Sons.

Weiner, Lynn Y. 1985. *From Working Girl to Working Mother: The Female Labor Force in the United States, 1820–1980.* Chapel Hill, N.C.: University of North Carolina Press.

Wenger, Jeffrey. 2001. "The Continuing Problems with Part-time Jobs." Washington, D.C.: Economic Policy Institute Issue Brief. 155.

West, Candace, and Don H. Zimmerman. 1987. "Doing Gender." *Gender & Society* 1:125–151.

Wharton, Amy S. 1991. "Structure and Agency in Socialist-Feminist Theory." *Gender & Society* 5:373–389.

Wharton, Amy S., and Mary Blair-Loy. 2002. "The 'Overtime Culture' in a Global Corporation: A Cross-National Study of Finance Professionals' Interest in Working Part-Time." *Work and Occupations* 29:32–63.

White, Harrison C. 1970. *Chains of Opportunity.* Cambridge, Mass.: Harvard University Press.

Whittier, Nancy. 1995. *Feminist Generations: The Persistence of the Radical Women's Movement.* Philadelphia, Pa.: Temple University Press.

Whyte, William H., Jr. 1956. *The Organization Man.* New York: Simon & Schuster.

Williams, Joan. 2000. *Unbending Gender: Why Family and Work Conflict and What to Do about It.* Oxford and New York: Oxford University Press.

Williams, Joan, and Cynthia T. Calvert. 2001. "Balanced Hours: Effective Part-Time Policies for Washington Law Firms." Washington, D.C.: Project for Attorney Retention.

Wolf, Naomi. 2001. *Misconceptions: Truth, Lies, and the Unexpected on the Journey to Motherhood.* New York: Doubleday.

Wolfe, Alan. 1997. "The Moral Meanings of Work." *American Prospect* 8(34):82–90.

Women's Bar Association of Massachusetts. 2000. "More than Part-Time: The Effect of Reduced-Hours Arrangements on the Retention, Recruitment, and Success of Women Attorneys in Law Firms." A Report of the

Employment Issues. Committee of the Women's Bar Association of Massachusetts.

Wrigley, Julia. 1995. *Other People's Children.* New York: Basic Books.

Wrong, Dennis. 1961. "The Oversocialized Conception of Man in Modern Sociology." *American Sociological Review* 26(2):183–193.

Wuthnow, Robert. 1996. *Poor Richard's Principle: Rediscovering the American Dream through the Moral Dimension of Work, Business and Money.* Princeton, N.J.: Princeton University Press.

———. 2001. "Moral Inquiry in Cultural Sociology." In Karen Cerulo, ed. *Culture in Mind: Toward a Sociology of Culture and Cognition,* pp. 123–134. New York: Routledge.

Wylie, Philip. 1942. *Generation of Vipers.* New York and Toronto: Rinehart & Company.

Zelizer, Viviana. 1985. *Pricing the Priceless Child: The Changing Social Value of Children.* New York: Basic Books.

Zerubavel, Eviatar. 1997. *Social Mindscapes: An Invitation to Cognitive Sociology.* Cambridge and London: Harvard University Press.

ACKNOWLEDGMENTS

I began this project while in graduate school in the Department of Sociology at the University of Chicago. I thank my dissertation committee chair, Andrew Abbott, for his extraordinarily generous gifts of time, attention, support, and perceptive criticism during the initial development of this manuscript and long after. I acknowledge the insightful contributions of the other members of my dissertation committee, Wendy Griswold, Gerald Suttles, and Mary Brinton. Members of the culture workshop at the University of Chicago, led by Wendy Griswold, offered useful comments. Harrison White and David Gibson graciously provided hospitality at Columbia University during my time in New York City.

Data collection was supported in part by a Dissertation Improvement Grant from the National Science Foundation. Later writing and revision was supported in part by a Completion Grant from the College of Liberal Arts at Washington State University. I thank the journal *Gender & Society* for permission to base Chapter 4 on my article "Cultural Constructions of Family Schemas: The Case of Women Executives," *Gender & Society* 15(5): 687–709 (October 2001).

Jerry A. Jacobs, Paul Lindholdt, and Linda Waite offered invaluable encouragement at key junctures. These chapters have benefited from critical commentary from numerous colleagues, including Michael Allen, Marin Clarkberg, Alison Cliath, Penny Edgell, Cynthia Fuchs Epstein, Julie Goldsmith, Gregory Hooks, David Jacobson, Arne Kalleberg, Michele Lamont, Anne Lincoln, Barbara Risman, Louise Roth, and Amy S. Wharton. I acknowledge Judy Hennessy and Gretchen DeHart for providing expert research assistance. I thank the wonderful editorial staff at Harvard University Press, especially Michael Aronson, Elizabeth Collins, and Christine Thorsteinsson. I thank the women I interviewed for sharing with me their life stories, dreams, and regrets. Without their openness and generosity, this book could not have been written.

I thank all the friends and family members who enveloped me during this adventure. This cloud of witnesses includes Shari Young, Erin Collin, Mark Melickian, Bonnie Perry, Susan Harlow, Barbara Anderson, Steve Witt, Carol Huneke, Roger Peven, Jolanta Drzewiecka, and my dear family, Joan and Alexander Blair, Peter Blair, John Blair and Rebecca Coolidge, Anne, Michael, and Carla Romero, and Dorothy Brown Wagner.

I extend my most intense gratitude and appreciation to my husband, David Blair-Loy. David has upheld me in every way during this book's long incubation and delivery. He provided brilliant and unsparingly candid commentary on draft after draft. He helped me meet numerous deadlines by providing emergency clerical support and hot meals and speeding the manuscript to the last Fed Ex pick-up location in town. Most important, he has always believed in me. I dedicate this book to David.

INDEX

acquisitions, corporate, 37
adoption, 12–13, 57, 75, 76
African-American women, 193, 208
age cohorts, 16, 25, 184; careers and child-bearing rates of, 115–116; definitions of, 117–118; oldest (World War II era), 121, 122, 124–126; middle (1947–1951), 122, 126–133; youngest (1952–1958), 122, 133–140, 142, 144, 183; family status of, 122–123; age at marriage, 150–151
agency, human, 18, 106, 172–175, 182, 191; creativity and, 185; cultural schemas and, 186; shaping of, 204
Alford, Robert R., 188
alienation, 86
allegiance, 23–24
ambivalence, 45–46
American Dream, 195
autonomy, 25, 26, 174

baby boom, 16, 25, 115, 140, 142; family devotion schema and, 19; age at marriage and, 150
babysitters, 54, 136, 164
Baker, Carol, 30
Becker, Gary, 71
Bem, Sandra L., 176
betrayal, 36, 40–45
billable hours, 21, 196
biological clock, 79
biology, 82–87, 167, 179
bonuses, 22, 98

boredom, 75, 80, 86, 107
bosses. *See* employers
boundary work, 63
bread-winning role, 35, 52, 67, 75, 89, 192
brokerages, 9, 207
Buckingham, Jane, 40–42, 44
bureaucracy, 20
business firms: as "greedy institutions," 19; allegiance to, 102–106; "family friendly," 172, 196, 197

calling (vocation), 1–2, 13, 35, 54, 164, 194
capitalism, 1, 2–3, 7, 180; work devotion schema and, 7, 20, 21; institutions and, 188, 189
career-committed women, 9, 12; age cohorts among, 16; work devotion schema and, 20, 35–36, 46, 181; financial rewards and, 24–25; household chores and, 34–35; definition of childhood and, 61; education and, 88; with children, 115–116, 210; age at marriage, 150; contingency events and, 159, 161–162; without children, 182; networking organization of, 203, 206–207, 209; characteristics of, 207–208; interviews with, 208–210, 215
caregivers, full-time, 7, 35, 136, 140. *See also* nannies
Carpenter, Jen, 119
case studies, 203
change, cultural, 112–114, 139–140